STD

ACPL ITEM
DISCARDED

S0-CBG-201

9-1-59

MANAGEMENT'S MISSION
IN A NEW SOCIETY

MANAGEMENT'S MISSION
IN A NEW SOCIETY

Edited by
DAN H. FENN, JR.
Assistant Editor of the Harvard Business Review *and Member*
of the Faculty of the Harvard Graduate School of Business Administration

McGRAW-HILL BOOK COMPANY, INC.
New York   Toronto   London   1959

MANAGEMENT'S MISSION IN A NEW SOCIETY

Copyright © 1959 by the McGraw-Hill Book
Company, Inc. Printed in the United States of
America. All rights reserved. This book, or parts
thereof, may not be reproduced in any form
without permission of the publishers.

Library of Congress Catalog Card Number: 59-10707

1079091

PREFACE

VIEWING THE CONFERENCE on which this book is based from a vantage point outside the business community, one observer recently commented: "It was an exciting and impressive sight; here was a group of professional men thinking seriously and deeply together about the most basic questions touching their lives and their role in the world."

He went on to point out that this meeting was not called to deal with the "hows" of day-to-day managerial life, but rather the "whys." Any man finds himself occasionally stopping for a moment in the middle of a busy life and, fleetingly, asking: "Why am I doing all this? What is the purpose? Are there other directions I ought to be taking, other values I should be using as guides?" At the Fiftieth Anniversary Conference of the Harvard Business School, 2,000 businessmen took two days out to ask these questions in an orderly, organized fashion.

What lay behind this soul searching (which took place, incidentally, before the November landslide buried the first businessman's government in this country in twenty years)? How did the Conference ever come to adopt such a theme in the first place? It boiled up out of the experience of a number of top business executives, members of the

Conference Committee, who felt themselves increasingly hemmed in by government regulation, labor union restrictions, and the pressures of public opinion. They felt that the businessman was being discriminated against in legislative halls, union offices, classrooms, and around the cracker barrel.

This hostile climate seemed all the more difficult to understand considering that business was at the peak of its achievement in the production of goods and services. "We have done our job and done it remarkably well," the men said. "Why, then, are we out of favor with the public?"

Dismissing the opposition as radicals, rascals, and/or nincompoops did not seem to be a very helpful or constructive solution. The techniques of communication offered a fruitful possibility, but saying the right words through the right media at the most popular viewing hour somehow did not seem to cut to the heart of the issue. After all, if no one is listening or believing, the best-planned advertising program will be barren of results.

At this point, someone began asking whether or not we were *doing* the right things. Are we clear on what our function really is in this kind of world? "Fifty years ago," said one man, "it was agreed that if countless businessmen looked to their own economic interests, the aggregate of all these efforts would produce a rough balance and would work out best for everyone. This is no longer true. Perhaps we should take another look at the kind of capitalism we have today and the type of society in which we live, and find out what the job of the businessman actually is in this part of the twentieth century."

Thus the Conference theme developed out of the questions and concern of practicing executives. They wanted to open up some issues that had been disturbing them, issues they saw as directly relevant to their performance as managers. And from the start they made one assumption: this Conference was not to be a purely academic survey of the situation. It was to serve as a guide and a prod to businessmen, urging them to set the boundaries of their jobs beyond the lot lines of their plants. The businessman, they felt, has a responsibility and an opportunity to make a mighty contribution to the shaping of the political and social climate within which he will live and work.

They left to the speakers the task of setting the dimensions of that responsibility. In the pages that follow, a group of distinguished managers, statesmen, teachers, and observers do just that. In closing his speech, Charles H. Malik, then Minister for Foreign Affairs of Lebanon and later President of the United Nations General Assembly, quoted from Alfred North Whitehead: "A great society is a society in which its men of business think greatly of their functions." The Conference provided some definitions of "thinking greatly" in a dynamic and dangerous world.

I hope the words of the participants as recorded on paper will stimulate the thinking of readers to the same degree that their spoken thoughts aroused the Conference audience that heard them.

Many people have helped in the publication of this volume. First, of course, I want to express my appreciation to the authors, who took the time to prepare their material initially for the Conference and then, later, for the book. Secondly, I am deeply grateful to Mrs. Louis E. Bertoni, without whose skillful editorial and managerial assistance this volume would never have found its way to the presses. Finally, my thanks to Miss Joan E. Foster, Mrs. Willis M. Hunt, Miss Diana Lees, and Mrs. Alan Lebowitz for indispensable assistance along the way.

Dan H. Fenn, Jr.

CONTENTS

INTRODUCTION OF THE THEME

Stanley F. Teele

DURING THE 50 YEARS that have passed since 1908 when the Harvard Business School was established, the American business system has made tremendous progress. The details are too evident to need rehearsing. They are highlighted by the vast speed-up in production and the almost miraculous changes in communications; by the spectacular development and application of technology; by the steady reduction in the amount of human effort required to produce goods and services and the consequent increase in leisure time that has become available to all of us; and by the dramatic flattening of the income pyramid. But to concentrate on these material signs of progress would be to overlook another aspect of the drama of the last 50 years for which business is also importantly responsible. I refer to our cultural progress—to the mounting educational opportunities which are available to everyone, to the high degree of economic mobility which characterizes our system, and to the increasing attention which is devoted, on all sides, to the dignity of the individual.

One glimpse at the record makes it clear that the American business system has created a new economy in these 50 years. And this new economy has been of major consequence, along with other significant developments, in the evolution of a new society. It is this new society and the relationship of business to it which we shall

Note: Mr. Teele is Dean of the Harvard Business School.

examine. What are its principal characteristics? Why have they developed? What role has business played—or failed to play—in creating them? What, in the parlance of today, is the public's "image" of our new society, and what is the "image" of business in relation to it?

We should, of course, acknowledge at once that in a two-day conference we could not possibly have answered all these questions. But in view of our concern with the need for the assertion of constructive business leadership in our society today, we hope that, first, we shall provoke grave concern about this new society and the role that business should play in it; and, second, that from these chapters some thought-provoking and constructive ideas will emerge which will help make you a more effective manager in this new society, one who is better prepared to play the role already demanded, one who can participate effectively in the shaping of the world in which we find ourselves. When I consider the extraordinary degree of interest stirred by the Conference and the wide consideration given to the specific suggestions put forward, I am confident that the ideas generated will travel on for many years to come. It is not too much to hope, indeed, that the concepts so eloquently developed will become a part of the bedrock thinking of the businessman of tomorrow.

As we look to the future it is of utmost importance that all of us understand and treasure the forces which have been so helpful in the past in order that we shall not lose their effectiveness for the future. Not only should we understand and treasure these forces, but we should constantly proclaim their importance to ourselves and to the rest of the world. It is no less important, however, to look at new forces and new problems. We must define for ourselves management's mission in a new society—and then proclaim it to our whole community and to the world.

Part One

MANDATE FOR A MISSION

HOW DID WE GET THIS WAY—
AND WHERE ARE WE GOING?

Arnold J. Toynbee

LOOKING BACK over the last half century, we can see that the associations of this word "business" in our minds have been changing perceptibly. What further changes are the next fifty years likely to bring? And the next fifty after that? It is to these questions that I want to turn in this chapter.

WHAT IS "BUSINESS"?

Let us remind ourselves of what we mean when we use the word "business." We do not, I think, mean anything so general as just working to earn one's living. That is something that we all have to do, but that does not make all of us "businessmen" in the ordinary usage of the word. For example:

Note: Mr. Toynbee is Professor Emeritus of International History in the University of London and was formerly Director of Studies at the Royal Institute of International Affairs in London.

We do not usually think of agriculture as being business, though agriculture has been mankind's fundamental and staple economic occupation for the last seven or eight thousand years. An agricultural enterprise may be conducted by a corporation which has invested capital, employs wage labor, and produces crops for sale instead of for the subsistence of the producers themselves. These are some of the principal characteristics of what we call business when it is not concerned with raising crops from the land; but when we find agriculture being run as a business, we think of this as being something a bit unusual.

In describing it, we should probably call it "farming run on business lines" rather than just "business" without any further explanation beyond that.

By business, in fact, we do not ordinarily mean farming, nor do we mean the professions. We mean trade, finance, and industry; and in industry we do not think of the workers in the factories as being businessmen and women. We think only of the workers in the offices from which industries are managed.

Business traditionally means gainful employment in which the work is done primarily for the sake of the remuneration rather than the remuneration following as an incidental, though of course indispensable, consequence of work done for its own sake. We also think of business as being work in which the remuneration takes the form not of a salary received from an employer but of a profit won by the worker from his own personal enterprise. These traditional connotations of the word business still cling to it. Yet, among businessmen of the present day, how many still actually work for profit? Is it not true that the great majority of them are employees, and, in this respect, are in the same position as their fellow employees in the factory?

From Pillar to Post

The self-employed man or woman has now become a rarity, and even something of a scandal:

> In Britain today the word self-employed has almost become a term of reproach. On the official forms that the government sends one to fill in, under the usual threat of dire penalties if one neglects to obey the command, there is a standard blank space

for entering the name and address of one's employer. In a foot-
note in small print, there is an instruction that one is to enter
one's own name and address if one is self-employed. If the form
is a national insurance form, the self-employed person finds, when
he comes to the figures, that he is condemned to pay a larger
premium and to receive a smaller benefit than if he had been working for someone else.

This penalization is the price of abnormality. The normal worker
now is an employee, and his employer is required by the government to make a contribution toward the employee's insurance. If
one chooses to be so peculiar as to be self-employed, one must expect to suffer financially for one's eccentricity.

At first sight it may seem surprising that the self-employed person should be penalized in Britain today. Employees are a by-product
of capitalism for which capitalism is censured by socialists; Britain
is a semisocialist country; so surely the self-employed person, far
from being penalized, ought to be encouraged and rewarded. This
would perhaps be logical, but it is not the way things have worked
out in practice.

A semisocialist country is, perforce, a more than semibureaucratic
country, and one of the tricks of the civil servant's trade is to save his
master, the government, time and money by making other people
work for the government gratis. Employers of labor, especially if
they are large-scale business corporations, are convenient victims of
the civil servant's purpose. In requiring them to return all the relevant particulars about their employees, and to pay directly to the
government the tax and insurance contributions that the government claims from the employee, the government is getting its own
business done more efficiently than it could if it were to deal with
every citizen directly instead of through his employer. The government exacts this valuable administrative assistance without any cost
to itself at all.

The civil servant in a semisocialist state approves of employers
because they can be made to do a substantial part of his work for
him. If the state were to become a 100% socialist state, the civil
servant would have to do the whole of his work for himself, and
the state would then have to pay for these extra man-hours.

This is a revolutionary change from the days of the drafting of

the American Constitution and the passing of the United Kingdom
Reform Bill of 1832. In those days the self-employed person was
assumed to be the typical citizen, the pillar of democracy. Today
he is being driven from pillar to post and from democracy to fascism.
While governments penalize him, big corporations put him out of
business. In desperation he becomes a National Socialist or a
Poujadist; disgraces himself by the savagery of his behavior when,
for a moment, he scrambles back into power; and then swiftly goes
down in inevitable defeat, having gained only infamy, a tragic fate
for the descendants of the self-employed democrats who made the
American and French Revolutions.

This tragedy is in store only for a minority of the men and
women who are in business today. The majority are now ensured
against being put out of business by their sheltered position as employees; and, at the same time, the connotation of the word business is changing. Instead of its original association with the notions
of enterprise and profit, it is coming to be associated more and more
with the very different notions of administration and organization.

These are, of course, the notions which people have always associated with government service. Business and government service
once stood at opposite poles in the conventional picture of the spirit
and the conditions in which the different bits of the world's work
were done. Nowadays, business and government service seem to be
becoming less and less unlike each other. This rapprochement is
taking place not only in Communist countries, where business is
a government monopoly, and in semisocialist countries, like those
of Western Europe, where business is the government's drafted
deputy and therefore its unloved but valued protegé. It is also happening in the United States and Canada. From the standpoint of
the employee, it is coming to make less and less practical difference
to him what his country's official ideology is and whether he happens to be employed by a government, by a commercial corporation, by a cultural foundation, or by a university. In this age, universities, as well, are becoming complex administrative organizations in which the teacher and the researcher feel more and more
severely the tyranny of the machine.

The World of Civil Service

Disliking institutions as I happen to do, I have been lucky in my normal working life to find niches and crevices to work in where the growing weight of organization has sat fairly lightly on me. But during the two wars I spent the best part of ten years working as a temporary civil servant. This is grist for a historian if he is interested in current history as well as the remoter past. Still, ten years is a considerable slice out of a working lifetime, and, for an old-fashioned student of human affairs, an inside view of civil service methods and the civil service spirit is horrifying as well as highly instructive.

In the realm of scholarship, as we know, free enterprise is freer than it ever has been in the realm of business, even at free enterprise's mid-nineteenth century peak. The scholar does not have to ask any man's leave to set to work, and nothing can stop him from reaching his goal except the inadequacy of his own ability and energy. He has only to find pen, ink, paper, and a cubicle to work in, and he can do his stuff up to the limits of his capacity. Transform him into a temporary civil servant, and he will find himself in a strange nightmare world in which his energies are inhibited and his faculties are paralyzed. In the world of civil service plunging into action is the archcrime. When you sight an objective you must not head straight for it. You must consult a thousand colleagues who have a right to file objections in the names of a hundred other government departments that are all great powers, and you must not feel frustrated or guilty when you find yourself bogged down. The civil servant's duty is not to achieve desirable results; it is to follow the correct procedure.

Whether the civil servant makes a success or a failure of the particular job on which he is engaged at the moment will make no appreciable difference to the public weal, because this is only one of a hundred thousand other jobs of no lesser and no greater importance on the public agenda. But it will damage the public weal, and perhaps damage it seriously, if, in an unprofessional eagerness to get some particular thing done, he incautiously creates an unfortunate precedent. This may affect adversely the hundred thousand other transactions in the same category that are going to come on

the agenda in the course of the next generation or the next century.
It is one of the fundamental rules for doing government work
that no particular piece of work may be dealt with on it own merits.
Every decision must be determined by its possible bearing on in-
numerable other decisions that other people will be taking at some
future date.

No doubt that is something of a caricature of the way in which
things are done, or not done, in government service. Yet, though I
may have exaggerated the reality, I do not think I have misrepre-
sented it. And this, if I am right, is the way of doing things which
business is now approaching rapidly. Moreover, the civil service is
not only asserting itself in business; it is also asserting itself in
technology, the sciences, the humanities, and religion—in fact, in
most branches of human activity. Here we seem to see a world-wide
tendency affecting almost all sides of life, which, I suppose, was
hardly foreseen as recently as 50 years ago when the Harvard
Business School was inaugurated. Whither will this current have
carried mankind, say, 50 years from now?

A LOOK AT THE PAST

In human affairs we cannot predict the future. We can only peer
into it and make guesses about it. The only light that we can throw
on it is light from our experience of the past. Analogies from the
past are never exact, and may be misleading; but we have nothing
better to go on, so we must use what we have, though we do this at
our peril. One episode of past history in which I had the good
fortune to be instructed, as part of an old-fashioned fifteenth-century
Italian education at a fourteenth-century English school, is the history of the Greco-Roman world during the two centuries before the
establishment of the Augustan Peace and the two centuries after
it. This story has been running in my head ever since I was invited
to participate in the Fiftieth Anniversary Conference of the Harvard
Business School. The earlier chapters of that story show some remarkable points of resemblance to the earlier chapters of ours. But
our story is a still unfinished one, whereas we know how the Greco-
Roman story ended; and this makes it interesting for us when we are
wondering how our own story is going to turn out.

Rise of Roman Business

The story of Roman business is part of our historical background. The English word business is a literal translation of the Latin word "negotium." Negotium means "the opposite of leisure," and the Latin word for businessman is "negotiator," which of course means not a negotiator in our English sense of the word, but a man who denies himself leisure in order to get business done.

Marxian critics of our modern Western businessmen have had some hard things to say about them. To many of us in the West, some of these things seem to be untrue, or at least to be overstated. The worst that the severest critic has ever said about our modern businessmen would hardly be bad enough for their Roman predecessors. When modern business is accused of being exploitative, it can afford to plead guilty because it can point out that, in seeking its own economic advantage, it has enabled the human race to achieve an unheard of increase in productivity.

Roman business, however, was mostly predatory and parasitical. Large-scale industrial production, e.g., the manufacture of crockery or of clothing, played a minor part in it. A bigger affair was the introduction of cattle ranching and plantation farming into areas in Sicily and Southern Italy that had been devastated in the second and worst of the three wars between Rome and Carthage. The Roman businessman made profits by stocking these areas with manpower in the shape of slave shepherds and slave plantation hands. Their energy and efficiency in running the slave trade can hardly be placed on the credit side of their account. The bulk of their business, and the most lucrative items in it, consisted of contracts with the Roman government and loans on outrageously extortionate terms to conquered and subject communities that could find no other source of ready money for paying the war indemnities and taxes exacted by the victorious Roman government. The Roman businessmen's opportunities came from the subject peoples' economic distress and the Roman government's administrative inefficiency.

When the Roman government carried the Roman commonwealth into its second war with Carthage in 218 B.C., its administrative organization was that of a small peasant state. In other words it was almost nonexistent. Within little more than 50 years, Rome had made herself militarily and politically supreme around all the shores of the Mediterranean, but her administrative machinery still remained rudimentary. Faced with the problem of managing a vast empire, the government helped itself by farming out every possible branch of public activity to private business enterprise. It farmed out the collection of customs duties, the collection of the grain tithe in the provinces, the collection of the fees for maintaining livestock on the public pastures, the operation of mines confiscated from the governments of conquered states, and the provisioning of Roman armies, which were now campaigning overseas at long distances from home.

The rise of the Roman businessmen was as sudden as the spread of Roman rule, and was indeed a consequence of it. They made themselves conspicuous at an early stage of the second Romano-Punic War in an incident that was characteristically discreditable. After a few years of conducting this tremendous and, at the outset, disastrous war, the Roman government went bankrupt. With an empty treasury, how was it to keep up the all-important flow of food, clothing, and supplies to the Roman armies fighting far away in Spain?

The contractors who had been supplying these armies offered to continue without asking for further payments until the war was over. This offer to supply on credit was accompanied by two conditions: the contractors must be given personal exemption from military service, and their shipments must be insured by the government against risks on the voyage. The government had no choice but to accept these terms; and the contractors then augmented their deferred profits by lading a certain number of rotten ships with rubbishy cargoes, valuing them for insurance purposes as if they were good cargoes and sound ships, and arranging for these vessels to be wrecked on route.

This would have been shocking behavior, even if the fraudulent contractors' country had not been fighting for her life. When the knowledge of what they were doing leaked out, there was public indignation. The government, however, was afraid to prosecute, for fear that this might stop the flow of such supplies as *were* being duly delivered, and the government had no other source of supply to which it could resort. When a magistrate did finally institute legal proceedings in the national assembly, the guilty contractors organized a gang and broke up the meeting. This was too much, and several of them evaded being brought to book only by taking asylum in allied states where they were secure against being extradited. But most of the profits from this discreditable business were eventually collected from the government by the contractors, and this was one of the sources of the capital with which the new Roman business community operated during the following two centuries. This was an ominous beginning for an economic system.

From Wolves to Shepherd Dogs

Those next 200 years were an age of agony for the countries around the Mediterranean. The Roman businessmen exploited them mercilessly, and the Roman government intervened only halfheartedly and ineffectively to protect its subjects from its agents. How could the government afford to do justice when it was dependent for the receipt of its revenues on the businessmen's unprincipled activities? Halfway through the first century B.C., civilized society at the western end of the Old World seemed on the brink of dissolution. Society was then snatched out of the jaws of destruction by two great statesmen, Caesar and Augustus. They conceived and executed a number of constructive reforms which gave the Greco-Roman civilization a reprieve that lasted two centuries. One of the key reforms was the transformation of wolves into shepherd dogs: they converted the children of the predatory businessmen into dutiful civil servants.

Like many strokes of genius, this one was based on a simple idea, obvious in retrospect, but not so easy to think of and not at all easy to carry out. Rome had conquered the Mediterranean world and overthrown or hamstrung all the previous states, but had failed to set up any adequate substitute for them. The consequence had been two centuries of chaos and misery. What the world needed was an efficient, honest, benevolent world government; what it had been getting was efficient, dishonest, and heartless exploitation by Roman businessmen. The point on which Augustus seized was that the efficiency was there, and that his problem was to redirect it and to harness it to constructive rather than destructive activities.

To judge by the record of the Roman Republican government

during those last two centuries, it might have seemed as if the
Romans were incapable of organizing public administration on a
grand scale. The lie was given to any such verdict by the record of
the Roman businessmen during the same period. This record was
morally disgraceful, but it was impressive by the criterion of material
achievement. Under the stimulus of the opportunity for making
lucrative profits, the businessmen had improvised large-scale organizations that worked. It was beside the point that they had been
working havoc. Their effectiveness in accomplishing the purposes
for which they had been set up demonstrated that there was a fund
of first-rate organizing ability in the Roman people. The fact that
the Roman government's own official organization had remained
rudimentary was evidence merely of the conservatism, unimagina-
tiveness, and callousness of the Roman governing class. It could have
found the men to staff a world government if it had chosen. It had
not cared to try, but Augustus intended to achieve this. He had to
achieve it or see civilization collapse and himself meet the same fate
as his adoptive father, Caesar.

The business community was the tool lying ready for him to use,
and Augustus made the Roman businessmen serve his enlightened
purpose by diminishing their opportunities for making business
profits, and at the same time offering them a new career as salaried
civil servants. By establishing a world-wide peace, which lasted,
with some short lapses, for 200 years, he struck at the slave trade's
source of supply and so reduced the trade and the profits from it
to less monstrous dimensions. By taking over the collection of the
public revenues from the the companies that had been farming them,
he forced the children of the tax farmers to become employees of
the state. He could do without the farming system because he could
draw on the business experience of the tax-farming class to do the
same work as efficiently as, but more honestly and humanely than,
government officials.

Orderliness versus Dullness

This administrative reform was an immense success. It was perhaps the chief reason why life in the Mediterranean world for the
200 years after Augustus was less insecure and less unhappy than it
had been during the 200 years immediately preceding. But all

things, and especially good things, have to be paid for; and, in the Mediterranean world under the Augustan Peace, the price of orderliness and justice was uncreativeness and dullness.

Under the Augustan regime, creativeness was deliberately discouraged and in extreme cases was victimized, because the activities of creative personalities are a disturbing factor in society. That is the price of creativeness, but Augustus and his successors were intent on "freezing" society as a precaution against the resurgence of disorder and violence. They looked askance at all manifestations of independent-mindedness and private initiative. They frowned on aristocracies; they frowned on private associations, even those as remote from politics as burial societies; and they frowned, for the same reason, on inventors. For instance:

⟨ There is a thrice-told tale of the horrid fate of an inventor of unbreakable glass. The foolish fellow proudly reported his invention to the authorities and suggested to them that he deserved a reward; and the junior officials concerned were sufficiently impressed to send the case to the Emperor.

"Sir," said the Emperor's secretary to his master one morning, "I have been directed to inform you that a man has made the astonishing invention of unbreakable glass, and to ask what action it pleases you to take." "Oh, have the man put to death," said the Emperor, without raising his head from the pile of papers on his desk. The secretary supposed that he had misheard. "I do not think, Sir," he went on, "that I can have managed to make quite clear what I have been instructed to tell you." "You did make it perfectly clear, so have him put to death." "But, Sir," the kindhearted secretary persisted, "the poor man has made a most remarkable and most useful invention, and we were wondering whether you wouldn't think him worthy of a reward."

At this point the overworked Emperor lost his temper. "How dare you plague me," he snapped out, "by forcing me to explain the obvious when it is your duty simply to carry out my orders. Don't you see that if this man's invention is put on the market, it will throw the makers of ordinary glass out of employment, unemployment will lead to unrest, and unrest to revolution and civil war? My predecessors' and my own immense labors for bringing happiness to the human race will run the risk of being undone. You will understand that we can't have that, so I tell you for the third time, see that the man is put to death, and, still more important, see that the blueprint of his invention is incinerated."

⟨ About this time, Heron, a man who lived in Alexandria, the greatest industrial and commercial city in the Mediterranean world of the day, discovered the principle of the steam turbine engine. In an age in which the whole Mediterranean basin was united under a single government, the application of steam power to locomotion would have done wonders for long-distance trade and still greater wonders for the defense of the Roman Empire's dangerously extended frontiers. But Heron's invention never came to be treated as anything more than a curiosity and a plaything.

The inventive genius was there, as no doubt it is present everywhere at all times; but in the Roman Empire the seed fell on stony ground. The will was lacking to turn inventions to practical account for improving the material conditions of life.

The imperial government's success in making life static had the unintended effect of making it dull. In an imaginary conversation, the historian Tacitus, writing in the second century of the Augustan Peace, raises the question why the public speakers of his own day made such a poor performance by comparison with those of the age before the establishment of the Augustan world order. The explanation that he offers rings true and is illuminating. We have the good fortune, he says, to find ourselves in our day living in such a well-administered and respectable world that there is really nothing to make speeches about.

Cicero, living in that terrible pre-Augustan age, was less lucky as a man (he met a violent death), but he was luckier as a public speaker as long as he escaped assassination. Sensational cases in court and shattering public events were everyday occurrences in his time, so his genius as a pleader and as a political speaker had full scope. He never had to search for a theme. During the Augustan Peace, public speakers did have to search for themes, and they usually had no better resource than to hunt up academic ones drawn from wellworn commonplaces of past history and older literature.

In the eyes of generations that had not forgotten their grandparents' tales of a dreadful age of anarchy and oppression, dullness and uncreativeness seemed a small price to pay for good government and social justice. Yet the price turned out to be greater than they realized. When society stifles human creativeness, it deprives man of the use of his fundamental asset. Unless man sets his creative powers to work on his environment, he cannot unlock the cupboard in which all his other potential assets are stored. If there is no zest in life, there will be no impulse to make the most of those creative achievements that break out here and there in spite of all the well-meaning impediments that a paternal government may devise.

One reason why the Augustan Peace eventually broke down was that it failed to arouse enthusiasm in the hearts of its beneficiaries. In addition to this psychological reason, there was an economic one. The elaborate and expensive Greco-Roman civilization placed too heavy a burden on the agricultural economy on which it was imposed. This economy might have been made much more productive in the Greco-Roman world, as it has been made in our modern world, by a practical application of technological inventions. But under the Roman Empire, the climate of opinion was as adverse to this as it has been favorable to it in the modern world. So eventually the static agricultural economy broke down under the burden of civilization, and the house of cards collapsed.

I have suggested that society cannot afford to stifle human creativeness. Fortunately, it is also true that it cannot succeed in stifling it in the long run. Whatever you may do to suppress it, it will break out sooner or later, and the history of the Augustan Peace illustrates this truth. While most of the men and women living under the Augustan Peace were content to "get by," there were awkward and irrepressible minorities that insisted on devoting themselves to ideals, to the point of giving their lives for them if necessary. There were the Roman soldiers, holding the frontiers of the world state, and there were the Christian martyrs. Of these two sets of earnest, exalted, unmanageable people, the martyrs were the more surprising, because they came out of an unheroic social setting in the sordid overgrown cities of the interior. Life was not dull for the martyrs or for the soldiers; so these two minorities made history and, in making it, undid Augustus's shrewd and painstaking work.

THE ROAD AHEAD

I have ventured to take you back with me into this episode of past history because of the bearing that I believe it has on our own situation and prospects. Our situation today is not unlike that of the Greco-Roman world just before it was salvaged by Augustus. Here and now there is a crying need, as there was then, for peace, harmony, teamwork, organization, administration, and efficiency on a world-wide scale. We are in the same danger of seeing civilization destroy itself by revolution and war. Indeed, in our case, the degree of the danger and the urgency is considerably higher. Our modern society has surpassed the Greco-Roman society in scale and complexity. It has become literally world-wide, embracing all sections of the human race from the richest to the poorest. And it is now armed with atomic weapons. For us today, world order, peace, and social justice are literally necessities of life. We know that we shall destroy ourselves if we do not achieve these goals, so there can be no question of haggling over the price. We have to pay it, whatever it may be; and I think it is going to be the same price that the Greco-Roman world paid in and after the generation of Augustus. Knowing how that story ended, can we use our hindsight to save ourselves from stumbling into the pitfalls in the road that we, in our turn, have perforce to take?

This brings me, in conclusion, back to our starting point: the changes in the last 50 years and the kind of world that lies just over the horizon. The businessman of the future, I believe, will be one of the key figures in a world civil service. This does not necessarily mean that many of tomorrow's business executives are going to be employees of the United Nations or of any of the other organs of world government that are being and will be set up. Only a minority may take service even with the national administration; the majority may still find employment with nongovernmental corporations and foundations. All the same, I believe that whatever their official labels may be, most of them in the next generation will be employed in building up and maintaining the new world order that seems to be our only alternative to genocide.

This would be a very different career indeed from the typical business life in this country at the time when the Harvard Business School was founded. The evolution of society during the last 50 years has restricted the field of private enterprise for personal profit. In the dangerous age into which we have moved, all-out competition in economic affairs would have to be restrained even if it were still practicable.

We can no longer tolerate the evils of private enterprise, but can we ever afford to do without its benefits? If we have to restrain it in the fields of economics and politics, can we find compensatory outlets for it in the fields of art, science, scholarship, and religion? The one thing certain is that we shall defeat our own purposes in the long run if, in the cause of security, we try to close all outlets for enterprise, ambition, and creativity in any field of human activity. If we make this mistake, human nature will take its revenge, as is witnessed by the episode of Greco-Roman history that I have cited.

Is it possible to foster freedom in some fields when one is compelled to restrict it in others? This, I believe, will be the burning question for the human race, if and when we succeed in building a world government that will save us from destroying ourselves. Here, I feel sure, is one of the problems with which businessmen will be wrestling during the next half century.

THE BUSINESSMAN AND NATIONAL SECURITY

John L. Burns

IN DISCUSSING the subject, "The Businessman and National Security," I feel strongly that I must speak not as a businessman but as a citizen. Partisanship for business, government, or political party is unthinkable in dealing with a problem of such towering importance to our nation, our families, and ourselves.

As a citizen, I believe that the period just ahead of us is the most critical in our history. For the first time, we are in danger of nuclear annihilation.

The question is: *how do we meet this deadly peril?*

THE THREAT

Like it or not, we must face up more realistically to the fact that today we are in a cold war with Russia. At this point, no one can say how long we can expect it to stay cold.

Note: Mr. Burns is President of the Radio Corporation of America.

Among our best-informed military and civil authorities, there are two principal schools of thought on the paramount threat to our national security:

⟨ One group holds that the danger is immediate. They argue that the Russians will mount a sneak attack as soon as they are confident they have the capability to knock out our key cities and destroy our retaliatory power. They claim that the Soviets have some 500 submarines as compared with our 100, and that they are building undersea craft at a rate ten times as fast as ours. Some experts put the critical period between the fall of 1959 and 1963. During this fateful interval, they say, our own capabilities in missiles, aircraft, and Army and Navy forces will lag so far behind those of the Russians as to place us in grave peril.

⟨ A second school of thought contends that the greatest threat to our security lies not in the immediate situation but in the long-range challenge. The adherents of this view argue that the Russians will continue, for an extended period, to apply moral, political, economic, military, and social pressures short of all-out war. They point out that economic warfare is cheaper, subtler, and more penetrating for the Russians, and their success to date has been such that they have been able to use their military power sparingly. This economic approach is one that is difficult to get people excited about. The feeling is that the Russians will keep on waging a ruthless cold war, probing for soft spots in the free world's defenses, in the hope of eventually accomplishing their aims without having to resort to a hot war. President Eisenhower has said that we may be in for as much as 40 years of cold war.

You and I are not in a position to judge the merits of these two arguments, but we do know that we cannot gamble with national survival—even when the odds might be only a thousand to one! Common sense, therefore, dictates that our country must take all reasonable precautions against *both* the short-range and the long-range threats. We must be ever mindful of the total threat—moral, political, economic, military, and social.

The challenge to the business community in this situation is clear. The security of our country is at stake, so business must live according to a revised set of rules:

(1) It must have the courage to speak up, to take a constructive position on controversial issues.

(2) It must do the job the best way it can until the government makes the necessary changes.

(3) It must look seriously and candidly at its own situation and keep its stockholders and other interested parties informed of our country's needs. Likewise, it should listen attentively to criticism and be prepared to act promptly.

In peacetime we have permitted our free enterprise system full play. In wartime we have become a modified dictatorship, mobilizing our manpower and industrial capacity for an all-out effort. Now it is up to the government to tell us whether we have a national emergency, and, if so, to spell out the specific requirements.

Against this background, let us look at some of the major factors that should be taken into consideration in planning for the future. I believe there is an overriding need for changes in our nation's defense posture—both short-range and long-range. To meet this need will require bold new approaches in many areas, especially on the part of business and government as partners in preparedness.

SHORT-RANGE SOLUTIONS

In facing up to the short-range threat, the government, and particularly the Department of Defense, must stimulate and encourage our free enterprise system. The competition between ourselves and the Russians is a new kind of competition with a new society. It is a classic test of the free enterprise system versus Marxian socialism. Our task is to put the creativity and productivity of American industry to work as effectively for the military as we have for the consumer.

In our defense effort, we have not taken full advantage of the superb strengths inherent in our free enterprise system. We have tried to operate with insufficient incentives and with highly centralized governmental control. In short, we have tried to whip the Russians with one hand tied behind our back.

If there is to be a free enterprise approach to our defense requirements, the government obviously must be guided in its dealings with business by the factors that make the system work. These factors include incentive, teamwork, decisiveness, initiative, and careful planning.

Lack of Incentive

When I talk about incentive in connection with the defense effort, I do not want to be misunderstood. I am not suggesting that business exploit the threat to our national security in order to increase industry's earnings. What I am proposing is something that would be an incentive to industry and would also save the government money. And above all, it would help strengthen our chances for survival.

In our present system, the basic weakness in the lack of incentives is not so much that many people in many companies are not working in defense. There are many talented people working, and, of course, with proper incentives there could be more. But the real losses to us are these:

- Some of the most effective people in our country are not working on defense, or are giving only a portion of their time and thought to it.
- The profit incentive is insufficient to enable companies to devote a major effort to research and development work originated by the company itself. Therefore, the full potentialities of free enterprise in this field of creativity are not realized.

Under the present system, there is a depreciation in incentive even below the level provided by law. There are two major laws that regulate defense work now. One is the Armed Services Procurement Act of 1947, which authorizes the services to pay contractors their costs, plus a fee up to 15% of their costs, as profit on research and development contracts. The second law is the Renegotiation Act of 1951, which authorizes the government to take a second look at a company's defense business after one year to see if the profit has been excessive.

The 15% fee, stipulated in the Procurement Act, has been cut back to 10% by the individual services unless the Secretary of the Army, Navy, or Air Force makes an exception—and this does not happen very often. In practice, moreover, military contracting officers seldom agree even to 10%. It is difficult to negotiate a fee of more than 7%. Even this is subject to further reduction because many of the costs which contractors incur in the course of a job are disallowed. When the contractor gets all through, his earnings before taxes average about 4% of his sales, and after taxes may run as low as 2%. During World War II there was a compensating factor. Companies got production contracts which, because of their large repetitive volume, made up for the low return on research and the meager percentage allowance on production. Now there is rarely any large-scale production, and the allowance figures are the same.

Throughout the present contracting procedure, renegotiation hangs like a sword over the contractor's head. Let me give you an example of what I mean:

> Suppose that an efficient producer manufactures a defense item and sells it for $900, making a profit, say, of 15%. Then, suppose that an inefficient producer sells the same item for $1,000 and makes a profit of only 5%. Even though the efficient producer sold the item at a much lower price, it is he and not his inefficient competitor who stands to have his defense profits renegotiated, on the ground that they are "excessive."

What we have here, in effect, is a case of a company's being penalized for actually saving the government money.

The purpose of the Renegotiation Act is highly commendable. It was drawn up originally during World War II to provide for a review of contracts that were being hurriedly executed under the pressure of a war emergency. But modification of the law is long overdue. The chief danger today lies in having too many checks rather than too few.

Businessmen, of course, recognize the need for some controls on defense work. But the control procedure must be tempered with judgment and adjusted to meet varying conditions if we are not to weaken incentive. The practice of checking, in some instances, has been carried to harmful extremes. For example:

> One aircraft company estimates that fully one-third of its technical staff is needed to cope with government paperwork. It devotes upward of 400,000 man-hours a year to preparing reports for a long list of federal agencies. Instead of writing reports and serving on reviewing committees, these scientists and engineers could be far more productively employed in gaining new knowledge through active programs of research.

Of course, this concept of incentives applies to those working in government and the armed forces as well as to those in business.

When George Washington came to Cambridge to take over the Continental Army Command, he understood very well the principle of paying men to fight. However, it remained a continuous problem with him throughout the Revolutionary War to convince Congress and the states that they should live up to their pledges of providing pay, equipment, supplies, and special benefits for soldiers.

Prior to World War II our military services were predicated on the traditional lines of land and sea forces operating relatively independently. The services were made up of a comparatively small corps of professional personnel, on the assumption that these people and the meager resources furnished them would provide a nucleus around which our fighting forces could be rebuilt in an emergency, as they were in World War I. The advent of modern weapons such as the airplane, the ballistic missile, and the atomic weapon has changed all this. We now find it necessary to maintain a very large standing Army, Navy, and Air Force, comprised in each case of highly skilled personnel, with the majority of them serving on a career basis.

Today our military career men are not paid what they should be, with the result that some of the most competent officers are resigning from the services. Many in the prime of their years are leaving to join the major corporations because of the financial situation in which they and their families find themselves. The new military pay law, based on the recommendations of the Cordiner Report, represents a step in the right direction, and one for which Congress and the Department of Defense deserve congratulations. But a great deal more remains to be done if we are to match the Russians in providing incentive for our key people.

Role of Business

To achieve maximum effectiveness in defense, the role of business —both large and small—must be better understood.

In our free enterprise system, we need big and small business working together to turn out the goods that each produces most efficiently. We need big business for its massive scientific and technical resources and its ability to produce in large volume. We need small business for its specialized skills and its initiative in developing new ideas. Without the one, the other would wither on the vine.

Both are especially necessary in our defense effort. The large companies perform a valuable function by taking on major projects, then breaking them down into segments that are manageable by smaller firms. In two world wars large companies have been one of the basic sources of American strength. During World War II, the 100 largest contractors handled two thirds of our critical defense production. In the present age of ballistic missiles and hydrogen warheads, when it costs anywhere from $50,000 to $150,000 just to make a proposal on a major defense contract, only companies with large budgets can afford to go after the big prime contracts. How could we prepare our defenses without the aid of the top three or four companies in steel, motors, electrical equipment, chemicals, aircraft, and other key industries?

David E. Lilienthal, in his book, *Big Business: A New Era,* tells how the government turned to big business for help in mass producing atomic bombs. Then he makes this comment: "To the extent that the principle of Bigness, in our economic life, contributes in an affirmative and an indispensable way to the strengthening of our national security we should, by an explicit and affirmative national policy, encourage and protect that kind of Bigness." *

A multitude of misconceptions has developed about the relationship between big and small business. The charge has been made that big business has prospered by stifling small business. Nothing could be further from the truth. The Rockefeller Report on the American economy points out that the total number of businesses in this country has grown by 40% since 1929, while individual business units have become larger. We now have 4.2 million nonfarm businesses in the United States, the largest total in our history. This is a pretty good indication, I think, that there is no stifling of small business and no shortage of the spirit of enterprise that has made America great.

I am not for big business or for small business as such—I am for maximum effectiveness. Whatever it takes—if it is good for the consumer and our people generally, and if it is good for our defense —let's do it! Let's do it with big *and* small business!

* New York, Pocket Books, Inc., 1956, p. 97.

Reducing Lead-time

To attain maximum effectiveness in our defense program, we must exert every effort to reduce lead-time—the lag between the conception of a weapons system and its actual production.

A Pentagon study group found that, on the average, it takes us ten years to conceive and produce new air-weapons systems—about twice as long as the Russians.* The group also found that half of our time is spent trying to decide whether to go ahead with the weapon or not. In other words, it takes us as long to plan a new system as it takes the Russians to plan and produce it. The problem is complex, but improvements can—and must—be made.

Business's approach should take into consideration all the elements of sound management—planning, organization, integration, and measurement. There is a natural tendency to keep doing things the way we did them yesterday. Business must be willing to experiment constantly with new techniques and adopt them whenever they can improve on existing methods.

On the other hand, government should give business greater authority and responsibility for making decisions on materials, components, and techniques. There have been some encouraging advances in this direction in recent months, and it is to be hoped that this trend will continue. One of the prime strengths of the private enterprise system lies in the creativity of individual contractors working on particular projects.

We must remember that any decision about new weapons carries with it a certain risk. We must accept this risk and use our best judgment about when to "freeze" major product designs and go into production. There are bound to be some mistakes. But this is part of the price we must pay to close the gap between ourselves and the Russians on lead-time—and this gap *must* be closed.

LONG-RANGE DEMANDS

In facing up to the long-range threat to our security, we must adapt ourselves to a situation which, for us, is entirely new. Throughout our history as a nation, we have grown accustomed to

* *Report of the Ad Hoc Study Group on Manned Aircraft Systems,* February 9, 1957, p. 2.

looking on war as one thing and peace as another and adjusting our national policies accordingly.

Now we find ourselves confronted with a situation that is neither full war nor full peace but cold war—or hot peace. One difference between cold war and hot war is that no one has quite pulled the trigger. Furthermore, recent hot wars have been of limited duration; cold war may last for generations—a throwback to the days of the fourteenth and fifteenth centuries when the Hundred Years' War and the Wars of the Roses raged on seemingly without end.

Because of the permanence of the crisis and the complexity of the problems inherent in it, this cold war situation calls for a new approach to over-all, long-range planning. We must establish far-sighted objectives and plans which will not be affected in a major way by short-term considerations.

How can we accomplish these aims without giving up those things we hold dear? This is the most important question of our time.

While I do not claim to be an expert on the subject, I believe we need fresh approaches to the solution of our cold war problem. We must lift our eyes to a more distant horizon.

A Permanent Council

In this spirit I would like to suggest a possible approach to this problem. I believe we should establish a fourth major branch of our federal government—one that might be called the Permanent Council on Plans and Policies. This new branch, ranking in importance with the legislative, executive, and judicial branches, would have responsibility for over-all planning.

The legislative and judicial branches have reasonable continuity, but the executive branch does not. The President has, at most, 8 years in the White House. The average term of a cabinet officer in the last three administrations has been 3.7 years. In these circumstances, there is little chance for continuous study and analysis of the fundamental problems that will confront us 5, 10, or 20 years from now—or the best policies for coping with these problems.

This would be the task of the Permanent Council on Plans and Policies. Council members would be appointed for extended terms, in much the same manner as our present Supreme Court members, by joint agreement of the executive and Congress. Hence they would not be subject to the varying fortunes of political parties. They would be selected from among top-ranking leaders in education, the sciences, business management, defense, labor, and other important segments of national activity and would be supported by an adequate staff of specialists.

The primary function of this Permanent Council would be to formulate our long-range objectives, policies, programs, and strategy as related to the total needs of the nation. Unlike the other three branches of government, this new one would look primarily to the future.

The difference between this Permanent Council and existing planning groups like the National Security Council, the Office of Defense Mobilization, and others, would be that the latter are all arms of the executive branch and are concerned with a particular area rather than with the over-all picture. The proposed new Permanent Council, being in itself a fourth arm of government, would have the independence and continuity that existing bodies lack. It would also encompass the whole broad range of government activity.

Although it would have the right only to evaluate programs, to recommend their implementation, and to persuade the other three branches of government, it is my deep conviction that, in time, the new concepts and ideas emerging from such a top-level group would stimulate greater leadership and direction at all levels of our society. The Council would serve to inspire and coordinate long- and short-range planning in all branches of government.

While it is true that the Russians pose the primary threat, I believe this program should be implemented because of the over-all needs of the country. The increasing complexity of our moral, political, economic, military, and social problems requires that we be ready to modify our methods and programs when necessary.

Because of their own experience, business executives have the utmost sympathy for government's tremendous problems in adjusting methods and programs. Nevertheless, this sympathy must not retard our efforts to point up and solve these problems.

I realize, of course, the time and effort involved in establishing such a fourth branch of government as I am proposing. It would require action by Congress as well as by the individual states. However, so urgent is the need for a coordinated policy on every cold war front that I would make one further suggestion as an interim move. I would urge that an over-all planning group be set up immediately by executive order. In that way we would begin to benefit at once, while steps were under way to make the Council a constitutional agency.

THE NEXT STEPS

There are other specific steps that could be taken promptly by both government and business. These steps would contribute materially to achieving the changes needed in our defense posture, both short-range and long-range.

Business should:

(1) Become acquainted to the fullest possible extent with the nation's military establishment to the end that national security requirements, present and future, are understood.

(2) Take the initiative in identifying, defining, studying, and solving the problems now facing our military establishment.

(3) Come up with better equipment and better procedures to meet our military needs.

(4) Make better use of industry's engineers.

(5) Make available more and increasingly better scientific, technical, and managerial people for service with the Department of Defense and the Armed Forces, and allow them to serve for more than the one-year period that has become standard.

(6) Offer training programs in technical and managerial skills for military personnel, to help develop a better understanding of the way business operates.

(7) Voluntarily go after cost reduction with resolution, even though it may mean less profit.

(8) Do the best job possible regardless of any limitations on incentives which may exist.

The government should:

(1) Devise defense contract terms that will offer genuine incentives for cost reduction, early delivery, and peak efficiency.

(2) Allow defense contractors the reasonable rates of profit which were intended and provided by the law in order to make defense work adequately attractive in a free economy.

(3) Reimburse contractors for all legitimate costs incurred on a job, instead of ruling out such charges as interest, accelerated amortization of facilities, and similar items.

(4) Encourage business to do independent research and development of its own origination, thereby releasing the great forces available through the decentralization of brain power and genius.

The new approaches I have suggested—both for the short run and the long run—must be made within the exhilarating framework of the free enterprise system, a system that has brought about remarkable advances in our material welfare.

In its propaganda, Russia has boasted of its economic approach as a great triumph of advanced thinking. In practice, our system is the one that has brought about the highest standard of living in the world. As a matter of fact, it is one of the dramatic ironies of history that Karl Marx's socialist goal of abundance for all in a classless society has been achieved by the very capitalist system whose collapse he forecast as "inevitable."

While we in America want plenty for all, we must remember that this will never be permanently achieved by reducing the rewards to our most skilled people, whether worker, manager, soldier, or engineer.

The Communist Manifesto of Karl Marx and Friedrich Engels opened with the portentous words: "A specter is haunting Europe —the specter of Communism." Today this specter grimly haunts not only Europe but the entire world—a world weary of cold war and worried about hot war.

The challenge to us is plain and pointed. We must set ourselves resolutely to the task, for in this competition we must stay ahead if we are to stay alive.

THE BUSINESSMAN AND
THE CHALLENGE OF COMMUNISM

Charles H. Malik

WESTERN SOCIETY today faces three formidable challenges. There are first the problems and laws of its own inner development. Can the clamor for social and economic justice be fairly satisfied without loss of higher values? Is there no natural end to the drive after ever-higher and higher standards of living? How is the great value of freedom, which is in the end probably the most characteristic hallmark of Western life, to be reconciled with and preserved against the ever-mounting pressures of society and government? How is economic process to be related on the one hand to the government, and on the other to the conflicting economic demands of society itself? Does democracy, does the rise of the common man, necessarily entail for Western society a tragic attenuation in creativity, in excellence, in distinction, in rank? Does the amazing

Note: Mr. Malik was formerly Minister for Foreign Affairs of Lebanon and subsequently President of the General Assembly of the United Nations (Thirteenth Session, 1958).

abundance of material goods which science, technology, and the Western genius for organization have produced help or hinder the Western soul from scaling the real heights and plumbing the real depths? Amid the distractions and seductions of modern life can man still believe, really believe? Is the realm of freedom free enough and resourceful enough to prevent its enemies from taking advantage of the amenities of freedom in order to destroy freedom? And finally, what about the overriding problems of security and survival? These are some of the questions which Western society poses for itself from the very logic of its own inner development.

Communism presents another set of challenges to the West. Purely economically, it is difficult to prove that, where Communism has struck, the concentration of all the factors of production in the hands of the government has not produced better results than the systems it has replaced. Militarily, there is the so-called "balance of terror." Socially, Communist society has taken precautions by which it appears to have successfully resisted the incursion of alien ideas. Scientifically, there are the Sputniks and the ICBM's; and nobody in the West has not been profoundly jolted by the sudden realization that the rate of production of first-class Soviet scientists, engineers, and technicians is greater than that of the West, so that in a decade or two the Soviet Union, at the present rate, will have outdistanced the West in this field.

In the matter of foreign languages alone, there is no comparison, for example, between the number of Soviet students not only learning but also going deeply into the languages of the Middle East and the number of American students doing the same. Ideologically, there is a point-to-point conscious challenge and contradiction of the dozen or so fundamental Western beliefs about God, man, freedom, society, history, and the ends of life. And with respect to competition with the West in the unaligned areas, it appears that Communism is more resourceful and successful in penetrating the ideas and systems and allegiances of these peoples than the West. It follows from all this that the West can no longer be smug and self-satisfied about itself, that it must undergo an experience of profound humility, and that it must honestly search into the strengths of Communism and the causes of its own present predicament.

The third set of challenges comes from the newly awakened

peoples of Asia and Africa. These peoples have three basic things in
common: most of them were until recently ruled or dominated by
Western peoples; their countries are for the most part underdeveloped; and their ancient and profound cultures are quite distinct both from the culture of the West and the culture of
Communism.

What do these peoples really want? They want to rule themselves;
they want sovereign equality; they want to develop their countries
economically and culturally; they want national freedom so that
they can develop their own national genius in their own way. They
do *not* want to be embroiled in great power conflicts; they crave an
international order of peace, because only under such an order can
they realize their national aspirations.

The challenge which Asia and Africa pose to the West is this:
can you really leave us in peace to develop ourselves as we please?
Can you really treat us—juridically, morally, humanly—as your
equals? If it were a matter of choice for us, could you really
compete on every level with the Communist ideology and technique
in the solution of our problems? Even if we are unable to articulate
them, even if we should rebel were they to be articulated for us,
are you really able to meet our deep intellectual and spiritual needs?
In all these matters, therefore, it is not a question of vague wishes
and fraternal sentimentality; it is a question of fundamental
existential ability.

These three challenges mutually determine one another. Thus, the
inner problems of Western development determine the development
both of Communism and of Asia and Africa; the development of
Communism brings about necessary responses both in Western and
Eastern societies; and the rise of Asian and African nationalism
presents both opportunities and challenges to Communism and the
West alike.

The businessman is thrown into the midst of this threefold
challenge. He must adjust at once to the forces of his own society,
to the dynamic character of Communism everywhere, and to the
rapidly growing requirements of the underdeveloped world, which
constitutes at least two thirds of humanity.

THE INNER CHALLENGE

The businessman—in the widest sense, not only of middleman, but also of producer and of servant—is primarily interested in the production of good products or services that will sell. On this depends his profit or remuneration. The goodness of the product or service presupposes some objective standard. This objective standard of excellence is not found everywhere; it is found only in the living traditions of science, technology, the professions, and the arts. The cumulative tradition of craftsmanship goes back in some cases thousands of years. But the public, on whose tastes and wants business depends, can be counted on in the long run to discriminate, through some innate capacity, between the good and the poor performance, between the good and the cheap product. There are two tyrants over all business: the objective standard of excellence embedded in the nature of things, and mankind's natural ability not so much to discover as to discriminate and recognize this standard when it sees it in actuality.

When, therefore, business speaks of itself as the servant of the public, it is too modest about its claims. In truth, both it and the public are servants of the objective standard of excellence which business, through its accomplished art, discovers and actualizes, and the public, through its innate power, recognizes and is grateful for. We are all servants not of one another but of the good.

"Then What?"

The production and improvement of goods and services is in the nature of the case endless, so there will never come a time when new and better things in all fields will not be created. With respect to the multiplication and perfection of material things, there seems to be no limit to human inventiveness.

This unlimited power of man to invent and create, this infinite capacity of the material world to be reformed and redirected, this perfect readiness of the forces of nature to disclose themselves in all their beauty and usefulness and terror to the disciplined mind— all this bespeaks a profound and great mystery. He who misses the religious significance of this fascinating material civilization, with its multifarious goods and gadgets, misses the heart of the matter.

For man and nature are perfectly made for each other: nature to serve man and man to exploit nature.

The Communist stops there. But those of us who belong to the older traditions cannot possibly stop there. For we say: it is wonderful in itself that nature is so perfectly suited to serve man; it is wonderful in itself that man is so inventive, so remarkably the master of nature. What is even more wonderful is the question: *after* nature has completely yielded all its secrets to man, *after* every human want and desire is fully satisfied, *after* man has fully exercised his powers in the understanding and mastery of nature, then what? Then boredom, ennui, futility, utter loneliness, absolute darkness? The culture in which business has flourished to such an amazing degree cannot possibly accept this answer.

The question "then what?" does not refer to a far-off event. It is fundamentally the question as to whether business is its own end. If nature is for the sake of man, the question naturally arises, then man is for the sake of what? Is he for the sake of himself alone? This is the answer of Communism and of Western secularism. But if the Western businessman is fully aware of his own roots and the roots of his culture he cannot possibly give this answer. It is at this point that the total perspective of Communism's challenge to the businessman really begins to open up.

THE COMMUNIST CHALLENGE

Here I rule out war as a means of meeting the Communist challenge. I speak only of peaceful competition. Unless one understands the challenge as a peaceful one—as one that cannot and should not be settled by war—and unless one is certain of meeting it and in fact plans to meet it under conditions of peace, one is not entitled even to think of war. If there is such a thing as a right to war, we can lay down the maxim: he alone has a right to war who has made full use of his right to peace.

Western business, in the widest sense of free enterprise, has created an exceeding abundance of consumer goods. Western society has a much higher standard of living than any other society in the world. Whether Communist society can overtake and surpass Western society in this respect remains to be seen.

But in the field of scientific and technological development and research there is a most serious competition with the West. The challenge here appears to be that unless the effort at the formation of scientists and technicians and at the promotion of pure and applied research is considerably intensified, the West is heading toward an inferior position in the foreseeable future. This is then the first dimension of the challenge: the field of sheer scientific research and development. This may, of course, be due more to the great scientific genius of the Russian people, who can boast of one of the richest of scientific traditions, than to any creative merits of Marxism and Communism.

A second dimension arises from the question of coordination. There are strict principles of coordination imposed and observed in Communism. The state plans the economic development according to a system of priorities and assigns productive tasks to the diverse sectors of the economy. There is on the whole no such overriding, unified, conscious planning in the West. The Western businessman carries out his planning with four considerations in mind: the inner, autonomous laws of development of his own particular skill; the possibilities of the market; the requirements of competition with other branches of the same skill; and the requirements of competition with other sectors of the economy. In all this there is of course a principle of coordination at work, but it works in an atmosphere of freedom without imposition from the state.

The challenge of coordination consists in whether the requirements of the whole—and "the whole" in a fast-shrinking world must mean more than the whole of the nation; it must mean and it will increasingly mean the whole of the world—should not be actively kept in mind, whether or not it is the government that "actively keeps them in mind" or some independent agency in which all businesses participate voluntarily. A tendency has been developing toward closer consultation and association among diverse businesses, and at times even toward agreement. Governments everywhere are taking greater interest in and placing greater orders with private businesses of one kind or another.

If the moment should come when the strict rigidity of Communist state planning relaxes into autonomous business associations (there is some evidence that this rigidity is relaxing), and if the tendency toward closer business coordination in the West continues (it appears that there are compulsions working in that direction), then at some indefinite point in the future the two systems, so far as what is strictly economic in them is concerned, might approach each other. Because freedom is ultimate, the ideal is not for the state to dispense freedom as a grant and a gift, for then it would have the right to withdraw it; the ideal is for original freedom to limit itself in the interest of the whole. This is the real challenge of Communism to the businessman as far as the matter of coordination is concerned.

Is Business Enough?

The ideological challenge is deeper and greater than either the technological or the economic. The Communist has a revolutionary vision of society; it is a potent vision of which he is fully conscious, and it colors all his actions and thoughts. The question therefore arises whether the businessman should not have a revolutionary vision of his own, whether business alone is sufficient for the human being who is a businessman.

A Communist may be an engineer, a physician, a technician, or a manager of some business; on top of all that he is, perhaps primarily, a Communist. He believes firmly in something concerning the nature of things: concerning man, society, the process of history, and the things that, according to him, ultimately matter. He tries to live what he believes and to relate everything that he does to it. The question therefore arises: beyond engaging in business, what else is a businessman? This is a very important question, for in this fearful age the real competition is not so much in material things as in fundamental convictions. He alone has a right to be heard and respected who really believes in something, something fundamental and deep and true.

The Communist claims that his interpretation of life embraces everybody, so he articulates a message for the man in the jungles of Africa, for the peasant in the heart of India, and for the worker in Boston. Can the businessman claim that he has a universal message? In this fearful age it is not enough to be happy and prosperous and secure yourselves. It is not enough to tell others: look at us, how happy we are; just copy our system, our know-how, and you will be happy yourselves. In this fearful age you must transcend your system; you must have a message to proclaim to others; you must mean something in terms of ideas and attitudes and a fundamental outlook on life. This something must vibrate with relevance to all conditions of men.

It will be remarked that one is expecting too much from the businessman; that after all he is engaged in a very modest undertaking; and that this message, this radiant outlook of which I speak, should rather devolve on other members of society, on the thinkers, the educators, the statesmen, the men of religion. This is partly true. But business is one of the main pillars, if not the main pillar, of Western society. America is as much known abroad by its industry and its products as by anything else. In fact, business is so dominant that the thinker, the educator, the statesman, and the man of religion often use business terms in the articulation of their message.

Hence the question whether the businessman should mean something beyond his business is most important. The challenge which Communism poses to the businessman is a challenge not only with respect to the quality of the product and the nature of the national economy, but a challenge with respect to the quality of life of the businessman himself. The day when the American, the European, the Asian, or the African can live by himself is gone. Today we all live more or less uncomfortably in one another's presence, and in the silent accounting which we thereby give of ourselves, we necessarily disclose what we really are, what we really believe. Nothing is more important in this age in which we are all really on the spot than to probe deeply not only into our worth as professionals or specialists but also into our worth and our meaning as human beings. Thank God our essential humanity is pressing, pressing from every side to assert itself.

Laying the Foundation

There are only two sources for the formation of mind and character: formal education and general experience. This is as true of the businessman as of any other person.

If the businessman is really to cope with the comprehensive Communist challenge, both of these sources must provide him with the necessary equipment. First, he must be grounded more deeply in general education. There is increasing recognition of this necessity in the curricula of the business schools. But the challenge is so big that the time and effort devoted to these subjects is not enough; about twice as much time and effort is needed. History and government are, of course, necessary topics, but in addition the businessman must receive a firm grounding in international relations, philosophy, geopolitics, and what might be termed comparative culture. The important thing is so to enlarge and deepen the mind, so to sharpen it in the power of argument, so to furnish it with generic true ideas, as to enable it to confute error and sophistry and to lay hold on what is true in every situation and relate it to first principles. Nothing is more needed than a consummate power of articulation, both in thought and action, with respect to the fundamentals of life.

General experience takes one into the open spaces of Western free culture: into its movies and television, its books and magazines, its religious experience, its family traditions, its general mores, its national and social customs, the whole conscious and unconscious tonality which constitutes the spirit of an age. Does Western culture provide the businessman with an adequate outlook to meet the challenge of Communism? If the businessman and the Communist meet a neutral, that is to say, one who is equally open to both, which will impress the neutral more? This is a crucial question, but the argument forces us to raise it. Everything about Western culture is in the balance today.

I believe there is such an infinite wealth of truth and being in Western culture that it will be only the fault of the businessman or of his upbringing if he does not impress the neutral more.

THE CHALLENGE OF THE NEUTRALS

It is in the non-Western, non-Communist areas of the world that the battle for the souls of men is most intense. These areas cover more than half of the human race. It is among these uncommitted peoples that the culture of the West is particularly called to assess its worth.

Economic and technical assistance, both governmental and private, is desperately needed all over these areas. No country in history has been more generous in this respect than the United States. The reward has been some stability, some advancement of human welfare, some friendship, some economic advantage. And in certain cases the alternative would have been something close to chaos.

It is true that the concept of the Marshall Plan may not be quite adequate to these regions. In this case, a new concept suited to local needs must be developed. There is no reason why the Middle East, for instance, should not work out much bolder schemes of development for itself than it has done so far. There are five conditions for the possibility of any Western participation in these schemes: the Middle East—I am using the Middle East only as an example— must be its own undisputed master in the planning and execution of these schemes; the West must come to a stable understanding with the vigorous nationalism of the area; the Western countries must not undermine and intrigue against each other; room must be left for possible Soviet participation; any participation must be politically unconditioned. Valuable suggestions have been made in this respect by President Eisenhower in his July 1958 speech before the United Nations.

There are continuities of culture, race, and economic conditions between the Communist realm and the adjacent areas. Such continuities do not exist between the West and those areas. Herein lies one of the greatest handicaps for the West and consequently for the businessman. The whole notion of business does not apply: what applies is total planning on a national scale. In many instances the Communist is one of the people, whereas the businessman is alien. How to develop men who will not go to these cultures to establish purely external relations with them and then retire abroad, but who either arise from native soil or completely identify themselves with the destiny of these countries and die in them and with them and for them, is one of the deepest problems facing the Western world today. Imperialism means primarily alienism, the relationship of a man who exploits you and does not identify himself with your condition and fate. This is the great problem of whether the West is sufficient unto itself, or whether it has a genuinely universal message.

The principle of freedom and independence is one of the most dynamic principles in the world today. This is partly an American contribution. People most certainly desire to be free and independent, but they also crave fellowship. And they care only for that kind of fellowship in which they are respected as human beings and treated as equals, in which they remain free and independent. Freedom, independence, respect, equality, fellowship—these spring from the inmost soul of the Western tradition. The question is whether the West can be existentially true to them. There is in the faithful observance of these things all and more that is needed to meet the challenge of Communism.

The New Materialism

The businessman is judged by more than his product and his performance: his humanity is at stake. Rising above his individual interests to the proper consideration of the common good and soaring even beyond the common good to the spiritual significance of his wondrous material civilization, the businessman can clothe his humanity with a shining new splendor. He will put to shame every culture that ends in boredom, self-sufficiency, and human pride. His spiritualized materialism will have something profound to say and give to all men. He will identify himself with their human state. He will be proud of his business and its achievements, but he will be even prouder of that which is beyond business in his culture. He will say, "Let others compete with me in material things and let them even excel, but there is one thing in which they cannot excel because they do not know it and are not even seeking it. That is the power and depth and freedom of the spirit in which man is fully himself." In this way Communism's challenge to the businessman will turn into the businessman's challenge to Communism.

Twenty-seven years ago, Alfred North Whitehead delivered a lecture at the Harvard Business School. All I have said in this chapter is mere commentary on one sentence from that lecture, and this sentence has been my text. "A great society," said Whitehead, "is a society in which its men of business think greatly of their functions." *

* *Adventures of Ideas* (New York, The Macmillan Company, 1933), p. 124.

THE BUSINESSMAN OF THE FUTURE

Stanley F. Teele

IN THE YEARS AHEAD many issues and problems will confront Western man in general and the American businessman in particular. The risks and dangers which we face are widely different in character and range around the entire world. What kind of businessmen do we need to meet these challenges?

Many highly competent and well-informed people hold that the businessman of the future should not charge himself with responsibility for much beyond the competent, profitable operation of his individual enterprise. The reasoning of those who hold this view runs in essence as follows:

(1) The successful long-run operation of our individual business enterprises is of the utmost importance to our society.

(2) The successful long-run operation of the modern business enterprise is so complex and difficult that it calls for the very highest competence available.

(3) Therefore, the risk of diversion of skill and highly valuable

Note: Mr. Teele is Dean of the Harvard Business School.

talents from the internal problems of an enterprise to the broader problems of our society as a whole is too great to be accepted.

While I agree completely with the first two steps in this analysis, I find myself unable to accept the conclusion. Asking businessmen to take on broader problems and broader responsibilities while continuing to improve and develop skills in internal management is expecting a great deal. It does, in fact, involve real risks, but the stakes are so high, the potential value to our society in a time of succeeding crises so great, that I am prepared to face the risks. To me, better solutions to the problems of the decades ahead represent just such high stakes.

Nor do I believe that wider responsibility for businessmen entails as great a risk of poor internal management as is sometimes alleged. When I consider how much the businessman has developed during the past 50 years, how many added complexities in business operation he has absorbed, I find myself greatly assured as to his capacity to undertake still more.

THE THREE R'S OF MANAGEMENT

Shortly after the establishment of the Harvard Business School, President A. Lawrence Lowell first used the phrase: "Business— the oldest of the arts and the newest of the professions." Fifty years ago the element of fact in this statement was small—the element of hope large. Over this half century, a great deal has happened, and the amount of fact has grown considerably.

One important distinction should be made here. Business encompasses a host of activities, and to some degree all the professions— medicine, law, engineering—play prominent parts in business. Many men function in business by exercising a particular specialty; they make their contribution by reason of their specific knowledge or experience. We are indebted to the General Electric Company for a full exploration of this important distinction with the consequent classification of all employees as either "managers" or "individual contributors." What we have in mind when we speak of the profession of business is really the profession of business management, excluding the very large number of people who make their contributions as individuals rather than as managers.

What then do we need to do to move further toward a profession of business management? I believe we must move toward more rational managers, more responsible managers, and more religious managers. These are the three R's of professional management.

Rational Managers

More rational managers should be the product of three major developments: more use of research; more adaptation of the methods of the sciences; and, most important of all, greater use of the tools of the discipline of logic. In the whole managerial process of detecting problems, gathering facts as to their nature, formulating alternative courses of action, gathering testimony as to their relative effectiveness, ordering and weighing evidence, reaching conclusions, transforming conclusions into decisions, and putting decisions into effect, these three developments can and should make major contributions which will be of real help to managers.

There are, of course, in business, a great array of problems and issues. With respect to some of these, facts lie close at hand. With respect to others, facts are available if sought diligently and skillfully. And with respect to still others, few facts can be obtained, at least within tolerable limits of time and money.

The utilization of mathematical-statistical methods, the rapid refinement of equipment for high-speed processing of information, the adaptation of a variety of research methods in the physical sciences to problems in business management are all important parts of the process to which I refer. Nevertheless, the steady increase in the habit of seeking facts and ways to relate facts to each other and to the whole situation will be far more important. Repeatedly in recent years when I have investigated the process of arriving at decisions in forward-looking companies, I have been struck by the extent to which major new developments have been adaptations from the discipline of logic. These adaptations have provided new and helpful ways of organizing and weighing pertinent available facts.

The push toward more rational management in the years ahead will take place within the framework of developments which obviously will affect the job of the manager in several significant ways. For example:

> An accelerating rate of change characterizes many parts of our life. We are accustomed to think of change with respect to industry

and technology. We often see the effects of new products, new processes, new sources of power, new methods of communication and transportation. But it is not only by technological changes that the job of the business manager will be affected. It is probable that the rate of change in American agriculture is even greater than in industry. The population explosion common to almost all parts of the world and the world-wide trend toward metropolitan areas also provide constantly new circumstances within which the business manager must operate.

In the years ahead, therefore, there will be an added premium on imagination, flexibility, and the capacity to devise answers to questions which have never before been asked. The effective business manager will need to find ways to operate in a team while at the same time preserving conditions which encourage individual imagination and mental flexibility. This will be no easy task, as Arnold J. Toynbee points out.*

Responsible Managers

During the last business generation we have seen a widespread acceptance of the concept that business managers have responsibilities toward stockholders, employees, customers, suppliers, and society as a whole. This has undoubtedly resulted in part at least from the steady and extensive separation of ownership from management over the last 50 years. It is a fact that a very high proportion of American business activity is directed and guided by men who do not hold their managerial positions because of ownership of the enterprise. To some observers this development of the manager divorced from ownership is one of the most important economic and social developments of our period.

The more responsible manager accepts his responsibility to his company but goes on to accept still further responsibilities with respect to the goals and methods of our society as a whole. Here, of course, the businessman blends into the citizen. But, since business is central to our society, it seems to me that the businessman has a special and central responsibility as a citizen.

At this point I should like to propose an attitude which should

* See the chapter entitled, "How Did We Get This Way—And Where Are We Going?" p. 3.

characterize the responsible business manager. Successful American business enterprises have uniformly approached their problems with a few basic principles to which they hold tenaciously, while preserving a flexible, pragmatic attitude toward the definition and solution of problems. It seems to me that the businessman should use this same approach when thinking about the problems of government or of a society as a whole. We shall face dozens of new questions of relationships between government and business and between business and other organized segments of the society. The budding space agency alone will give birth to dozens of such questions, just as the Atomic Energy Commission did. Similarly, our continuing contest with Russian Communsm will repeatedly pose problems where novel arrangements between government and business will be called for. Donald K. David has described such an imaginative development.* The responsible business manager of the future should not let his attitude toward such problems be completely governed by shibboleths and slogans but should take a hardheaded, practical, realistic look at the nature of each problem, at the gains to be secured, at the risks to be run, and then make his judgment and exercise his influence in the direction of that judgment.

Religious Managers

I have used the word religious in describing the third R of professional management with some trepidation. I know I run the risk of being misunderstood, for the word may call to mind either denominational dogma or a picture of a wishy-washy do-gooder seeking to escape from the realities of business life. Yet I can find no other term which conveys the thought important to me.

Two pressing concerns account for this emphasis: our competition with Communism and the Soviet Union and our own long-range national goals, which stand quite apart from any immediate crisis. Since I am convinced that this competition will continue to be the decisive fact of the world for many years to come, it seems clear that no one can think about the future and the men who will manage it without making some presumptions and drawing some hypotheses about that relationship.

* See the chapter entitled "The New Relationship of Business to Society," p. 66.

I believe that Russia will take major military action only if she finds herself in one of two situations: either the odds on her victory are so heavy as to reduce the element of risk to a very low level, or internal difficulties make a foreign war appear the lesser of two evils to the men in the Kremlin. Since I see little likelihood of that kind of internal crisis or of such overwhelming odds on a Russian victory in a war, the focal point of the competition will be in nonmilitary areas. Our policy, in fact, has been to keep it there, and we shall continue to pursue such a course, staying close enough to the Russians in military capacity to keep the odds on their victory narrow and the ultimate outcome of a war in doubt. This, then, is our policy in the military area. It is clear-cut and understandable.

But what is our strategy for the nonmilitary competition with the Soviets?

We talk about "besting" them, but besting them at what? What constitutes a victory—a success—in this field? What are we trying to do better than they? Personally, I am troubled by our apparent continued emphasis on material progress alone as the measure of success or failure in this kind of competition. Is it really true that our system is better only because it turns out more goods, or has created a higher standard of living, or is further advanced technologically? If so, Sputnik, Soviet accomplishments in a host of scientific fields, and the extraordinary rate of recent Russian economic progress should stir real doubts in our hearts and our minds about the supremacy of this pathway.

We are falling into a trap of our own making; we have become so impressed by the world's reaction to our tremendous material progress that there is risk that we shall consider this the true measure of our greatness and the most important contribution which we have made and can make to the world. In our hearts we know better; we know that the demonstration of how 170 million people can live together in peace, with basic goals of human dignity, morality, and justice, is our real contribution.

What does the danger that we shall misinterpret our role to ourselves and to the world mean to the business manager? Since national goals are the bundling together of the goals of individuals and organizations, it means a great deal. It means that the objectives which the business executive of the future establishes for his company are going to be the raw material from which the nation will fashion its own purposes both in the competition with the Russians and in its constant forward movement into territory the like of which man has never seen.

Already we are groping toward these new beacons. We have not yet clearly formulated or articulated them, but we have reached the point where we are not entirely satisfied with the ones we have been using. We shall find what we are seeking when we begin to realize and admit to what we are already doing, to the direction the great changes of the last 50 years have taken, and to the kind of future to which they point. For we have been shifting steadily toward a reversal of the words we have continued to use in describing ourselves. We say that our system is great because it has created an incredible standard of living and has thus provided each individual with the possibilities for personal development to the outer reaches of his own abilities; but what we have been doing in our businesses is increasingly attempting to provide each individual with the possibilities for personal development to the outer reaches of his own abilities, and thereby creating an incredible standard of living.

The evidence seems to me to be accumulating that the very great strength of Russian Communism rests on what is essentially a religious attitude, calling for unity, for the development of common purpose, for effort and self-sacrifice with the resulting satisfaction that comes from the sense of making a real contribution to the achievement of an important goal.

With a completely different concept of the purpose of life, a completely different economic, political, and social system, and an ideological framework which exalts rather than degrades the individual human being, we need today a corresponding fervor on the part of our business managers. The plain and simple fact is that the truly effective business manager in our society makes a major contribution to the welfare of both individuals and the society as a whole.

Thus, we need even more business managers in the future who will see clearly what has been happening and step forward to proclaim it with pride, who will sharpen their goals and those of their companies in terms of a society based on the dignity of the individual, and who will work for and speak for their beliefs and their purposes with truly religious zeal and fervor. In short, we need businessmen who will reassert the traditional American national purpose and work to implement it with skill, energy, and enthusiasm.

AMERICA'S MISSION IN A NEW SOCIETY

Richard M. Nixon

IN THE CRITICAL YEARS that face us, years in which the destiny of the world will be shaped for decades to come, our success or failure will be determined in the realm of ideas. If this is to be the area of decision, it is essential that we constantly re-examine our fundamental beliefs to see if they actually can prevail.

Judging the worth of our American idea solely in terms of results, we can point to a record of economic progress unsurpassed in world history. In the last 50 years our gross national product has quadrupled. Translating this dramatic figure into individual terms we find that:

- Per capita income has increased from $188 to $2,032 a year.
- The number of home owners has risen from 7 to 30 million.
- The annual production of automobiles has increased from 4,000 to as many as 7 million.

Note: Mr. Nixon is the Vice President of the United States.

48

- The number of refrigerators in use has climbed from 23,000 to 47 million.
- Primary and secondary school attendance has increased from 7 to 40 million.
- Child labor has been abolished.
- Eighty-six per cent of our labor force has been covered by the Social Security program.

We have not reached the goal Theodore Roosevelt set forth 50 years ago, in his Square Deal speech at Osawatomie, Kansas—to give every American an equal place at the starting line—but we have made more progress toward that objective than anyone dreamed possible. Ironic though it is, of all the great industrial nations, the strongest defender of private capitalism is the one that has come closest to achieving the socialist goal of prosperity for all in a classless society. We have achieved the benefits of wide distribution claimed by socialism, while avoiding the controls and restrictions on freedom inherent in a socialist system. And this happened not because we took from the rich and gave to the poor, but because we gave everyone an opportunity to share in a constantly increasing pool of wealth.

IDEALISM VERSUS MATERIALISM

I recognize that among some of the critics of our much-maligned "affluent society" it has become something of a fashion to deplore and condemn the mere conveniences of living as though these necessarily precluded the successful achievement of our real and proper aim—the full realization of the physical, mental, and spiritual capacity of every individual. Self-examination of this character is healthy and constructive in a free society, but I submit that few Americans are actually interested in material things as ends in themselves. We know that material well-being and spiritual and cultural achievement are related (it is as true today as when the Roman poet said it 2,000 years ago that man must first eat before he can become a philosopher) but we could make no stupider blunder than to rest our case on materialism alone. This is all that our opponents have to offer. We have much more.

The Soviet tourists now visiting our country may be impressed by our skyscrapers, our beautiful automobiles, and our comfortable and even luxurious homes. But they will see more than this if they wish. They can see the throngs that go to our churches to worship God in freedom. They can observe the evenhanded justice of our courts of law. They can read our free press, attend free trade union meetings, and watch our preparations for free elections. They can visit our schools and universities, where the only restraint is the restraint of conscientious searching for the truth.

Unfortunately, they can also see and read things that will confirm some of the charges that have been leveled against us. They will read of gangsters in some labor unions, of the bitter struggle for racial justice, of our concern over rising rates of crime and delinquency. But if they read wisely they will see that these events are news precisely *because* the moral conscience of America is rebelling against injustice and discrimination. We believe it is morally wrong for hoodlums to rob the American worker. We fight for racial justice because our religious faith, our traditions of freedom, and a decent regard for our fellow man cannot tolerate discrimination against any minority group.

No one can objectively view these struggles for right and justice without concluding that ours is a nation in which idealism rather than materialism is the dominant national characteristic.

The Spirit of Nationalism

If our case is basically so good, why are we on the defensive in so many areas of the world? It is superficial and inaccurate to contend that if it were not for the Communists we would not have this problem. Communism is one of the major forces opposing us in the world today, but confusing it with other and different forces does not help us in fighting it. One of those drives is the powerful spirit of nationalism in the developing countries of the world.

It is ironic in the extreme that the United States should ever be cast in the role of opposing legitimate nationalist movements. Many of the ideas which motivate today's nationalists stem from American history and have been taught in American universities at home and abroad. These ideas of freedom, democracy, and independence are now at work in other parts of the world, but unfortunately we find that they are sometimes used against us. There is no reason why this should be so; on the contrary, *we* rather than the Soviet Union should be the natural champion of legitimate nationalist movements.

Through all our history, America's leaders have recognized that the principles on which the United States was founded—freedom, equality, and constitutionalism—have universal validity and applicability. The rights we have defended are natural rights which come from God. In this sense, America indeed has a mission and a destiny: to defend, preserve, and extend the rights of man. If America makes this clear we shall receive the support of most of the people of the world.

The ideas of our Bill of Rights and our Declaration of Independence are the most exciting in history. It is time we recognized that these ideas are still on the march. Let us make sure we are marching with them and not against them.

What, then, is the major reason for the Communist appeal in the world today? Its appeal does not lie in the Marxist philosophy as such, but rather in the fact that Communism appears to be on the march, advocating and promising change, despite all its evils.

Our answer then must be to talk less of the threat of a Communist revolution and more of the promise of the American Revolution. This is what the world wants to hear. We have nothing to fear if we remain true to the best elements in our tradition.

The Communist world has made gains, but at the cost of inhuman sacrifices and of moral and spiritual values. It is significant to note that they are sending their experts here to learn our methods. The most recent changes in Russia, Poland, and Yugoslavia have been in the direction of increased incentive and decreased state controls. They have gained partly because they are moving our way. If we lose it will be because we move their way.

Our Living Heritage

The course we should follow if we are to win the ideological battle is therefore clear. We must revive to the fullest our pioneer spirit of adventure and growth—the vision that developed a continent. We must give the lie to the Communist charges that we are a decadent people, that we are going down while they are going up. We must make known throughout the world the exciting fact that the American Revolution, which captured the imagination of the world 180 years ago, did not end at Yorktown but is a living, vital idea today, an idea which we believe can best satisfy the aspirations of people for economic progress, individual freedom, and national independence.

The solution to the problem we face is not to be found simply in better information and propaganda. In the words of Hegel, "Nations are what their deeds are." And a nation is strong only when it is engaged in realizing great objectives. Once it loses its sense of mission, its days are numbered.

I suggest that we examine the American idea in the light of these considerations to see if it has the vitality and drive to prevail. In so doing, what are the dangers we must guard against and the goals we should seek to attain?

Let us recognize at the outset that we shall not win this battle by standing still. We are ahead now, but the only way to stay ahead is to move ahead. Let it not be said of our generation that we set as our goal simply holding our own. Let us resist the temptation to be satisfied by merely putting another guard on the cash box. Let us, on the contrary, boldly expand our heritage to new heights both materially and spiritually. Standpat, defensive thinking is not adequate for the challenge we face either at home or abroad.

TOWARD A DYNAMIC ECONOMY

To carry on this battle in the world market place of ideas, however, we must maintain the growth and stability of our domestic economy. There are three specific economic problems in which government must play a part if we are to push forward with the vigor and boldness the times require.

Alleviating Unemployment

A dynamic and growing economy is bound to cause hardships to some of the people involved in the process of change. As new businesses come into being and others grow, some will be replaced. In a free economy we must expect readjustments from time to time, which will mean temporary unemployment for some American working men and women.

With these facts in mind, consideration should be given to instituting permanent reforms in our system of unemployment insurance. Specifically:

- To the extent feasible, the 12 million workers who are not now covered should be brought under our unemployment compensation system.
- The prolongation of benefit periods now in effect as a temporary measure should be made permanent.
- The federal and state governments should work together to establish higher minimum standards for the level of benefits, their duration, and their coverage.

These proposals are sound not only for reasons of plain humanity, but also because the flow of income provided by more adequate unemployment compensation serves to cushion the impact of the business cycle. The faster we carry out this basic reform, the greater our assurance that occasional setbacks in economic activity will remain brief and mild.

Curbing Inflation

A second major economic problem is inflation. When we look into the causes of inflation we find three main areas that must be watched closely: the monetary and fiscal policies of government, the cost and price policies of business, and the impact of wage demands on costs and prices.

The $12 billion deficit in the 1958–1959 federal budget is a major inflationary factor. We must learn that we cannot add new programs to the federal budget unless we are prepared to levy the taxes to pay for them. Inflationary pressures are also created by the excessive use of private credit. We must follow credit policies which will prevent these inflationary excesses to the extent possible.

It is completely unrealistic, however, to assume that inflation can be controlled entirely by the monetary policies of the Federal Reserve System or the spending policies of the federal government. Business also has a job to do. It must resist upward pressures on cost, it must redouble its efforts to cut down on waste and to find real economies in production and distribution, and above all, it must have the daring and imagination to price for volume sales with low unit profits.

Organized labor has a responsibility in this area, too. During the postwar years labor sought and received large wage increases in order to keep up with inflation. The momentum of this process continued during years when the consumer price level was stable, and produced the upward push of costs on prices that was an important factor in the inflationary trend starting in late 1955. The remedy for this situation most consistent with our free institutions is self-discipline at the bargaining table. Unless we apply this medicine the pressure from consumers for government action to control inflation will become irresistible. There will also be strong demands to control by law those union activities that are monopolistic in character. This can be avoided if our union leaders are guided in their contract negotiations by the basic principle that wage increases which force price increases are not in the best interests of union members themselves.

Decreasing the Tax Burden

Our third major economic problem is that of tax reform. In the light of our expected continuing need for funds, this appears to be a completely academic question. But here we are faced by a dilemma. If we wait for needed tax reform until we believe we can afford a tax cut, our economy will have been denied a vitally needed stimulus for growth.

The importance of economic growth to our fiscal position is indicated by the fact that if our economy were to grow at the rate of 5% a year we would have $10 billion more in tax receipts in 1962 than if it were to continue to grow at the recent rate of 1½%.

Consequently, I suggest the following proposals not as administration policy but as areas that should have top priority for consideration by the administration and by Congress:

(In this day of rapid technological change we need more liberal treatment of depreciation for business taxation purposes. Only in this way can we stimulate businessmen to take risks by investing in new plant and equipment.

(We should consider the economic effects of downward adjustments in business taxes. There are strong reasons to believe that the stimulus of even a small cut in the corporate tax rate of 52% would lead to more, rather than less, revenue.

(Consideration should also be given to a complete overhauling of the present hodgepodge of excise taxes. If the taxes on liquor and cigarettes are left as they are, a general manufacturers' excise tax of approximately 1½% would bring in as much revenue as we presently realize from all other excise taxes.

❡ In the area of personal income the almost confiscatory rates in the highest brackets stifle and prevent risk taking and encourage tax dodging. The small loss of revenue caused by some reduction of these rates would inevitably be offset by the new investment and business expansion which would result.

The charge will inevitably be made that such reforms will benefit business and not the people. But let us understand once and for all that "business is the people." The people own it, and their ownership is becoming ever more widely diffused. They make their living out of business. They depend on business for progress, for opportunity, for their mutual well-being, and for the development and production of the military equipment which shields the nation against aggression.

Prosperity for the American people is inseparable from prosperity for American business. We cannot raise the floor of security unless we raise the ceiling of opportunity. The best way for the American people to improve their living standard is through policies that promote maximum business growth.

In summary, we must not allow the fear of a temporary budget deficit to put us in a strait jacket that will keep us from doing what we ought to do to ensure economic growth. Our goal should be to fashion a tax structure that will create more jobs, more income, and genuine security.

NEW FRONTIERS

The exciting potentials of a dynamic, growing American economy are almost unbelievable.

A $750 billion gross national product is within our reach by 1975 if we grow at the rate of 3%, and by 1968 if we can increase our growth rate to 5%. Completing our 41,000-mile interstate highway system, doubling the facilities of our colleges and universities, eliminating the pockets of poverty that trouble the conscience of a rich nation, restoring the vitality and beauty of our cities through urban renewal—all these goals are attainable within this generation. And when we consider the explosive progress which will result from expanded research in industry, medicine, and other areas, the prospects are breath-taking.

But exciting as these prospects are, the greatest goal of all lies in the international area. Arnold J. Toynbee wrote in 1951 that 300 years from now this bloody twentieth century will be remembered not for its splitting of the atom, or for its diminutions of distance and disease, or even for its shattering wars, but for "having been the first age since the dawn of civilization in which people dared to think it practicable to make the benefits of civilization available to the whole human race." * This is the ultimate challenge for us in the last half of the twentieth century.

Modern-day Malthusians to the contrary, if our statesmen and businessmen can keep pace with the breakthroughs of our scientists, the last half of the twentieth century will see us approach the realization of this objective. The critical question is: will this progress be achieved in a climate of freedom or in a climate of slavery?

No people could have a greater mission than to play a part in seeing that the decision is made on the side of freedom. It is not enough to say that this responsibility rests with our statesmen and diplomats. It is not enough to increase, as we should, our pitifully inadequate appropriations for developmental loans, technical assistance, and information. To win this struggle, our national effort must be as total as the Communist effort.

No effort in a free nation can be total without a maximum contribution from the business community. The Harvard Business School can be proud of the contribution its graduates have made to the nation in the School's first 50 years. If the American businessman takes to heart Donald David's admonition "to weld to his economic prowess a similar drive, skill, and creativity in his dangerously neglected social and political function in society," † 50 years from now we may realize the ultimate dream of America and of mankind.

* *New York Times Magazine,* October 21, 1951, p. 15.
† See the chapter entitled "The New Relationship of Business to Society," p. 66.

THE NEW AMERICAN CAPITALISM

H. Gardiner Symonds

ONE OF THE UNIQUE FEATURES of our American capitalism lies in the fascination it has for all kinds of people. Countless specialists and laymen both here and abroad have our economy under their magnifying glasses. The American system is studied with intense interest and unwavering, fixed attention, as if it were a new germ or chemical element. Its temperature is taken. It is graphed and charted. Facts are accumulated on the gross national product and the productivity index of such key items as steel. Continual indices are put together on the cost of living, the number of employed and unemployed, and the stock market. Even the voters get into the act, for national elections are won or lost by whether times are good or bad.

CAPITALISM—THEN AND NOW

Yet it is not our economic system itself which generally gets the major attention, but its results. So first let us take a fairly brief and

Note: Mr. Symonds is President of the Tennessee Gas Transmission Company.

panoramic look at what we might call the results, or visible aspects, of the Old Capitalism as it was when the Harvard Business School was founded in 1908. Then let us compare them with the results or visible aspects of our 1958 economic system, the New Capitalism.

To Those Who Have . . .

In 1908 business was capitalistic in the old sense of the word. The owners of companies, who had put up or obtained the capital to start their enterprises, in a great many cases ran them personally. While there were many corporations, some of which had several thousand stockholders, partnerships or family-owned businesses were much commoner. There was little in the way of either custom or law to restrain the proprietor from running his business as he pleased. It was a day of scanty reports to stockholders, or even in some cases no reports at all for several years at a time. Much of the information that corporations make public in a routine manner today was withheld 50 years ago as trade secrets that would benefit competitors. Capitalism was a free-swinging contest between opposing groups of owner-operators who sought the quickest possible profit without regard for the interest of society.

Government played a minor, almost negligible role in business. Although the Sherman Anti-Trust Act was in effect, it was narrowly interpreted and little enforced. The government was small in men, money, and powers. It was not the government but the great bankers of Wall Street, headed by J. Pierpont Morgan, who stepped in to restore confidence and end the 1907 bank panic; for in that day of unrestrained capitalism and individualistic, personally dominated businesses, bankers had much more power and prestige than now. Morgan, the most influential figure in the national economy 50 years ago, has no counterpart today. The great captains of industry, men like Rockefeller, Carnegie, and Harriman, dominated and enlivened the business world. Entrepreneurs, financiers, empire builders, they were renowned and admired for their drive, boldness, and creativeness. The Old Capitalism also had its inventive geniuses like Edison, Bell, and Ford. As a matter of fact, it was the year 1908 that saw the birth of the famous Model T.

In a day of the utmost business and economic freedom, even the most honest and morally upright of these great industrial leaders

appeared to believe in, and often acted to bring about, greater concentration of the fruits of the economic system. One of the most
striking features of the economic scene 50 years ago was this great
chasm between the small number of wealthy people and the many
poor ones.

The gap between the two classes was wide indeed, and we had
no large, moderately well-to-do middle class to serve as a bridge.
To illustrate:

> Some of the princely individual incomes of the time ranged
> above $20 million per year—and there was no income tax until
> 1913, so this was all "take-home pay." In contrast, the average work-
> er's wages were $400 to $500 a year by various estimates, although
> reliable statistics are lacking—and that was for a 10-hour day and
> 6-day week. Child labor was common. Immigrant labor, hitting a
> peak in 1907, flooded the country in excess of available jobs, put
> into operation what an early economist called the Iron Law of Wages,
> and tended to minimize wages. This flood of immigrant workers
> was one of the reasons why such organizations of labor as existed
> had little influence or power.

Viewed by today's lights, this all added up to a maldistribution
of the fruits of the economic system.

The Great Leveling

One of the most striking results of our economic system today is
that our citizens enjoy the most widely and probably the most equi-
tably distributed abundance the world has yet known. The years have
greatly narrowed the gap between rich and poor. Our economic pie
is being sliced more evenly, and its size has grown enormously, out-
stripping population growth. So, even in terms of constant dollars,
real income has grown and the national standard of living has risen.
This narrowing of income differences has been accompanied by an
even greater narrowing of ways of life. For example:

> In 1908 the rich man often lived in a magnificent mansion tended
> by a retinue of servants, entertained lavishly, went abroad, spent his
> vacations at spas. He wore silk hats, cutaway coats, and other attire
> of quality and good tailoring. He and his equally well-dressed wife
> were like beings from another world when they moved among
> groups of people with low incomes. The latter wore clothing ob-

viously inferior in material and cut, often with little regard for style.
Differing widely in background, education, customs, and thinking,
the rich and poor had little common meeting ground.

Today, the head of a company does not stand out in the crowd.
His employees' appearance is much like his own. His secretary's
frocks may be less expensive than his wife's, but they may well
follow the latest fashion more closely. Present-day Americans in
great numbers have not only the necessities but all the conveniences
of life and many of its luxuries within their reach. Good homes
with modern appliances, late-model automobiles, vacations in Florida
or California, even trips to Europe, are not exclusive prerogatives
of the wealthy. Rather, they are enjoyed by, or are within the reach
of, a very large part of the population.

This wiping out of differences in appearance and in other aspects
of life was more important than it might seem, for it presaged the
elimination of the classes themselves. In this respect as well as in
others, we have moved not toward socialism but on past socialism,
toward something better.

What has closed the chasm between the ways of life of the rich
and poor? I will list seven causes, and there probably are more:

(1) *The mass production and distribution of goods.* Makers and
sellers of luxury goods find it impossible to compete for the consumer dollar, luxury goods tend to disappear, and we all end up
buying the same thing—with certain exceptions, of course.

(2) *The spread of education.* We are witnessing a mass movement
of our youth into schools and colleges. Where fifty years ago only
one out of ten boys and girls of high school age went to high school,
eight or nine out of ten now do so, and there has been a 700%
increase in the number of students in college. This joint education
of students from homes of all income levels is itself a great leveler.

(3) *The universality of travel.* Country boys, traveling all over the
world in World Wars I and II, came back noticeably broadened
and educated.

(4) *The mass-communication media.* Magazines, movies, radio,
and television carry the same news, entertainment, and advertising to
practically everyone in the country, and make Americans more alike.

(5) *The disappearance of the servant class.* This has tended to
make every woman her own housemaid. (I might add that before we
bemoan our housewife's fate we should note that she often needs

to hire a mechanic or engineer to maintain the labor-saving devices in her home.)

(6) *The disappearance of "Society."* In its place is a fluid, rapidly changing number of little societies, groups of people who gather socially, bound by ties of occupation, religion, participation in social work, or other shared experiences. Change and informality are the rule of the day in most of these groups.

(7) *The trend toward informality.* This has almost become the common denominator of today's living. It is notable in men's and women's attire, in entertaining, in home life, and to some degree in business life. The wealthy have adopted it nearly as widely as those of lesser means.

WHAT'S NEW ABOUT IT?

We have taken a look at some of the most visible *results* of the Old Capitalism of 1908 and the New of 1958. Now let us turn to our New Capitalism itself. What are some of its essential new characteristics which we can identify?

The Young Giant

Sheer bigness of the economy is one of the New Capitalism's main characteristics, particularly in the market for goods. There are more people able to buy the things they need, or think they need, than in any country anywhere before. From a businessman's point of view, this means that if he invents a better mousetrap, and is tooled to mass production, he is likely to find himself moving an astronomical number of mousetraps.

Hand-in-hand with this bigness goes the marked complexity of the typical large business today. It is especially true of firms with diversified products and activities and with geographically widespread operations.

In such firms specialists are a necessity over a wide spectrum of operations—in fields such as taxes, accounting, finance, and economic forecasting; in law; in labor relations, public relations, and employee relations; and in dealings with government.

Team Operation

This leads me to my next characteristic of the New Capitalism: teamwork. We hear a great deal about the professional manager,

that interchangeable executive whose ability and skills are such that
he can switch from the top of Company A to the top of Company
B and run both equally well. There are such men, I know. But without detracting from their credit or reputation, I feel that perhaps
they are like the albino buffalo: famous, but uncommon.

Much more the mode in today's business is team operation. It
is the very antithesis of the personally run, one-strong-executive
business of the past. Today's company head leads and inspires, but
does not drive. He puts together a skilled management team and
builds it in depth. He manages, referees, pushes for unanimous
decisions, and sometimes has to cast the deciding vote.

Government in Business

We not only have a big, complex economy, but we also have an
equally big, complex government, which touches on and influences
the course of business in ways too numerous to count. Big government, like the New Capitalism, is different from anything we ever
had before. It is larger, more powerful, and continually growing.

That is partly due to the requirements of the cold war, our huge
defense effort, and the current competition to explore and perhaps
to occupy outer space. The complexity of our social system and our
increasing population and urbanization have brought problems
which seem almost insoluble except by a central government. For
example, the government has taken on, at least by implication, such
tasks as the prevention of depressions and the maintenance of employment on the one hand, and the stemming of inflation on the
other. Government maintains controls over business as a whole,
which it quickly extends in time of emergency or war, and somewhat less speedily relinquishes afterward. An example is price controls, kept in effect for about a year after World War II, each
month less successfully.

Our firm's business is almost continually involved with government on a broad front. We encounter many dedicated, able men in
government who are doing the best job they can and very likely the
best job anybody could do, but government is essentially politics,
and politics has been defined as the science of compromise. A natural
consequence is indecision, inaction, and complexity. For instance:

A tremendous volume of paper work is involved in projects which require applications to the government for authorization. At Tennessee Gas several groups of specialists, 30 or 40 people in all, work 10 to 14 days on the final stages of one of these applications, nearly day and night as the deadline approaches. As many as 3,750,000 sheets of paper have been used for a single multiple-copy filing and the required supporting exhibits, contracts, and studies. Furthermore, we have waited three years and more for decisions on major projects.

Today government extends so far, and the national debt is so huge, that questions with a vital bearing on the health of our New Capitalism arise. For instance:

(1) Can we keep running up deficits and increasing the debt and the debt limit without impairing the national credit?

(2) Can we raise our already high taxes without stifling production or causing widespread tax evasion?

So today government does many things. But there is one thing it does not yet do, and this fact is important to the New Capitalism: it does not really run our private businesses. We who wear the hair shirt of regulation may sometimes feel that it does. But when you get right down to it, even in closely regulated companies or industries, management makes the decisions, has the authority, and must shoulder the responsibility for success or failure.

Based on my experience, government has four main obligations to business if it is to help further the New Capitalism of today:

- It must provide a favorable climate in which to work. After all, the sound operation by business of our economic system is the foundation on which all our edifices of government, culture, education, and even national defense and existence as a nation are built. Business does not need or expect any *carte blanche* for its actions, but those companies that keep their house in order—and they are in the vast majority—deserve to know there is government understanding of their teamwork and approval in principle of their goals.
- It owes business farsighted policies that will encourage initiative and stimulate putting capital to work.
- In its national and state labor policies, government should

foster the right to work, the opportunity to work, and the right to benefit from such work. It should not condone lassitude or featherbedding.

• Its rules for business should be simple, clear, and as stable as possible. Changes should be evolutionary, not whimsical or revolutionary. And with it all, government owes fair and equal treatment to all business.

IS IT CAPITALISM?

Given the great contrasts between 1908 and today both in the results and the characteristics of our economic system, many people have questioned whether the modern version is really capitalism at all. To some experts, this is a brand-new economic machine, as yet unnamed; to others this is *real* capitalism, finally and for the first time working as it was meant to.

Maybe it is just a matter of semantics, that rather inexact science of word meanings, but personally I do not think that the bare word "capitalism" is adequate to describe what we have today. The term carries negative connotations of cartels, restricted production, high-unit-profit operations, and wealth held in a few hands.

Adding the qualifying adjective "new" provides another and truer concept. For we have tinkered with and modified our economic system; it has been affected greatly by government and importantly by organized labor. Yet basically it is still capitalism as defined in Webster's Unabridged Dictionary:

> The established economic system of most modern civilized countries in which ownership of land and natural wealth, the production, distribution, and exchange of goods, the employment and reward of human labor, and the extension, organization and operation of the system itself, are entrusted to, and effected by, private enterprise and control under competitive conditions.

Today's professionally managed corporation, with its broad ownership, complicated structure, and vital relations with government and labor, is a far cry from the simple business of 1908. Sizable, complex businesses today cannot achieve their full potential without public good will, sound labor-management relations, and advanced administrative techniques. All of these are new, at least by those names.

Basically, however, our economic system is still the same system, which works because it is psychologically sound, because it developed from peoples' desires and needs. Despite the inroads of Social Security, private business still provides modern pension plans, thrift contributions, and long-time job security on a private enterprise basis.

To me, our economic watch keeps getting a different style case, a new face, and different hands. We add gadgets, poke at it, clean it, and repair it. Generally it runs better afterward.

But the important thing is that it tells time, because we have not removed the jewels nor eliminated the mainspring. In our system the jewels correspond to the free competitive market. There, price levels and the volume and nature of commerce are determined in trading between buyers and sellers on the sensitive and flexible scales of supply and demand. And we have not replaced the mainspring—the free enterprise incentive to work, save, invest, and take risks in order to make private profits and acquire private property. As long as we maintain these two intact, we will have the same watch—and it will keep on running.

THE NEW RELATIONSHIP OF
BUSINESS TO SOCIETY

Donald K. David

THE LAST 50 YEARS have seen great changes in business and the climate in which it operates. In that period the American economy has grown to be the dominant economic force on this planet. Today, our 6% of the population produces more than one third of the world's goods and services.

Interwoven with this progress has been the development of the professional point of view that is now so largely characteristic of American businessmen. This sense of professionalism—and of responsibility—must become dominant if business is to achieve the relationship to society that these swiftly changing times require.

Solutions must be found to the issues in our society and in our world that seem to defy solution. And in the search none will be

Note: Mr. David is Vice Chairman, The Ford Foundation; Chairman of the Board of Trustees, Committee for Economic Development; and former Dean of the Harvard Business School.

held more accountable for success or failure than those who are in, or aspire to, positions of business leadership.

BUSINESS AND THE COMMON GOOD

It seems wise, therefore, for us to begin by recognizing that all is not well with the climate in which business operates. The distrust and conflict which still characterize relations between labor and management, for example, are indictments of both. There remain many on both sides who have not yet seen that the purposes of both can be realized only through the growth resulting from the mutually profitable operation of American enterprise.

Some of the problems they share will be solved only in the political arena, and it is here that business encounters some of its most serious shortcomings. For this, business has mainly itself to blame. Businessmen have not been articulate in expressing their hopes and desires for their communities. Too few have realized that the profitable operation of their enterprises is linked with the healthy growth of their communities. Too seldom are public problems given anything that approaches the attention accorded to private concerns. Too often the community views the businessman's aims as selfish gain rather than advancement of the general welfare. And even when such suspicions are baseless, the wisest of counsel makes little headway in a swamp of distrust.

The *prime necessity* for the businessman today is to weld to his economic prowess a similar drive, skill, and creativity in his *dangerously neglected social and political functions.*

The Crisis in Education

In facing this necessity, there is, it seems to me, an obvious place to start. The problems of education in America call for the attention of every citizen, including—most particularly—the businessman. Here is a place, too, in which corporations as such can play a big part. Already, almost 90% of our 500 largest corporations sponsor educational programs of their own. But these are largely refresher courses or specialized training programs which have nothing to do with the higher educational system on which our business organizations depend for their executive personnel. Today more than two thirds of the country's key business executives have

had at least an undergraduate college education, and the percentage
is growing every year. To illustrate the problems:

⟨ Despite the importance of the independent, privately supported
colleges in the field of higher education, they are pinched for funds
with which to keep abreast of their responsibilities. The question
here is how these colleges can maintain their independence and
keep up their standards if they are to take care of the same proportion of college students when, by 1970, there will be 70% more
young people in the college-age group. If they are not adequately
supported financially, the tax-supported state universities will have
the field to themselves. This raises the question of whether a tax-
supported system can provide the caliber of education required for
our specially gifted youth—the kind you must have to provide a
reservoir of talent for top-management positions.

⟨ Another puzzler arises from the estimate that about half the
labor force will have college degrees in another 15 years or so. Will
business be able to absorb these people and avert the frustrations
which, in the Germany of 1930, caused such people to look for a
national superman to solve their problems?

These questions are simply samples of the kind of educational
issues to which businessmen must give their best thought. They
would be tough enough even if they could be dealt with in a
vacuum, sealed off from the rest of the world, but this is not the
case. We confront very wily and determined competition from
abroad as we know full well.

The group of American educators, led by Chancellor Edward H.
Litchfield of the University of Pittsburgh, who returned from a
survey of Soviet education in July 1958 reported that the Russians
dedicate themselves to higher education with "deadly seriousness."
Sparing no expense or effort to give their youth the best they can
provide, the Soviet efforts must, according to the Litchfield group,
"give very serious pause to any nation which finds itself in a
competitive position."

Since the fall of 1957, when a Russian word became a synonym
for scientific and technological progress, we have been engaging in
a great deal of critical self-examination of our educational shortcomings. This has all been very useful, but it would be tragic,
indeed, if our action in such a fundamental field of national policy
and purpose were to be dominated by mere responses to Soviet

practice. Many thoughtful Americans were calling attention to the urgent problems of education in this country long before we ever heard the word "Sputnik." Men like James B. Conant from the world of education and Roy E. Larsen and Devereux C. Josephs from the world of business perceived the basic issues long ago.

What businessmen do or fail to do to strengthen the educational underpinnings of our society will be, I am convinced, a decisive element in the judgments that are certain to be passed on the place of business in society.

If the energy, ingenuity, and public spirit of the businessman do not lead him to assume a position of leadership in this obvious and open arena of social responsibility, there is little hope that business can ever attain respected and effective positions of leadership on the broader fronts of human affairs.

Developing a Conscience

The relationship of business to the educational crisis underscores the *general need* for management to take a good, hard look at internal corporate organization and policies as they affect the public interest. Those directing American enterprise must give more careful, top-level consideration to public attitudes and needs. This is more than a matter of public relations; it is a matter of public responsibility. Management should consider having someone in the organization who acts as its public "conscience." He should be a major officer, reporting to the head of the organization, and able to influence policy when and where it is made.

The outside members of boards of directors should be increasingly conscious of management's responsibility to the public. They should encourage and support the development of criteria for measuring corporate policy against public needs and responsibilities. Some experiments in this field are already being carried on for various companies. I trust the day is fast approaching when most corporate boards will conduct periodic and systematic reviews of corporate policies and practices from the standpoint of the public interest. Building such sensitivity toward public needs and interests into the corporate organization is bound to stimulate management to find more effective ways for working with and through the political structure of our society.

I should not have to stress further how important it is for

businessmen to become effective operators in our political as well as our economic life. What does need examination is the question *how* to achieve effectiveness. It is ironic, indeed, that men who are extremely alert to opportunities to improve procedures and techniques in their corporate life seem to atrophy when they turn to the machinery for political action. The clarity of analysis, the articulate formulation of solutions, the flexibility, the willingness to adapt, to merge, to experiment, and to diversify that are used to make economic progress are rarely found on the political front.

Labor, farmers, and veterans, for example, have shown far more skill in selling their points of view. The contrast, however, should only pose the challenge to business and not suggest the adoption of similar techniques. Business is not a mass movement and should never behave as one. Nor should it be identified with a particular partisan approach to political action. Moreover, in today's world, the organization of pressure groups to achieve self-serving goals is outmoded as an acceptable or even an effective political practice. *The political future belongs to those who are recognized as seeing in the advancement of the general welfare their own opportunities for progress.*

TOWARD A NEW PARTNERSHIP

This example of partnership between business and government leads me to what I regard as the first priority for business in forging a new relationship to society. Of course, it is important to make our democracy work better. And it is important for business to have a part in the process. But *the first necessity is for our society to survive.*

This generation is engaged with the Soviet Union in a contest of civilizations. Survival of human life on this planet may well be at stake. Certainly survival of the values central to our civilization face a deadly challenge. The threat has been stated clearly by Khrushchev in these words: *"We declare war.* We will win over the United States. The threat to the United States is not the ICBM, but in the field of peaceful production. *We are relentless in this and will prove the superiority of our system."*

The warning is clear, but I am not sure that its real meaning has registered. Certainly we have not even begun—as we would in the case of armed conflict—to mobilize the productive power of our private enterprise economy. We *must* find methods that will enable us to throw into this unavoidable economic war our major economic strength—the ability of private businessmen to conceive, to organize, to direct, and to deliver. We have always found ways to do this in other wars, and I think we can do it again in this new and equally deadly conflict.

We need to bring business and government together in a new partnership to promote economic development abroad, for such a working relationship can help us win the economic war and safeguard our national existence. Moreover, the successful operation of this partnership, I am convinced, can strengthen the whole fabric of our national life.

Several years ago at Harvard George C. Marshall initiated a program of economic aid that saved Western Europe from Communist captivity. The massive export of capital from this country to Western Europe that accomplished this feat is properly regarded as one of the most enlightened acts of statesmanship in modern times. But when we turn from industrialized Europe to the other continents, where two thirds of the free world's people subsist on per capita incomes ranging from $30 to no more than $300 per year, the pattern of the Marshall Plan is neither appropriate nor adequate. The background of education, skills, traditions, laws, political structure—the whole complex of managerial and entrepreneurial as well as production operations that make the mere infusion of capital a constructive act—is limited or nonexistent. It is in these areas that the crucial battles of the economic war for survival of our society are already beginning. Our failures in these battles are apparent. Barely yesterday they jolted us in Latin America and the Middle East. Tomorrow they could plague us in Africa and Asia. In fact, wherever primitive economies and poverty create political unrest and invite Soviet intervention we are involved in mortal combat with our opponents.

Why We Have Failed

What we have thus far thrown into this conflict is, essentially, a program of government-to-government aid, *most of which has not even been economic aid*. This approach is ill-adapted not only to the needs of emerging nations and economies but also to the capacity of our own economic structure to respond effectively to those needs. The continued pursuit of economic development on a predominantly government-to-government basis could well be self-defeating.

The Soviet Union has now embarked on a large-scale program of economic aid and penetration. It, too, is conducting this program on a government-to-government basis. But this similarity of approach carries within it a basic difference which it is urgent to recognize. When the Soviet government undertakes a program, it has at its direct disposal its entire economic system. Not only can it apply capital, but it can also commandeer machines, plants, skills, and talents from any part of its economic structure, because that economic structure is owned by the state and by no one else. Our own society, on the other hand, places less value on service to the state. Government does not have the best talents and skills at its direct disposal, because, unlike the Soviet Union, the productive and managerial genius of America is located in the private sector.

Without regard for the discouraging effect of government-to-government programs on the growth of private enterprise in the recipient countries, consider the implications of this situation for us. In competing with the Soviet Union on this basis we enter the race against their best and without the help of our strongest runners.

It is unreasonable to expect that in a society in which economic enterprise is in private hands, government is suddenly going to develop procedures and attract people capable of performing the most difficult of all jobs—organizing and carrying out the economic development of whole countries. How, then, do we enlist the leaders of industry as commanding officers in the economic war? Merely to urge that they become more alert to opportunities for foreign investment and development as a private venture will not win many battles. The risks of private investment in many areas that need help most are too great to attract the massive-scale development that is required. Moreover, many countries, through past experience or propaganda, fear private development as the instrument of exploitation. And in some countries, notably in the Middle East, it is not capital that is lacking but the knowledge of how best to employ it.

What We Can Do

We have solved problems like this before. Making munitions on the massive scale needed in wartime, for example, has always been accomplished by government contract with private industry with remuneration for the costs involved. When economic development represents the explosive element in this new war, we should be able to adapt a similar technique. Basically, *I suggest that we mobilize the full resources of our private enterprise economy as we do in war by having responsible government agencies contract with private companies and private management to do a massive and effective job of foreign economic development.*

Let us suppose, for example, that the economic development plans of a country call for the creation of a farm equipment industry. Instead of undertaking this task with advisers employed by governments for short-term assignments, is it not possible to conceive of an appropriate contractual arrangement being concluded with, say, International Harvester Company, J. I. Case Company, or Deere & Company, that would put the organized talents and resources of the entire corporation to work on the problem?

We have supported surveys, we have made grants and loans, and we have even joined in construction projects. But what we have *not* done on any significant scale is to *organize the complete package* to bring into being part of any successful economic development plan. This means starting with the organization of a company, securing its financing, and moving on through the design and construction of its plant, the organization of its management, the development of its market, and the recruitment and training of people within the company's marketing area to carry on the management of the developing new enterprise.

Such an approach recognizes that when a country needs to develop a particular industry or other economic activity, the best talent and experience is to be found in private American enterprises operating in the same or similar fields. This approach also recognizes that an operating firm can provide certain elements of entrepreneurship which government simply cannot hire. These are the initiating, organizing, capital-mobilizing, and policy-making functions which are the essence of private enterprise activity. As things now stand, we may provide capital or hire a technical adviser to do a particular job. We must provide the entrepreneur who sees what needs to be done and brings together the whole complex of elements needed to make the enterprise succeed. This approach would permit us to apply the best talents we possess without expecting the best to re-

move themselves from the escalator of corporate advancement. And
it means finding the way to harness the power of an economic
machine that has millions of pistons to the attainment of an essential national goal.

Obviously, there are many difficult problems of equity, of procedure, and of government and corporate policy that must be
solved. For instance:

❨ There should be no obligation on the part of the contracting
company to make an investment of its own. But if the country concerned agrees, neither should the contracting company be prevented
from taking at least a minority position in the enterprise it establishes.

❨ Fears, on one hand, that such a close relationship with government will undermine free enterprise, or, on the other, that free enterprise will take unfair advantage of government are ill-founded. A
correct accommodation will be found once the facts are recognized.
And the facts are that we are engaged in fighting an economic war
for survival which thus far we have waged mainly with untrained
troops and virtually none of our officer corps.

❨ There will be problems, in some cases, arising from the creation
of competitors. But the economic development opportunities in most
of these countries will be in noncompetitive lines and in supplying
the needs of their own and neighboring countries. Moreover, the evidence is clear that wherever living standards and purchasing power
rise, so does the over-all demand for American goods and services.

Despite these problems, if we want to bring about development
on the massive scale required and within the short time allowed to
win this economic war, we must devise methods and institutional
arrangements for bringing the full scope of private enterprise to
bear. Such a partnership of business and government for waging the
war for development in freedom could help us regain the leadership
that saved the wavering Western world a decade ago. Unless the
great strength and varied resources of our private enterprise system
are harnessed to this task, Western civilization will lose the economic
war. But if the drive, the ingenuity, the creative talent, and the
dedication to human values that are present in American enterprise
can be focused on this essential national goal, we will win this war.
In winning, we will strengthen the processes of democracy both
here and abroad, and we will raise the well-being and the hopes of
men, wherever they aspire to be free.

FOR A REVISED SENSE OF VALUES

Erwin D. Canham

THE ROLE OF JEREMIAH is not particularly congenial to me; I am a notorious optimist. I can see thousands of things which are right about American business, and I believe our economic system has helped to achieve a great deal for people and can do much more.

But we cannot have strong faith in its future unless we recognize what is wrong with it today. Objectively, what is wrong is that we have a false sense of values—or, to put it more accurately, we do not recognize and act on the truer sense of values that underlies the gloss of materialism covering our lives. Unless we discern and restore a more accurate sense of values, our system is in the gravest danger of decline and fall. The problem was given allegorical expression recently by August Heckscher, who wrote, "In trying to create highways which would be perfectly safe, we have succeeded

Note: Mr. Canham is Editor of *The Christian Science Monitor.*

in putting the driver to sleep, thus raising new dangers more deadly
than the turns and crossroads, the hills and passing villages, which
we eliminated at so great a cost." *

I shall, of course, return to this point. Let me first look at some
of business's unfinished business at the more superficial level, and
work my way down.

THE DANGERS OF INFLATION

It seems to me that American business's most flagrant mistake in
this decade is its failure to do its part to maintain price stability.

It is correct to blame organized labor for part of the inflationary
spiral which has gone so far beyond maintaining an expanding
economy, and has helped to distort and to some extent destroy real
values. But business has also been guilty. Just to the extent that
business—and this applies particularly to the biggest and most
powerful industrial groups—has accepted higher costs for labor
because it knew it could pass them along to consumers, business
has given itself a grave handicap. This is not in the tradition of the
American competitive system, which has prided itself on reducing
costs and giving the consumer more for his real dollar.

Some measure of inflation is of course the price we must pay
for an expanding economy, but we have gone far beyond that point.
This may be remembered as the decade of inflation—of price instability—and that would be a fundamental blow to the purpose of
free enterprise, which is to contribute to the betterment of man
through a steadily increasing standard of living. For altogether too
many Americans, the standard of living is not now increasing.

We cannot so gravely weaken the value of fixed incomes, of
savings in most of the traditional forms, of pensions and annuities,
of professional incomes, of public expenditure for schools and other
community costs, and still feel that we are adequately serving
society. Again, wage-price inflation is by no means all the fault of
business or of all parts of business. It is more labor's fault, but
management will have to pay a large part of the penalty and management—particularly of heavy industry—could have done more
to curb the spiral. This will be remembered as a grave mistake.

* "The True Welfare: America's Continuing Quest," *Modern Age,* Summer
1958, p. 235.

Tailfins and Toasters

There has also been an inflation of goods, of ideas, of taste, of design—a burst of antifunctionalism which looks like materialism at its worst—for which business will also have to pay the price. Take the automobile industry, for instance:

> Tailfins, of course, are the commonest scapegoat. Does an expanding economy really require so swift a rate of obsolescence? Must automobile styles change every year, always getting bigger, longer, lower, more expensive? Is there not a happy medium somewhere between the Volkswagen and the 1958–1959 products of the American designers? Why should not functionalism really be the decisive criterion in the development of automobiles or of anything else? Do we need so much horsepower? Remembering Henry Thoreau, somebody said there should be a Walden-wagon—a simple, effective, functional, economical American automobile.

But let us not be obsessed with automotive marketing practices. The problem is much wider than that. The first electric toaster I ever owned back in the 1920's made better toast and took up one-fourth the space of any toaster I can locate nowadays. (I should be careful here. Maybe the toast just tasted better to me in the 1920's, and you know why.) I believe all business needs the tight, challenging pressure of a competitive market in which price is a dominant factor, so that it will again be producing for economy-minded customers. I think business does a more functional and efficient job in hard times than it does in soft times. And if we are to continue to have deficit-financed prosperity, we should create the disciplinary equivalent of hard competition, simplicity, and functionalism.

Credit and Debit

The excessive use of consumer credit is another serious problem which business must face realistically. Somebody said the 1957–1958 recession set in because too many people began living within their incomes. Perhaps, but I also think there is a danger point in the piling up of debt, personal or governmental or corporate. Insofar as business's sales techniques and pressures have artificially forced this mounting burden of debt, business will be held accountable.

Here I am protesting against the piling up of debt beyond the consumer's reasonable capacity to pay—the inflation of the debt structure. I cannot forget the part inability to repay debt has played in the political and social history of this nation. There are better ways to bring about social change than by forcing farmers into bankruptcy and violent radicalism, or by guaranteeing farm prices, for that matter.

The Bargain Merchant

In addition to prices, debt, and competition, perhaps I should say a word about two factors which have spread rapidly over the American economic scene. One is the discount house; the other is the disintegration of a firm price structure in such areas as the marketing of automobiles. Surely the tremendous growth of discount houses in recent years is evidence of something wrong in retailing; specifically, of adhering to fair-price practices too long and of fixing too wide a profit margin throughout too much of the retail field. Perhaps we apostles of competition should simply welcome the discount houses. Perhaps we should say they are the dynamics of a free economy operating in the vulgar way in which dynamic forces usually operate. But if I manufactured appliances, or if I sold goods in an old-fashioned store, I would not feel very comfortable about the discount house, and I would not think my methods had been altogether healthy.

Similarly, I do not wish to haggle for an automobile as if I were buying it in an Oriental bazaar. I like to think that I can get as good a bargain as my neighbor, who may be more talented at barter. A two-price system does not represent retailing at its best. "I can get it for you wholesale" is an indictment. The orthodox retailer will always have to charge the customer more, insofar as he is paying for service, reliability, an urbane clerk, an air-conditioned store, and a carpet. But the margin must not be too great, and it has been.

MIGHT AND RIGHT

On a deeper level than prices and competition, my next point concerns the basic control and responsibility of American business. I am inclined to believe that the great unfinished business of American business today is its failure to solve the problem of representative, responsible, or—if you will—democratic control. Power in our economic order is split: balanced, some will say. Some of this power, an increasing amount, resides with government. Some of it, also an increasing amount, though not temporarily so, resides with organized labor. Insofar as power over business resides in business, where is it today, and where should it be?

The Managerial Revolution

Who owns business? The stockholders. Who controls business? The managers, sometimes. The directors, sometimes. But neither executive management nor boards of directors have evolved an adequate system of accountability to the ultimate ownership. This is irresponsible. It may be benevolent and enlightened—heaven help American business if decisions had to be taken by vote of all the stockholders, in some sort of misbegotten town meeting—but present controls are simply not enough. It should not be beyond our organizational genius to work out a better system.

Business has sharply and rightly criticized unions for their frequent lack of democratic processes. Is it not time for us to move out of our glass houses and work harder than ever on the solution of this problem? Perhaps we should recognize that the board of directors composed entirely of company officials—and some of the finest and best-run corporations in the country are set up on this basis—is the most difficult to defend. This is the managerial revolution indeed. It is also the least hypocritical.

The board of directors without real power is just as indefensible. There are, of course, plenty of boards of directors, particularly in banks and fiduciary institutions, where the directors make up a well-balanced group, largely of outsiders who play a powerful role in the decision-making processes of the institution. But I think there are relatively few such boards where the system of electing the members can be readily defended. The best system I know about is the election of the directorate of the Federal Reserve Banks by a widespread membership. They effectively exercise control over the officers. But this is an exception.

Vast power is now aggregated in the controls of our economic enterprises, despite the dispersion of power to labor and to government. Decisions of the largest of our economic titans affect the well-being of every person in the land. Such decisions will be increasingly and gravely at the mercy of governmental interference and control if a more responsive system of private control is not attained. Already governmental power has gone deep. It can only be minimized by the fullest and the most responsive measure of private control.

I know, of course, of the assumption of voluntary responsibility by many leaders of business. Many of them feel a deep sense of accountability to their stockholders, to their customers, to the community as a whole. I know their feeling that the ultimate accountability is with the economic service of the enterprise: whether or not it makes a profit, whether or not it survives. This is very well and very important, but it is not enough.

What's Good for GM ...

This leads me to a related point: the danger of self-righteousness in American business leadership. If there is one thing that has brought businessmen-in-government to grief, it is the sin of self-righteousness. If there is a vice which stands in our light externally in the world today, it is self-righteousness.

The case-hardened professional politician is relatively free from self-righteousness. So, in a cynical way, is the lawyer. But the businessman often has a blinding and inhibiting sense of his own virtue. Of course, he may well be virtuous, but that is not enough. He does not see why it is wrong to say that what's good for General Motors is good for the country. He falls into ghastly traps that wary old politicians would have avoided. His skin is also oddly thin, for he cannot take criticism. This self-righteousness is the businessman's worst handicap in good public relations.

It is the sin of self-righteousness, then, which persuades a business executive that since he knows he has his company's interests at heart, no further controls over his decisions are necessary. Sooner or later, if we are to preserve our real freedom from excessive governmental controls, we must solve this problem of responsible democratic power.

PROFITS OR PROPHETS?

One of the most distressing facts about our economic order is that it is not really spreading into the rest of the world. It is not a dynamic, contagious system. There is indeed a "new American capitalism," but it is beleaguered on its little islands in a socialist sea. Where some of its attributes are imitated, they are likely to be the least desirable ones. Indeed, paradoxically, there is some danger that the baser elements of American life may infect much of the rest of the world. There is powerful contagion in the elements of our society and our economic order of which we are least proud. The massive programs of economic aid and tutelage we have lavished on the world during the last decade and more have not really laid the foundations of a free economic system as we understand it. Venality and corruption have poisoned many of the elements of private business which have sprung up or been revived in many crucial parts of the world. Little, indeed, of the social responsibility that helps redeem our system at home has emerged abroad.

There are, of course, good examples of American enterprise now operating in many parts of the world. I do not ignore the many individuals who have come to the United States and learned much from our concepts and the Americans who are diligently and effectively sharing our technical experience overseas. I am speaking, in broader terms than that, of the conflict between free enterprise in anything like the form we know it and statism and socialism as they exist nearly everywhere else, and of unreformed capitalism in its remaining manifestations. In relative terms, though, our free economic system does not possess the missionary zeal, the drive and force, the contagion, which it deserves to have.

Of course the American economic system should not be forced on other parts of the world. It could not be made to work in many of them, but more of the elements of freedom which are the virtue of our system should have been adapted by others to the needs of others. More of us could be proclaiming and exemplifying the liberating efficacy of a free economy. Marxism, or what passes for Marxism, is a powerful missionary force. It has zealous converts in every corner of the globe, fanatically spreading its conspiratorial practices. Where are the equally dedicated and indigenous missionaries of the free system?

Redefining Our Values

We lack a body of doctrine, and we lack a prophet. We lack revolutionary zeal. And all of this, it seems to me, stems from our failure to define our values accurately. We cannot concoct synthetic doctrine nor contrive a fustian prophet, but we *can* look deep into our hearts and consciences, for we are the heirs of a proud and noble tradition of political ideals, and we *can* redefine our values. Some of our leaders are already beginning to do so. Senator J. William Fulbright put it eloquently in a speech on the Senate floor during the last week of the 85th Congress when he said:

> Can anyone here deny that the distinguishing feature of American society during much of the decade of the 1950's was its weakness for the easy way? I remind the Senate that the influence of this country was never greater in the hearts of men throughout the world, nor the power of the words of its leaders to move men more potent, than when it had no machines or technological capacities to speak of. It was never greater than when its leaders, for the most part, were deeply religious men, when life was not easy but very hard, when men were judged more by what they were than what they had, by what they contributed of their thoughts and heart and labor to the community, when new ideas were as welcome as new peoples to these shores.
>
> What I am suggesting ... is that the problem is larger than what has gone wrong with our policies. Even more fundamentally, it is what has gone wrong with our society.

To put it bluntly, what has gone wrong with American business? What has inverted our values? For one thing, we have deified production for production's sake. There is nothing wrong with the increased production of consumer goods, but there is a great deal wrong in thinking and acting as if the mere production of goods were a justifiable social goal.

The only valid social goal is improvement of the lot of man and the better relationship of men to one another and to God, to fundamental truth. But we must define the lot of man; we must give priority to values. The classic illustration is that we should place education much higher in our system than entertainment. A teacher should be worth more than a janitor. The improvement of man's mind and heart is more important than the better satisfaction of his material wants. This thesis is incontrovertible, and once we tended to live by it.

There is nothing inherently wrong with the satisfaction of man's material wants. Shoes are not immoral, nor is there spirituality about a loincloth. But if the loincloth typifies the placing of spiritual values first, it becomes an important symbol.

In fact, the attainment of a better standard of living is itself a spiritual victory, insofar as it exemplifies man's mastery of his physical environment. Behind all our technological, industrial, or mercantile attainments lies this kind of true victory. But we do not often recognize it as such, nor have we made any progress in explaining to the rest of the world that the real American achievement is spiritual instead of material. On the contrary, the tawdry materialism of conspicuous consumption, spread by the mass media, accompanied by rock-and-roll, splattered by comic books, has become a symbol of America in most of the world. We have been on the whole our own worst missionaries. This is a disgrace, because the surface sensationalism is not the truth about American life.

You can argue that the battle of the twentieth century is a battle between two books: Karl Marx's *Das Kapital* and the Sears and Roebuck catalogue. In a way this is true. And I think the Sears and Roebuck catalogue may win, since I believe the human desire for the satisfaction of material needs may prove to be the stronger force. It may produce a modification of the system of the Soviet Union and perhaps of Communist China as well, though there the leaders are playing their cards much more skillfully and subtly. Anyway, the desire of people to improve their lot must be redefined for what it is or ought to be: not just the gratification of material needs, but the elevation of man to higher levels of life and service.

I have been much impressed by J. Kenneth Galbraith's *The Affluent Society.** Does he build a bridge between the immense and abiding importance of the free enterprise system and the realm of the public domain? Up to now, we have attained significant social values. We have liberated men and women and children from the worst degradations of toil. We have begun to lift the curtains of ignorance from their minds. We have enormously enhanced their standard of living.

BUSINESS AND PUBLIC SERVICE

Despite our great achievements, however, today we face new challenges. There is, of course, first of all, the task of assuring our national security and the security of the free world. This can be

---

* Boston, Houghton Mifflin Company, 1958.

attained only by efforts in almost every realm of national life, not by the piling up of more consumer goods. Coordinately, we have the problem of rescuing our cities, of conserving our natural beauty, of improving our general educational standards, of meeting all our other civil needs.

We are the beneficiaries of the greatest population explosion in the history of the race. We have the technological tools capable of meeting man's material needs munificently. We have the capacity and the margin to meet his social needs as well. We need better mechanisms for coping with these social needs. Just as I have urged that business needs better mechanics for internal democratic control, so the operation of the public domain needs immense improvement. Business can and must make a large contribution to the solution of the governmental problem if, as seems undeniable, the social problem can be met only by a large increase of public service, in short, by an expansion of government.

But business itself, without turning over all the problems to government, can do a great deal for public betterment. It is already doing a great deal. The amount of voluntary public work done by American businessmen and women is of staggering volume, far higher than anywhere else in the world. Though it still has a long way to go, it is one of the most impressive phenomena in our life today and is already carrying us forward. But perhaps even more than its concrete accomplishments is the evidence it provides that beneath our apparent preoccupation with false values and false gods there is a perception of truth on which to build.

SOME ADDED COMMENTS

At one point in the Conference Messrs. Symonds, David, and Canham participated in a discussion with a group of businessmen under the chairmanship of George F. Baker, James J. Hill Professor of Transportation at the Harvard Business School. The thoughts reported here came out of this session.

Mr. Baker: What is the mission of a corporation beyond the running of a good business that makes a profit?

Mr. David: Over a period of time, the test of our American private enterprise system will be whether it can provide spiritual as well as economic satisfaction to people better than the Soviet system can. Management has to realize that the really important question in the long run turns on this matter of the fulfillment of a whole range of human goals and aspirations. Can people achieve these purposes—material and nonmaterial—more quickly and more fully in a free society like ours, or a statist community like the Soviet Union? We are convinced that freedom is the answer, but we have to prove it again and again to make our point.

I am certain that we are on the right track, because American businessmen are rapidly developing a sense of trusteeship. The public is uppermost in the minds of most people who are running companies today. Of course, operating at a profit is our first responsibility. This is the guts of what we do. But beyond this, manage-

85

ment and directors increasingly look at their jobs as a public trust.

Mr. Symonds: Wouldn't you say that "the public" must be first measured by the public the company comes in contact with: its own customers and its own employees? Satisfy them first—and when you have done a good job there, you can then spread out into society.

Mr. Canham: I agree definitely with the emphasis on trusteeship, but I think we must make sure that this trusteeship really exists and that we have machinery to bring it to life. We must operate under an accountable system in which we have accepted and are living by this sense of trusteeship. The only way I know to do this is by electing to boards of directors a certain number of people who will support and give validity to this concept.

From the floor: At the same time that we are involved in a close race with Russia in the development of weapons, we are fighting an even stiffer battle on the ideological front. So far the Russians seem to have the upper hand in this battle of ideas. What can we do to beat them at their own game? Can we make our democratic ideas salable to everybody?

Mr. Canham: I think we need a deeper sense of the significance of the system in which we are living and which we are operating; we need to understand it and feel it more deeply. This is the obligation of the corporation and, in a broader definition of terms, its contribution to the well-being of man. The corporation must serve man and the inner values of his life, and enable him to lead a more fruitful life in which values are put right side up. We have, of course, considerably inverted our values by regarding *things* as important, when what is really important is what lies behind them.

We are proving the dominion of man over his material environment. This is a great thing, far transcending any concept that Marx developed in his London garret. This is a tremendous, potent doctrine, a truly revolutionary system of ideas. When we begin to understand more deeply and articulate and cultivate more fully a sense of values based on the fulfillment of man's individual potentialities and capacities, we will have a missionary force. I do not separate the building of steel plants from doctrine in any way. Neither would have any meaning without the other. All I am saying is that we must understand and articulate the true meaning of our technical achievements, which lies not in the provision of more goods but in what they do for people.

Mr. David: I think the best way for people abroad to understand what our private enterprise system is, what it means, is for them to operate it in their countries so they can see it in action.

Mr. Canham: Of course, there are many phases of our economic system that they couldn't operate, for they do not have some of the essentials. There are elements which they can adopt and adapt, but in the final analysis their economic system, like their political system is going to be the result of their capacity, their history, their climate, and all the other elements which have produced their way of life. Just as our way of life is the product of a long string of circumstances which have all come together, theirs will be innate to their capacities and their needs. We must not expect them simply to imitate us. This would be a futile effort.

But though the details of their economic system and their political system must be their own, we would like to share with them to their capacity and help them adapt to their capacity the central elements in our system—those which make the cleavage between freedom and serfdom.

From the floor: In discussing management's mission in a new society it seems to me that you gentlemen have pointed out very clearly that we are in an ideological conflict which is probably equal to the economic conflict. Today "ideology" means a group of ideas and a program to carry them out. My feeling is that the average businessman is not as well equipped as his Russian counterpart to engage in this ideological battle. What can businessmen do to strengthen our ideological position?

Mr. Canham: One of the greatest advantages of the Communists is that they work through the natives of the country they are trying to win. I think this is an enormous advantage and our greatest single handicap. Penetration and subversion take place largely through the nationalists of the target area.

How do they do this? They have been training their people for a long time: the first Asian Communist conference to equip experts to do this job took place in 1919, and they have been working on the project ever since. What do we do about it? We must work through our voluntary private organizations, such as trade associations, professional associations, and chambers of commerce. There we can gather important and significant ideas.

We have to go into the range of action. Collectivism is a horrid word, but we have a form of voluntary, free collectivism which we have built over the last third of the century. Meetings such as the annual business conference on which this book is based illustrate this kind of coming together and putting an edge on one's ideas. It seems to me that we can extend this principle of voluntary collective action into international channels by working with our counterparts in other countries. In this way we can create a *capitalist* international.

Part Two

A CLOSER LOOK AT THE
BUSINESSMAN'S ROLE

OVERSEAS BUSINESS, ECONOMIC DEVELOPMENT, AND THE COLD WAR

Lincoln Gordon, Harold K. Hochschild, and Hal J. Wright

IT IS PERFECTLY CLEAR that among the many explosive changes in the past 50 years has been the transformation of the United States into a large trader and major source of international capital. More recently, the shift of power in the postwar world has imposed still another kind of role on us.

Obviously there has been a change in the patterns of foreign trade and especially in overseas development. All this has taken place in a context of very rapid and occasionally violent change.

Note: Mr. Gordon, who makes the introductory remarks, is William Ziegler Professor of International Economic Relations, Harvard Business School; Mr. Hochschild is Honorary Chairman of the Board, American Metal Climax, Inc.; and Mr. Wright is Director, Creole Petroleum Corporation.

The problems that are caused by these developments are far-reaching. There is, for example, the very important issue which Donald K. David discusses: how can we get more constructive American private investment in the underdeveloped countries? * Another troublesome matter is how large investors, who are often the dominant figures on their local scenes, should conduct themselves in order to foster constructive change and oppose destructive change. I put it this way because it is perfectly clear that nowhere is the situation going to be static; the one thing that cannot last in any of the less developed countries is the status quo.

Here are questions that affect the corporate interests of overseas investors, the interests of the United States, and the prospects for the survival of freedom in the world at large.

THE COPPER MINING INDUSTRY OF NORTHERN RHODESIA†

In Northern Rhodesia, next to the border of the Belgian Congo, lies a strip of land about 75 miles long by 35 miles wide that has become known as the "copper belt." Thirty years ago the population of this sector consisted of some African peasants and a handful of Europeans. There was no industry of any kind. Today it produces nearly 500,000 short tons of copper per annum, about one sixth of the free world's supply of primary copper, and it has a population of about 400,000 of whom some 50,000 are white.

From the start, American capital and industrial leadership have played a considerable part in the development of the copper belt. There were four, and now are six, major mines there. From the earliest days their financing, development, and operation have been in the hands of two organizations: the Anglo-American group, which manages three mines, and the Rhodesian Selection Trust group, generally referred to as the R.S.T. group, which manages the other three.

The Anglo-American group, despite its name, has practically no American participation; it is owned mainly by British and South African investors. It also controls gold and diamond mines in the Union of South Africa, and its headquarters are in Johannesburg.

* See the chapter entitled, "The New Relationship of Business to Society," p. 66.
† By Mr. Hochschild.

The R.S.T. group, with headquarters in Salisbury, Southern Rhodesia, is owned largely by American and British investors, including primarily American Metal.

Growth of an Industry

Before its merger with Climax Molybdenum Company in December 1957 to form American Metal Climax, Inc., The American Metal Company, Limited, had been in the nonferrous metal business for 70 years—in mining, smelting and refining, and marketing. For many years it had owned or partly owned mines in Canada, Mexico, the Union of South Africa, and the Territory of South West Africa, as well as Rhodesia.

It was in 1927 that American Metal first became aware of the potential extent of the copper sulphide mineralization then being disclosed by prospecting and drilling directed by Chester Beatty, an eminent American-born mining engineer living in London. American Metal, in part by an exchange of shares with the Beatty group, by the end of 1930 had acquired its present holdings of a one-third interest in the Roan Antelope mine and over half of Rhodesian Selection Trust, Limited, which in turn owns two thirds of the Mufulira copper mine. American Metal thereupon assumed primary responsibility for raising the money to complete the development and equipment of the Roan Antelope and Mufulira mines. Roan began producing on schedule in 1931, but the starvation copper prices of the depression upset all calculations of profits and dividends. Thanks to the highly resourceful management of David D. Irwin, an American who had gone out to Rhodesia from Arizona, Roan—and later Mufulira—survived under these extraordinarily adverse conditions.

In the late 1930's conditions improved somewhat, and by the eve of World War II Roan and Mufulira had reached a combined output of 150,000 short tons per annum. During the war this was pushed to 175,000 tons. Again, profits shrank to small dimensions because of government-fixed copper prices and heavy wartime taxation in the United Kingdom and the United States. During the Korean War price controls were reimposed. In 1953 they ended. In the same year the companies were permitted to move their domicile from England to Rhodesia.

These developments, coupled with changes that had taken place in American tax regulations, substantially improved American Metal's returns from its investment. Including a third mine, the Chibuluma, the R.S.T. group's combined output has now risen to 225,000 short tons per annum, about 45% of the copper belt total. The group's total will increase further in a few years through development of a new ore body at Mufulira.

Let me make it clear that the R.S.T. group is not just an outpost of American business. While technically the holding company, R.S.T., Ltd., is a subsidiary in which American Metal has just over a 50% interest, a considerable portion of its shares represent British investment. Roan Antelope also has a large investment interest in Great Britain. Many of the members of the boards of directors of the R.S.T. companies are British or Rhodesian, and no Americans are now employed in their management. To consider the R.S.T. group as only a case study of private American investment abroad would be unfair to the farsightedness of the group's British investors and of its executives, particularly the progressive chairman of the R.S.T. companies, Sir Ronald Prain.

There are several lessons which can be drawn from the experience of the copper industry in Northern Rhodesia:

(1) It took a long time before this substantial investment in Central Africa began to justify itself, as it has now amply done. I sometimes wonder whether our management, if it had been aware of what the future held in terms of prolonged depression, two wars, governmental controls, and vastly increased taxation of corporate profits, would have had the courage to make or to carry through these Rhodesian investments, and whether it would have been considered good business to do so. This experience shows that judgment and patience are especially needed for investments that break the boundaries of the known and the familiar—and luck helps.

(2) Large amounts of capital are required today for new mining ventures, and it takes a long time to bring them into operation. Thirty years ago it took five years and roughly $25 million each to open up mines of the present size of Roan Antelope and Mufulira. Today it still takes five years to open up mines on this scale, but it requires capital on the order of $100 million for each such mine, to produce around 100,000 annual short tons of copper.

There is much talk of the need to open up Africa's mineral resources. The figures I have given on these two mines in one territory of Africa indicate that such development will require many hundreds of millions—even billions—of dollars.

(3) My third observation deals with the risks and effects of price fluctuations in a commodity like copper, known for its volatility. When American Metal assumed the major responsibility for completing Roan and Mufulira in 1930, copper was selling just above $.17 per pound in New York. Eighteen months later, as Roan was opened, copper had fallen below $.05.

During World War II copper was pegged by government orders at around $.12. During the Korean War it was pegged at about $.24. By the spring of 1956 copper had sold at above $.50; about two years later it sold at nearly as little as $.20.

The impact of such price fluctuations on company profits has been sharp. The effect on Rhodesian public revenues and development plans has been equally drastic, although Rhodesia has the advantage—on the down side—of a lag of one to two years because its tax system is not on a pay-as-you-go basis.

(4) British and American investors and capital markets have cooperated in providing the capital for these Rhodesian properties. Originally, the ventures were financed by British capital; they were brought to completion by American capital. Recently, investors in Britain, the United States, France, and other countries have contributed the money required for expansion. The multinational origin of capital attracted to Northern Rhodesia for and by the copper industry is also illustrated by the financing of the huge Kariba hydroelectric development, which not only will give the copper mines needed power but is also expected to bring about an industrial revolution in Central Africa.

The Zambesi River is being dammed to produce ultimately 1,250,-000 kilowatts of electric power in territory which only 100 years ago Livingstone was the first white man to enter. The first stage of about half that capacity is scheduled for completion in 1960. It will cost about $220 million. The largest single loan which the World Bank has made toward any project in the world is its commitment of $80 million toward this total.

The two groups of copper companies, although expected to have only 20% priority on the first 600,000 kilowatts, are providing an even larger sum, $84 million, of which $56 million will be in long-term loans and the balance in surcharges on power used. Other capital is coming from other Rhodesian private sources and British government agencies.

New Life for Africa

Let us look at some broader implications of the creation of this great copper mining industry in what had so recently been darkest Africa. The companies that opened up these mines had to start from scratch:

- Since there was no power, the companies had to build power plants.
- The area was malarial, so the companies had to dig drainage canals.
- Because there were practically no living facilities, the companies had to build whole towns for the European and African workers and provide schools, hospitals, recreational clubs, sewerage, and water supply.

Today the copper belt contains one of the largest integrated industries anywhere south of the equator, and one of the most valuable extractive industries in the sterling area. The growth of this industry had a considerable indirect influence on the birth of a state. In 1953, after many years of discussion, the self-governing territory of Southern Rhodesia joined the protectorates of Northern Rhodesia and Nyasaland to form the Federation of Rhodesia and Nyasaland, also known as the Central African Federation.

The Federation's population is made up of 7,250,000 Africans, nearly 300,000 whites, and 35,000 Asians and other peoples. Nearly all these 7,500,000 people have, in one way or another, felt the impact of the development of the copper belt.

Take transportation for instance. In 1957 nearly 1 million tons of coal were shipped 500 miles from the Wankie Collieries in Southern Rhodesia to the copper belt for its power needs, and over 400,000 tons of copper went 1,000 to 1,500 miles by train to harbors in Portuguese Mozambique on the Indian Ocean for shipment overseas. This traffic has played a major part in the growth and modernization of the Rhodesian railway system.

Local expenditures by the European and African workers of their earnings, which totaled over $50 million in 1957, have created businesses of many varieties in the copper belt and in Southern Rhodesia. The logistics of food supply for the population of the copper belt has led to large-scale local cattle raising. And every year thousands of young Africans from Northern Rhodesia and from overcrowded

Nyasaland, which has an inadequate agricultural economy, find work on the copper belt.

Copper accounts for nearly 60% of the exports of the Federation and over 90% of Northern Rhodesia's exports. It provides two thirds of Northern Rhodesian governmental revenues, and one third of the governmental revenues in the Federation as a whole. All told, nearly 50% of the gross profits of the copper mining companies flows directly and indirectly into the budgets of the Northern Rhodesian and Federation governments.

Social and Political Problems

This industry in Rhodesia was founded solely by private investment. Private companies and their stockholders located the capital and took the risks, waited many years for their returns, and regularly reinvested a portion of their earnings.

In the context of contemporary discussion of the role of private capital in backward lands, it may be useful to underline the fact that there were no political objectives in the minds of these investors who opened up the copper belt. They did not intend to help create modern political institutions; they did not intend to provide the revenue basis for great water power plants and large-scale expenditure on education and social services; they were not even concerned with the secondary economic effects of their own investments. They did not put up their money in answer to any pleas by the British government that its backward African colonial provinces be developed, or pleas from our government that American private capital play a responsible role in developing backward areas. This was a case of a private investment in its classic sense—in search of profit, and nothing more.

Regardless of this sharply focused purpose, however, the companies soon found themselves facing social and political problems. Chief of these was race relations, an issue which has become more acute in recent years.

The proposal to federate the three territories in 1953 was generally supported by the white residents and opposed by the articulate Africans, in particular those of Northern Rhodesia and Nyasaland. These Africans were reluctant to sacrifice the guardianship of the Colonial Office in London for rule by the white settlers, modeled on the government of Southern Rhodesia, in which Africans had virtually no say.

To allay the consequent misgivings in England and to gain approval by the United Kingdom Parliament and the Crown, the proposal for federation submitted to the white voters of the three territories included a declaration of the aim of partnership between the races and the retention by the Colonial Office of certain rights of intervention on behalf of the Africans for a period of years. These provisions were not popular with the white voters of the three territories, but they approved the plan for federation on that basis just the same. On that basis it was ratified by the British Parliament and Queen Elizabeth II.

Since the enactment of the Federation, it has become plain that, as to the pace and extent of implementation, "partnership" has different meanings for the African and the white settler. During these four years some progress has been made politically, and to a slighter extent socially, but in general the Africans of the Federation are still under political and social restrictions similar to but greater than those imposed on the Negroes of our deep South. Economically, the gap between the Federation's whites and most Africans is much wider than anywhere in our South. The one great difference between that region and the Central African Federation is that in the Federation the blacks hold a majority of 23 to 1 over the whites.

How does all this affect the copper companies? Let us look for a moment at the situation as they found it in the late 1920's. When preparation for mining began on the copper belt, the labor at hand consisted of utterly primitive Bantu natives. The companies therefore needed Europeans—that is what white men are called in Rhodesia—for every job of any degree of skill.

To persuade white workmen to expatriate themselves from Southern Rhodesia, the Union of South Africa, the United Kingdom, Australia, Canada, and the United States, and come to work in this primitive, unhealthy, and unknown corner of Africa, the companies had to offer extraordinary inducements. Without these men, the mines could not have been opened.

In this way, even jobs that demanded little skill came to be considered exclusively for Europeans at high pay and privileges. Today, working in a climate where the hot season is cool compared with

Boston in the summer, the European miner in the copper belt lives at subeconomic rent in a comfortable modern house, with one, two, or three African servants. He enjoys subsidized amenities and other substantial privileges. His living standard is higher than that of any group of workmen anywhere I know, including the United States.

The African Worker

Large numbers of Africans have also always been employed in the mines as unskilled labor. They come from rural areas. Today, Roan Antelope and Mufulira together employ 17,000 native African workers in addition to 3,100 Europeans. The copper belt totals are something more than double these figures.

Unlike the mines in the Union of South Africa, the copper belt mines encourage the African worker to bring his family to the mines; three fourths of the Africans now employed have their families with them. For the greater part—and it will soon be true of all of them—the married African mineworker, his wife, and his children live in a rent-free brick house equipped with electric lights, running water, and modern sewerage. They have medical facilities as good as those serving most people in Great Britain, and for their entertainment there are well-built movie theaters, libraries, recreational clubs, and sports grounds. This is a great change for a race of people who were living in semisavagery only 30 years ago; probably most of them had never even seen a wheel.

The Africans' progress toward European standards of industrial efficiency will inevitably be gradual. It is natural that there should be some who cannot easily cross the incredibly wide gap from primitive village existence to the complexities, dangers, and discipline of modern industry, many of them encountered in the mysteries of dimly lit tunnels and workings deep underground. Before the African can take the whole of a European job and give the same value as a European, he needs the intermediate training and experience that were denied him by the color bar until recently, and are still available only in a limited number of positions. And, for better or for worse, he must undergo certain psychological and physiological changes. For example:

- Because his copper belt pay is high compared to his traditional needs, the African has tended to work only long

enough to save enough money to return to his native village
and to live there in relative idleness for a year or two. At
the end of this time he returns to the copper belt to repeat
the process.

• The equalitarian tradition of the tribes makes the African
  reluctant to accept promotion to positions with disciplinary
  responsibility over fellow Africans.

• The African is better at repetitive work than he is at a
  job requiring resourcefulness.

While many of the African mineworkers still return intermittently
to the reserves, a process of slow change has set in. The African has
begun to find living conditions back on the reserves unattractive
compared with those on the copper belt, and he has begun to want
bicycles, radios, European clothing, and other conveniences for
which he needs money. Since 1950, in consequence, the average
continuous service of Africans at Roan Antelope has increased
from 2.75 to 6.6 years. And more Africans are now willing to accept supervisory responsibilities. As they gain experience, coming
generations of African mineworkers will no doubt develop the
faculty of thinking independently and will apply it to their work
problems, but this evolution will take time.

Subject to such limitations, the Africans have shown themselves
adaptable to industrial processes. On the copper belt it has long
been clear that many of them, if given adequate training, would
become competitive with the lower grades of European workmen,
if not prevented by a color bar.

Breaching the Color Bar

This color bar was not statutory; it became a tradition in large
part because of the close ties to the Union of South Africa. In the
British protectorate of Northern Rhodesia, in which the Africans are
wards of the British government, the color bar is in direct contradiction to the British government's professed policy that native interests should be paramount.

The color bar was imposed on the mining companies by the
European workers and their union during World War II, when a
strike was unthinkable because of British wartime requirements
for copper. Between 1940 and 1953 the Northern Rhodesian government appointed a series of Royal Commissions of Inquiry on this

subject, each of which recommended that the color bar be abolished. Their findings were ignored by the Northern Rhodesian government and by the British government under both Attlee and Churchill, because these governments feared the hostility of the white settlers and particularly the white labor unions.

In 1953, after racial partnership had been approved in principle by the Federation's voters, the R.S.T. group decided that if government would not take action, its companies would. R.S.T. proposed to the European mineworkers' union that the color bar clause be deleted from the union's contract with the companies. Some 15 tense months of intermittent negotiations followed.

From the start the companies pointed out that the normal turnover among European workers would take care of African advancement, and they offered to guarantee that no employed European would lose his job or suffer in any other way. This guarantee did not satisfy many European workers, who wanted to maintain the color bar in order to ensure the preservation of their own highly privileged status for their sons and grandsons. In addition, the companies demanded the right to divide a European job between two or more Africans at correspondingly reduced pay, pending the time when one African became capable of equaling the European's performance. The European union strongly opposed this so-called right of fragmentation.

At this juncture the government appointed another commission, which found that the abolition of the color bar had become imperative, and it upheld the companies on fragmentation. The union rejected the commission's report, whereupon the R.S.T. companies gave the union six months' notice of termination of the contract. This was at the end of 1954, a time of high copper prices and high profits. R.S.T.'s readiness to risk a strike under such conditions came to the European mineworkers' union as a great shock, and brought them to their senses.

Finally, in September 1955 a three-year agreement was signed. It transferred 24 categories of jobs to Africans at differential pay, leaving the companies free to give any remaining European job to an African at full European pay. Thus the color bar on the copper belt was breached. Since then several hundred African mineworkers have taken advantage of their new opportunities.

The policy of the other group, the Anglo-American companies, during these negotiations, was inevitably influenced by their South African associations. They followed R.S.T.'s lead haltingly and reluctantly. In the end, after R.S.T. had won its battle, the Anglo-American group joined in signing the new contract.

One Step Forward

Will African advancement raise or reduce costs? No one knows. The companies hope that in the long run it will reduce them, but they do not expect this to happen during the years of transitional friction and labor troubles. Beyond that, the outcome is still in doubt because the wage structure of the advancing Africans is based on the abnormally high European wage scale, in that every skilled African who can replace a European will get that European's wage. But the R.S.T. companies realized that regardless of the effect on profits, this change had to come.

Everywhere in southern Africa foreign business must deal with nationalism or race consciousness, but in no two countries are the problems alike. In the Belgian Congo, for instance, the great Katanga mining company broke the color bar many years ago when the company and the Belgian government, which runs the Congo with benevolent and complete autocracy from Brussels, decided to repatriate all white mineworkers to Belgium except for a few left behind to teach the natives. In Ghana the white residents, who are mostly temporary, have never amounted to more than 1% of the population. There, foreign business now deals with an independent, all-black state.

In the Union of South Africa, by contrast, the blacks have no say whatever, although they outnumber the whites four to one. African workers may not be advanced beyond the limits imposed by the government and the white labor unions, Africans are forbidden to organize for collective bargaining, and in the mines the color bar is statutory.

In the Federation of Rhodesia and Nyasaland the situation, as we have seen, is more complicated. In Northern Rhodesia the mining companies face: (1) the African workers, who have an active labor union and are theoretically encouraged to advance economically, politically, and socially; (2) the federal government, controlled by the white settlers, who resist African advancement on all these fronts; and (3) the Colonial Office in London, represented by the Governor of Northern Rhodesia, who usually stands somewhere between the other two forces.

There will be racial tensions in the Federation for years to come. The race problem has not been solved, but the breaking of the color bar in the copper mines was a first important step toward its solution. The event was unusual in that a great social change for the better was achieved by big business on its own initiative, with government watching from the sidelines. The British and American partners in R.S.T., working in harmony, brought about this change, which may have far-reaching effects throughout southern Africa.

Another interesting innovation pioneered by R.S.T. is the introduction of an employee stock purchase plan, open to all workers, including the Africans. This is the first such arrangement that I know of anywhere in southern Africa. Already, over 100 Africans have become stockholders under this plan.

If most representatives of business sent from the United States and other investing countries between, say, 1890 and 1940 to work in far-off regions had known more about those regions and their peoples, many of the later troubles there might have been avoided. Today there are heartening signs on this horizon. Here and in other Western countries more and more companies want their managers and chief technicians to have had some education in the humanities, and, if they work abroad, to have some knowledge of the language, history, and culture of the countries where they are to live.

Profitability is still the fundamental criterion for private capital attracted abroad, but among its essential safeguards are vision, tact, and courage on the part of its representatives in dealing with the problems that will arise from the racial and national sensibilities they encounter.

THE OIL INDUSTRY IN VENEZUELA *

A major theme of this book is the realization that the most difficult problem of the American businessman is no longer the production and selling of goods and services but the degree to which he is an asset to the society in which he operates. This problem is

* By Mr. Wright.

doubly difficult for the American businessman who lives and works abroad, for in addition to his responsibility as an *American* businessman, he must consider his responsibility to the *foreign* community in which he operates. Of course, the extent of the problem depends on the country involved and also on the influence he can exercise on the life of that country.

In this chapter I would like to concentrate on the experience of my own company, the Creole Petroleum Corporation, in Venezuela. I shall describe the political situation in Venezuela, which is the history of a difficult transition from dictatorship to freedom, and then discuss the steps that Creole Petroleum has taken to adjust to this change.

Politics in Venezuela

Although the climate for foreign investment has generally been favorable, in January 1958 we were faced with a change of government. A dictatorship was overthrown, and since that time nationalism has greatly increased. The oil industry has been a major target of this nationalism. This attack is quite understandable in view of the fact that the oil industry is foreign and represents 65% of the government's income. In effect, the criticisms range from demands for higher taxes on the oil industry and suggestions for more control over its operations and markets, to demands that the government itself enter the oil business.

The Communists have played an important part in the attacks. Although they did not originate these particular theories, they make a great deal of use of them as techniques to aggravate the grievances and feelings of the people. Their objective is very clearly to drive a wedge between Venezuela and the United States, and the best and quickest way to do this is by attacking the oil industry, which is principally American-owned. They have been able to strengthen their influence in the press, schools, and labor unions. Although a minority party, they have great influence in opinion formation.

Their attacks in Venezuela are reinforced by action in other parts of South America. Argentina, Brazil, and Uruguay depend largely on imported oil—mostly Venezuelan—to meet their internal demands. They usually pay for the oil in dollars. Recently, however, contracts have been signed between the Soviet bloc and these three countries to supply them with Soviet oil on a barter basis. In return, the Soviet bloc receives the products that those countries have been exporting and on which they depend for their dollar credit—wool, cocoa, and other products of that kind.

It is true that these contracts cover only a relatively small percentage of the entire need of these countries, but the Communists have managed to get their foot in the door. As usual, they have picked a sensitive spot and gone to work on it.

Since all three of these countries are in severe economic straits, these offers are irresistible on a short-term basis. First of all, the price is considerably below the going market price for oil. Personally, I doubt if the Russians could supply oil at these prices and under the conditions of the barter arrangement in any great volume for any period of time. But the fact remains that they are in, and there is not much that private companies can do about this economic situation. After all, we are in business to make a profit; we could not stay in business otherwise. We cannot meet the Russian prices, nor can we accept those products in exchange for oil.

There are perhaps ways in which the United States government could alleviate the situation. Technical assistance and economic aid are a step in the right direction, although the job of developing human and economic resources has been much more successfully accomplished by private capital.

The Latin American countries can also do more than they are doing today to create a favorable climate for private capital and foreign capital, which they need badly. Instead of that, however, the trend has been toward statism. In Venezuela, for example, a large share of the national budget is being spent to cover the losses of a steel company, a petrochemical company, an airline, and a chain of hotels. These costly undertakings naturally reduce the funds available for education, roads, and public health. On the other hand, Venezuela's new democratic government is most eager to improve and expand these latter services.

Serving the Community

In the face of this political situation, Creole Petroleum seeks to maintain its reputation as a good citizen and to fulfill its obligations to the community. Some of the basic rules we follow are:

(1) Under no circumstances does the company interfere in the internal politics of the country. All our foreign service employees must live under that same rule as far as their individual conduct is concerned.

(2) We always try to identify ourselves as a Venezuelan institution. In order to do that, we must identify ourselves with the cultural, educational, and economic progress of the country. Our foreign service employees are encouraged to learn and enjoy the culture of the country and to integrate with the community and be a part of its life. They must never forget that in everything they do they are guests in Venezuela.

(3) Every United States national who is employed there must learn Spanish.

(4) We always employ Venezuelans in preference to foreigners if we can, although the demand for technically trained people is so great that they are not always available.

We have implemented these rules in many ways. In the field of education, for instance, a couple of years ago we organized a Creole Foundation which spends in excess of $1,500,000 for scholarships, teacher training, vocational schools, and laboratory equipment. The Foundation also sponsors such cultural activities as the visit of the New York Philharmonic to Venezuela and exhibitions of Venezuelan art in the United States.

Our advanced management course represents another activity in the field of education. We decided to develop our own program, with the help of professors from the United States. The students lived, worked, and studied together for three weeks, and we invited a number of Venezuelan businessmen to live and work with them. We have now arranged for the local university to take over the course and run it on a permanent basis. I am glad to say that we were successful in setting up this plan. With the help of the local businessmen enrolled in the school, we were able to send three Venezuelan professors to the United States. They are back now, and the classes are being run in Spanish for the first time.

Our community integration program is another important Creole project. When we first went to Venezuela, our operations were in remote areas. In order to operate and keep our work force healthy, we had to supply all the services ourselves in company camps, mess halls, schools, laundries, garages, ice plants, and the like. Communities sprang up around these camps, and a few years ago, after some soul searching, we decided that we had better quit living behind gates and integrate with them as quickly as we could. We set out to do this by passing out a few of the services that we were performing, even lending money to help start a laundry or a garage, for example, and finally gave them all our businesses, virtually all our service activities.

We also lend money to our employees so they can buy lots from us to build their own homes. They are required to pay back only half of the loan. We lend money to merchants to set up shops; we build churches and schools. We try not to interfere in the community; however, it must stand on its own feet. When we are able to make the community operate successfully, we will have gone a long way toward eliminating the company camps, with all the social and economic pressures they generate.

Our help to the Venezuelan government in reorganizing its classification and salary system is still another project. (The government did not even know how many employees it had, so it asked us to give it a hand.) We put anywhere from six to twelve men on the job full-time and helped the authorities develop a budget through classification and salary work and administrative assistance. Now Venezuela has organized what might be called a Hoover Commission, headed by a Creole employee who devotes half of his time to this effort (at no cost to the Venezuelans).

These are some examples of how Creole Petroleum has faced the problem of being the biggest company in the biggest industry on which the nation depends. As a result of our size, the impact of our actions on the economic and the social life of the community is so great that it is frightening. But at the same time, this impact is a challenge, for it means that we have to take it into consideration in every decision that we make.

QUESTIONS AND ANSWERS*

Mr. Gordon: How strong is organized Communism in Africa?
Mr. Hochschild: It has achieved some foothold in the Union of

* Businessmen present at the panel session on which this chapter is based raised certain questions which brought about the interplay of ideas reported more or less verbatim in this section.

South Africa, where all the political organizations of Africans are infiltrated to some degree. In Rhodesia there is surprisingly little Communist influence, so far, despite their best efforts to develop strength. However, I don't think that this situation will remain as it is a great deal longer.

From the floor: If for political reasons the Soviet Union should attempt to disrupt the copper market by selling below cost, could they succeed in forcing your industry to sell below cost?

Mr. Hochschild: While the Soviet Union might do some damage in that direction, I doubt that it could keep it up for very long. I should think the Soviet Union would not want to sell its copper at a loss for any extended period of time. It is a tall order for even the most powerful producer to undertake to put another producer out of business by underselling him at a loss for an indeterminate period.

From the floor: The question as posed might better have been asked about aluminum than copper, because although we don't know how much aluminum the Soviet Union will have in the future, it could conceivably become a very large producer.

The policy of the company that I represent is pretty much a free trade approach, and it does not come naturally to us to suggest that artificial barriers of any kind be raised, even again Communist trade.

On the other hand, it is very easy to conceive that Khrushchev will sit in Moscow and have a marvelous time seeing just how much trouble he can cause between nations in the Western world with a very small amount of tin and aluminum. If he sold 30,000 to 40,000 tons of aluminum in the West, perhaps 1% of the aluminum used in the free world, the European countries and the United States would be setting up high tariffs against everybody else's aluminum. I think the right approach might be for some defense organization to be paid to work in reverse. Instead of letting the Soviet Union decide how much of the various materials the West will be allowed to sell in the East, this organization might turn around and say, "Well, now, how much of these materials will we allow the East to sell to the West?"

We wouldn't cut them off completely, maybe, but at least, we could put a ceiling on their sales.

From the floor: I believe that in the last Congress a bill was introduced to set up a corporation to produce goods and to sell in competition with the Russians. How feasible is this?

Mr. Gordon: I don't think that particular approach would help very much.

To go into a cutthroat competition with the Soviet Union by having aluminum purchased by a United States commodity corporation and selling it at a loss would be a silly game for us, because in the market where the cutthroat competition took place, the other competing suppliers, who presumably are friends of ours, would be even more badly hurt than they would be by the Russian competition alone.

I doubt if this would really be desirable. I had the impression that this proposal was partly designed to deal with cases where the Soviet Union seemed to be supplying capital goods at barter prices, or concessional prices of some kind, and where it was thought that perhaps we ought to be in direct competition with it.

One feasible solution, which would certainly work in the case of aluminum, where the main consumers are a fairly small number of countries, would be an agreement among the consuming countries that they would not permit the importation of Soviet aluminum at prices lower than ruling market prices in the West. This would make the price effective, rather than trying to limit the amount, and it would be enforceable.

From the floor: This kind of problem is becoming serious for the oil industry. Some Soviet oil is showing up in Sweden, Iceland, France—in fact, about everywhere—in relatively small amounts. But these small amounts are enough to disrupt markets and upset marketing and supply operations in these areas. We don't know how far this is going to go, and we are very much concerned about it.

Another approach is the one the Russians have taken in Iceland, Argentina, Brazil, and Uruguay, where they have set up a barter arrangement. We used to supply petroleum to Iceland, for example; today we supply petroleum only for our own military forces, because the Russians trade petroleum to Iceland for fish, and the United States government has been unwilling to buy fish.

Mr. Gordon: Do you sell the Russian petroleum for them?

From the floor: In some markets we are forced to do so. Certainly we would never do it unless we were forced to by local governments, but it has happened.

MARKETING: THE TWIN DANGERS OF SUCCESS AND FAILURE

Malcolm P. McNair and Theodore Levitt

MARKETING AND THE "SOLID SELL"*

IN RECENT YEARS the critics of our society—and of business in particular—have directed much of their attention to modern marketing and its goals. Marketing men find themselves the victims of a two-pronged attack. On the one hand, they are asked such questions as these: Can marketing really be successful in moving the output of industry and keeping our economic ship on an even keel? Can it really do the large and ever-increasing job that is ahead of it? On the other horn of the dilemma, they are confronted with these

Note: Mr. McNair is Lincoln Filene Professor of Retailing, Harvard Business School; and Mr. Levitt is a marketing and economic consultant. Edward C. Bursk, Editor, *Harvard Business Review,* and Professor of Business Administration, Harvard Business School, acted as moderator for the panel session on which this chapter is based.

* By Mr. McNair.

queries: If it can and does do that job, is not marketing going to debase our entire American culture by inducing us all to buy for ephemeral and emotional reasons and to throw things away before they are worn out? Is it not responsible for developing a false set of values, for the exaggerated worship of newness, material success, and conformity?

My position very briefly is that unless it mends its ways, marketing is not going to be able to accomplish either the task of successfully moving the output of industry over the long run and keeping us on an even keel or the job of promoting a truly good standard of living and a soundly based set of values. To get at the question of *how* marketing can reform itself, let us look at some of the current criticisms being leveled at it.

The Marketing Revolution

One criticism prevalent among economists parallels a fallacious but long-held theory about the creation of purchasing power. This notion, called Say's Law after Jean Baptiste Say, a French economist of the eighteenth century, held that purchasing power will always be ready to take the product off the market because production itself, through wages, creates the necessary purchasing power. This theory held sway down to the time of the late John Maynard Keynes, when the economists finally succeeded in putting their finger on the flaw: there are many circumstances under which production does not create the necessary purchasing power at all points or the purchasing power does not function actively in taking the product off the market. Many aspects of the Keynesian doctrine have now become orthodox economics, and the flow of purchasing power is one of the principal guides to the health of the economy.

One fallacy which is in many respects parallel to Say's Law still persists, however. The notion that the public is ready to take the products of industry as they come off the line, without any nudging, is still accepted by some economists. These economists take the point of view that marketing would not really be necessary in an ideal economy because consumers would be standing in line trying to buy the manufacturers' products. In other words, marketing does not perform any intrinsically useful service; it is an economic waste, and in a properly organized economy it would be, for the most part, unnecessary. These economists feel that in a very high-level economy we can probably afford this extravagance but we do not really need it.

My point of view has always been very different. I do not concede for a minute that marketing is not necessary. The theory that marketing is a social waste totally fails to take into account the contribution that marketing makes to the dynamic character of a moving economy, which goes forward toward an ever-increasing standard of living.

At any given time a substantial proportion of the products being sold to consumers are of relatively recent development. They were not dreamed of by our fathers, still less our grandfathers. Does the public stand avidly in line waiting to grab these new goods? On the contrary, the public resists them with great vigor. The fact is that people do not always rush to buy a better mousetrap; you have to educate them about it, or they simply will not buy. The opposition to new dress fashions is an example.

Hence, marketing has a tremendous educational job to do in paving the way for new products and higher consumption. In a high-level economy, marketing tends to become the primary business force. In a penetrating analysis of American business in this mid-century period, Saville Davis poses the question: How has American capitalism been transformed?* In my view, it has been transformed largely by what I call the "marketing revolution": the emergence of marketing as the primary force in American business. I am talking about something more than just an emphasis on sales promotion; rather, I mean the broad concept that products have to be continually changed and replaced in a moving economy, and that the marketing point of view, which rests on meeting consumer demand, tends to become the most important influence in American business.

There are, of course, many factors in this transformation. Unquestionably, the technology and the spreading of purchasing power to which Donald K. David refers have been vastly important in the changes that have been taking place in this half century.† But we

---

* "What's Happened to Capitalism?" *Harvard Business School Bulletin,* June 1958, p. 22.

† See the chapter entitled "The New Relationship of Business to Society," p. 66.

must not forget that the gradual rise of marketing to a dominant position in American business is likewise one of the very important forces that have led to the transformation of American capitalism. This is the opposite pole from the position of the economist who, looking at a static world, says that marketing is not really necessary.

Consumer Freedom

Another familiar complaint from the critics turns on alleged restrictions on the consumer's freedom of choice. If I do not want to buy an automobile with fins on it, if I do not want one that is 18 feet long, and if I would like to have one that is only 78 inches wide so that I can get it into my garage, I will have a hard time finding it; in other words, I cannot get what I personally want, but must take what some businessman imposes on me.

Another related target is the whole area of the "hidden persuaders." The idea behind this is that people buy because of subconscious motives, and that if you can just find out how to press the right button you can get them to pick out what you want them to, though they may not be conscious of why they are buying. Obviously very much in the forefront here also is the emphasis on gimmicks, trading stamps, gadgets, giveaways, and the very high volume of consumer credit. In his chapter, Erwin D. Canham brings up these points as criticisms of the American business system and, perforce, of the dominant position which marketing occupies in the American business system today.*

How serious are these complaints? Let us look at the other side of the coin. In the first place, demand is enormously more complex than most economists and businessmen realize. A variety of motives, both rational and nonrational, enter into consumer choice, and the pattern is becoming more and more complicated all the time.

As the standard of living and hence the amount of spending goes up—particularly the amount of spending for goods and services over and above necessities—demand keeps splitting. We no longer have simply a demand for automobiles or dresses as such, but people begin to want a great many different kinds of a particular product. The automobile marketers have missed this point in the last few years. The demand for automobiles has not lessened; rather, it has become much more complex and varied than it once

* See the chapter entitled "For a Revised Sense of Values," p. 75.

was. This varied demand means that many different selling efforts and selling appeals must be used.

Furthermore, the idea that consumer freedom of choice has been cut down is overstated. To be sure, here and there we may find that it seems to be somewhat curtailed temporarily. But in automobiles, for instance, the foreign cars have stepped in to meet a particular demand that is not yet being met by the American manufacturer. There is a time lag, certainly, but the need is being filled.

Retail marketing provides another example. Here the rise and fall of particular types of enterprises resembles the revolution of a wheel. When the department stores started out they were the discount houses of their day, but then they became affluent, respectable, and a little stodgy. Their prices rose, and the markup kept getting higher, until the wheel began to turn again.

Erwin Canham thinks that some aspects of this process are a little unlovely, but frankly I think that it is just a part of competition, of countervailing forces, of business evolution.

In defense of marketing, also, some of us would say that the criticisms are not really directed at Amercan marketing but rather at the fundamentals of American life and culture today. The present American way of life, in turn, stems from wishful thinking, education for life adjustment, continual stress on emotional factors and overemphasis on Freudianism, a disregard of the old-fashioned virtues, the cult of "togetherness" and conformity in human relations, and a decline in the sense of individual responsibility. Why blame marketing, then, for what is just part of the way in which American life has evolved?

To this the critics reply, "What is marketing doing to combat these trends in American life, which many people feel are not only detrimental to the long-run health of the American economy but also a real handicap in our battle with Communism? Is not marketing, by its modern practices, aiding and abetting the development of these less attractive aspects of American life?"

What conclusions should the American business executive, and particularly the marketing executive, draw from these attacks and counterattacks? It is my own position that marketing must do some things differently if it is to be successful either in continuing to move products or in helping to build a truly sound way of life.

Hard Road Ahead

For one thing, we must get back to what I used to call the "hard sell." Unfortunately, that term has become a bad word, synonymous with the aspects of marketing to which the critics object, so I have to use "solid sell" or "genuine sell" instead. But they all mean the same, and reflect the fact that selling is an important part of life.

Our critics complain about the search for the "easy way" in marketing. I agree. There is too much grabbing for panaceas and short cuts; there are too many attempts to sell by gimmicky changes rather than by fundamental appraisal of demand and good merchandising to develop a better product and, if possible, to produce it at a lower price. More emphasis should be placed on solid, constructive merchandising and less on the easy way.

Somebody recently made the very discerning comment that a product is essentially like an organism. It starts with a concept. It grows and is developed, perhaps on a drawing board. Then, after a period of change and experiment, it comes into being, but it has to be popularized and sold. Then it gradually must be modified to meet changing demand. After a while it reaches the point where it begins to become obsolete, and then finally dies and goes off the market entirely. I think we must increasingly accept this sequence in American industry and do a much more constructive and imaginative job of continuous product design and development. Let's forget trading stamps and frilly changes for a while and pay more attention to good solid merchandising.

Secondly, I think it is important for us to know a great deal more about our markets. To be sure, we have done an enormous amount of marketing research, and we have a lot of ideas on new tricks in the area of consumer research and consumer motivation. But the fact is that we have been developing a tendency to grasp at the superficial aspects, trying to pick up some clever psychological device in the hope that it will sell our product. Without ever getting into a lot of these modern doodads of one kind or another, American business can do a much solider job of study and analysis of its customers and thereby market its products more effectively.

Finally, we ought to re-examine the virtues of price competition.

Not everybody wants to pay several hundred dollars more for an automobile that has been dolled up with more chrome and a larger number of gadgets. Many people would like to be able to buy a good solid car, without the ornaments, for a couple of hundred dollars less. I recognize the many difficulties, including wage rates, which confront any effort to reduce prices; but business is much too prone to assume that demand is inelastic and that people will indefinitely pay higher prices for an allegedly superior product.

We must get back to real and basic price competition. Although sometimes price competition may have some of the unlovely aspects mentioned by Erwin Canham, that is the nature of the animal. What I am pleading for essentially is a return to the solid virtues, the hard work of marketing. We have been trying to evade the tough job in recent years. Only by giving real values to the consumer can marketing retain its supremacy.

THE EXAGGERATED DANGERS OF SUCCESS*

Many businessmen are now acutely concerned with the possible dangers of marketing success. It is natural enough for them to think about the consequences of their actions. In our more abstracted and contemplative moments we all ask ourselves some basic questions. Is it all worthwhile? Is not what we do for our daily bread trite, superficial, banal, perhaps even corrosive in its general consequences? For instance:

- If you sell antibiotics, perhaps you feel satisfied with what you do, although it may occasionally bother you that a lot of needy people cannot afford your asking price.
- If you sell switch-blade knives, you may have to think twice, but you do sell.
- What about the man who sells mudpacks to the aging matron in search of youth? The mudpack does not provide youth, though she is told that it will.
- If you have paid the hidden persuaders big money to manipulate people to buy things that they do not need and cannot afford and that perhaps are of doubtful utility, what will your soul-searching ruminations yield?
- Suppose you are a solid, devoted, church-going family man in

* By Mr. Levitt.

the automobile business. How do you feel, knowing that some people say that the car has debased American life and morals, that it is facilitating crime, vice, infidelity, adultery, and unchastity?

Whatever your business is, if you look deeply and sensitively enough, it is possible to see its wholesale contribution to decadence, self-indulgence, materialism, cynicism, irresponsibility, selfishness—a swelling galaxy of assorted social, economic, cultural, psychological, and ethical evils. You cannot escape them. The more successful your particular business, the more evil it generates.

The basis for this chapter is a list of penetrating questions raised by Professor Bursk. They were:

> Suppose we can succeed in endowing consumers with all the material goods, the necessities, the conveniences, the luxuries that our factories can produce and our stores can handle? There are still grave questions. What will happen to people as human beings? Will they lose their dignity, their culture, their appreciation of spiritual values? Will their standard of living be higher just because they can afford to obsolete their possessions quicker—continually buying new fancy models at the expense of economic waste? What is the psychology of unbounded satisfaction? What are the effects of manipulation—whether it be blatant persuasion or subtle motivation like the "hidden persuaders"? Will we become a nation of robots with mechanical appetites?

These are fundamental questions. Society must always ask itself where it is going, or it cannot know what road will take it there.

Business for Business's Sake

It is my contention, however, that the cultural, spiritual, social, and moral consequences of the businessman's actions are not his occupational concern. He is in business for his own personal good, not to save or to ruin souls. His job is perfectly neutral on the matter of the outcome of what he does.

The moment he becomes preoccupied with the deeper purposes and consequences of what he does, he becomes the conscious arbiter of our lives. He will try consciously to decide what is good or bad for us; what we should or should not have, should or should not see, hear, read, or think. He will throw the mighty weight of his great economic power behind the community-wide implementation of his own private values and tastes. Even if his values and tastes were the highest expression of God's will, the result could only be evil. Nobody can know better than the adult individual himself what his values and tastes should be, even if he is a congenital idiot. The fact that we put idiots away, it seems to me, is entirely beside the point.

The businessman exists for only one purpose: to create and deliver value satisfactions at a profit to himself. The test of whether the things he offers do, indeed, contain value satisfactions is provided by the completely neutral mechanism of the open market. The businessman's job is clear and simple. If what is offered can be sold at a profit, not even necessarily a long-term profit, then it is legitimate. The consumer has cast a favorable economic ballot.

If enough other consumers disagree and want to cast their more powerful political ballots against it, they can. That is the veto of democratic politics over democratic economics. And this ranking, I believe, is precisely the desirable and necessary order of importance, because the economic system exists only by consent of the political system. The political system creates the laws; it creates the environment; it makes possible the conditions under which the economic system operates.

Everything points to the fact that the businessman's greatest responsibility is to succeed as a businessman. He should pursue his own sense of workmanship with a singular purpose, unburdened by things that drain his vitality or cloud his objectives. He should feel free to probe wherever his instincts and talents lead, just as scientists and philosophers should be free in their fields, as neutral about the outcome as the goddess of justice.

Everything, of course, has good and bad consequences, depending in part on your values. Every thinking person should try to be aware of both. But what we want is less, not more, concern with the consequences of successful marketing. We should get away from normative considerations entirely.

The reason is purely functional. It is the same reason as applies when we say that the scientist should leave dogma and personal preference at the door when he enters his laboratory. Dogma restricts scientific development just as much as scientific development undermines dogma. Dogma also restricts marketing develop-

ment and performance. The businessman's self-conscious preoccupation with elevating the public is potentially very dangerous. When he
consciously uses his product to affect the spiritual, cultural, and
aesthetic lives of his customers, then he is playing God.

It is bad enough that he intimately affects our private lives in
the random process of doing his job as businessman. To affect them
intentionally and in a clearly manipulative fashion that has nothing to do with the object of selling as such is a compounded evil.
There are already too many institutions and individuals tyranniz-
ing us with their own private versions of God's will.

If capitalism learns to distribute and sell goods as well as it can
produce them, if marketing becomes successful enough to create
a Frankenstein loading people with superfluous goods, arousing
superficial and vulgar wants, and generating the kind of opulence
that turns luxuries into necessities and necessities into ceremonial
rather than substantive values—if this happens, perhaps we will
become soft and decadent and finally drift down into the quagmire
of decay that is alleged to have been Rome's fate.

The Puritan Voice

Let us not go overboard in an orgy of moral self-flagellation, however. A lot of this viewing with alarm is an irrational Puritan reaction against the good life, and it is well that we are aware of it.
We shrink from really having an uninhibited good time. We still
associate virtue with work and idleness with vice. Deep down inside,
somehow or other, we can not seem to shake off the guilt of Adam's
fall. "In the sweat of thy face shalt thou eat bread." We feel that
the easy life destroys the spirit. Spiritual purity is equated with hard
work and almost with physical discomfort. The prophets of the
Old Testament equated luxury and comfort with depravity and
vice, denouncing the "wearers of fine raiments" and those who
"idle on beds of ivory." Jesus said, "It is easier for a camel to go
through the eye of a needle, than for a rich man to enter into the
Kingdom of God."

None of us seems capable of fully enjoying his opulence and
leisure. We pride ourselves on not having had a vacation in ten
years, and think that one of the most commendatory things that
can be said of a man is that "he died with his boots on." There is

no greater example of the guilt frustrations that we associate with idleness than the way we refer to leisure. We call it "active leisure," a sort of euphemistic compromise with the stern Puritan voice within us that says, "Leisure? Maybe. Okay. But not idleness."

We feel that spiritual values can thrive only in adversity. Scarcity, hard work, poverty, challenge, unfulfilled social and economic needs—these are implied as the preconditions of human dignity, cultural appreciation, and cultivation of spiritual values. Anything else produces decadence.

If this is where spiritual values and dedication come from, one wonders if they are worth having. I see no merit in embracing spiritual values unless the process is the free, honest, uncoerced expression of a pure, private, and personal choice.

It is not at all a settled matter that luxury creates softness and decadence, that leisure produces sin and licentiousness, that material abundance corrupts spiritual values, that the hidden persuaders produce robot consumers and pander shamelessly to our basest instincts. For instance:

⟨ Which capitalist society is culturally and technologically more creative—the opulent, capitalist United States or hand-to-mouth, capitalist Spain?

⟨ Which condition has produced more statesmen, business leaders, writers, poets, scientists, and clergymen—the well-heeled breeding of the Marlboroughs, the Huxleys, and the Adamses or the mountaineer adversity of the Hatfields and the McCoys?

⟨ Which soldiers fought more successfully during World War II —the pampered, almost undisciplined Americans with their gum chewing and fleece-lined shoes or the arrogant Germans goose-stepping in ice-cold leather boots in pursuit of their intoxicating dream of historic mission?

⟨ What is better, for our wives to spend endless drudging hours scrubbing clothes half-clean on corrugated washboards and serving us half-done, half-digestible pies and cakes they have proudly made from scratch, or for the hidden persuaders to have banished their Puritan guilt feelings about using automatic washing machines and premixed cake flour?

To become excited about the social and human consequences of so-called successful marketing is know-nothing hysteria. It defies the

facts. After all, last year more Americans attended live perform-
ances of serious music than went to professional baseball and foot-
ball games combined. More good books are being read per capita
today than 50 years ago. I would say that our taste in furniture today is certainly superior to yesterday's mid-Victorian monstrosities.
Magazines like *Harper's Bazaar, Playboy, Esquire,* and *Holiday,*
which cater to so-called people of means, regularly publish some
of the best authors writing in the English language today, people
like the late Joyce Cary, William Faulkner, Kenneth Tynan, William Sansom, A. B. Guthrie, Jr., Anthony West, and Eudora Welty.
Why are these people not published in the comic books that go to
the people in the lower economic echelons, who are supposed to be
culturally emancipated as a result of desperate economic straits?

The Cake of Custom

As for conformity, we have always had it abundantly. The abiding quality of conformity during some of history's most flowering
times of creative uniqueness, whether in music, art, literature, science, or business, is illustrated wonderfully in a brief passage in
Aubrey Menen's witty and serious book, *The Prevalence of Witches.*
It tells about a group of Englishmen living in the mythical jungle
colony of Limbo. One of the older men, who has been there for a
long time, always carries a whippy stick. A new arrival, fresh from
the Home Office, asks why. The answer:

> "Everybody who knows how to live in the jungle carries a
> whippy stick."
> "What for?"
> "Why, to break the backs of snakes, of course."
> "Have you ever broken the back of a snake?"
> "Never. Whenever I see one I run like hell. But if you're going
> to be accepted here, you'll just have to carry a whippy stick. It's
> like swinging a tennis racket in the suburbs of London on a Satur-
> day afternoon. You must do the proper thing, you know." *

This was the late nineteenth century. Conformity is an ever-
present fact in history. Nothing emphasizes its venerability more
than the fact that every martyr, whether a Jesus of Nazareth, a

* New York, Charles Scribner's Sons, 1953, pp. 33–34.

Joan of Arc, or a Sacco and Vanzetti, is celebrated for having defied to the death some prevailing orthodoxy.

No matter how much people talk about the decadence of our society, no generation can completely judge itself. It simply does not know enough. It cannot know or predict the completed, worked-out, mature consequences of the forces that are currently in motion. The forces of challenge and response are in a perpetual state of dialectical ferment. They constantly create new reactions to new challenges, producing new syntheses of newly contending vectors of change. We must recognize that the cake of custom is always breaking up, particularly in the last half century. Change is a cost of freedom and threatens the rule of things we hold dear. This does not mean that the world is degenerating. It may be that something much more edifying will finally emerge—a higher synthesis.

We seem perfectly willing to take this optimistic view when it comes to material things. We believe that machines will become more versatile and more productive, that gadgets will be more plentiful and more serviceable, that even food will become more abundant and more nourishing. In other words, material change is equated ideologically with progress.

When it comes to the nonmaterial consequences of these changes, we become paralyzed with apprehension, fear, and doubt. Our attitudes toward changes in tastes, values, and human relations seem always to imply that things can only get worse, that we live in some sort of utopia, the best of all possible worlds. We ignore the terrible evidence of war, duplicity, mayhem, vice, and corruption that surrounds us every day. Perhaps we should assume that things cannot get worse, that they can only get better.

We do not have to accept the lugubrious prophecies of imminent disaster that have been made periodically since Isaiah. Such prophecies should be rejected, because each comes with its spokesman's own narrow formula for salvation. We are always being asked to trade away the pluralistic, competitive, multivalued, free world within which we live for some rigid spiritual doctrine which its advocates say will yield the utopian perfection essential for survival.

Such people always seem to value survival above all else—whether the rest of us like it or not. It is like the man who was against the revolution, even when he was told that after the revolution he could

eat strawberries and cream. "But," the man said, "I don't like strawberries and cream." He was told in no uncertain terms, "Comes the
revolution, you'll eat strawberries and cream, whether you like
it or not."

This is survival at any price. Is it possible that life is not worth
living under certain regimented conditions of survival? After all,
that is what war is all about. War is a condition under which we
agree that we would rather die than change our minds. We would
not have wars if we would change our minds.

The Double-edged Sword

The quest for perfection is a fine ideal. But when individuals
generalize their own notions of the beautiful and the true, when
they turn into inspired spokesmen intent on making converts, and
especially when the effort is sustained by the businessman's great
secular power, they are dangerous. Once you begin to second-guess
the nonmaterial consequences of the soundly materialistic functions
of business, you become involved in an endless and fruitless rhetoric.
If you are at all serious about these bigger issues, they will keep
you from doing the workmanlike job that your business demands.
Anyone who seriously dabbles with these higher values during
business hours inevitably finds that they engulf him, for they are
much more important than business. That is, of course, why successful operating men generally leave them alone.

No wonder this is usually the province of the chairman of the
board, the elder statesman who is tapering off and now cultivates a
garden that promises a different, more elevating kind of yield, a
yield that is written in the Great Book Beyond, not in the Great
Book in the financial vice president's office.

It is true you cannot as businessmen serve two masters, God and
Mammon. I suggest that you serve business and yourself. That is
your only function. Saving souls, promoting or preserving spiritual
values, elevating taste, cultivating human dignity and consumer
self-respect—these high-priority objectives are other people's business,
if that is what they want to make them. The businessman's job is to
do the things that are the pure, undiluted objectives of business—
to satisfy the materialistic and related ego objectives of those who
run it.

When business becomes involved in lofty causes it dilutes its own efforts and ultimately ceases to deliver the goods properly. Perhaps worse, it makes itself, or the business executive, a self-appointed arbiter—a Great White Father sanctimoniously and censorially meting out predigested standards of taste, thought, opinion, and material comforts to the childlike multitudes whose precious souls must be saved for another world.

Aside from the danger of this becoming a really powerful threat to our free and open society, I am forced to conclude that it represents the height of vanity on the part of its advocates. They are acting very much like lords of the manor. Of course, nobody really wants to return to this kind of feudalism. But from my observations, people who talk and write approvingly about socially responsible business behavior seldom think of anything but the positive values that might result from the effort. They seldom contemplate the possible nightmare consequences.

Moral and ethical standards are not reprehensible, but they are a double-edged sword. They can strike in unexpected and unedifying directions. Under certain conditions of powerful secular sponsorship they can, and historically have, led to the worst kind of tyranny —from inane censorship to witch hunts, inquisitions, and even blood baths of frightening proportions.

QUESTIONS AND ANSWERS*

Mr. McNair: Mr. Levitt has indicated the very grave dangers in trying to play God. I have great sympathy with that point of view, but it seems to me that he carries it almost to the point of disclaiming any social responsibility on the part of the businessman. There I do not go along with him.

I think that because marketing has become so central to American business in the last 50 years, and especially in the last 12 or 15, it is dangerous to disclaim social responsibility. Marketing is an important molder of tastes and values today, especially since its sales promotion aspect is so closely allied with the entertainment industry. Marketing cannot escape its social responsibility.

* Businessmen present at the panel session on which this chapter is based raised certain questions which brought about the interplay of ideas reported more or less verbatim in this section.

Mr. Levitt: Do you equate doing a good job as a businessman with social responsibility?

Mr. McNair: No, I am not equating business and social responsibility entirely, but I think that the marketer must look at some of the social consequences of what he does. When he takes the easy way out, when he places the emphasis on gimmicks and gadgets and does not really improve his product, when he does not really do a job of "hard sell," and when he does not do all that he can to lower costs and prices, he is fulfilling neither his social responsibility nor, in the long run, his business responsibility.

From the floor: Is it possible that our marketing people have done such a good job of selling the soft life that our people no longer can face up to the realities of our situation?

Mr. Bursk: I don't think that marketing has sold the soft life. On the contrary, life gets continually harder because of marketing selling. It is softer in the sense that we have more comfort, but we keep wanting more. Because of marketing, we are striving for things more than ever.

I also want to point out that a good marketing man isn't going to sell junk or poison, because, if he is wise, he knows that poor or harmful goods are not going to have a long sales life. Marketing men have found that the best way to sell is to offer something that serves a fundamental need. Then customers keep coming back for more.

I would like to submit that one of the functions of marketing— for which it does not get credit, incidentally—is getting people to want *something.* In other words, it stimulates them to look ahead to a better standard of living, improved social status, and so on.

This basic desire can be spurred and then harnessed to make it the dynamic behind the achievement of an ever-higher standard of living for all. Of course, the people who criticize this approach would argue that mankind should have aesthetic, intellectual, and spiritual values, satisfactions, and aspirations; but I would ask, in return, how you are going to reach these unless men and women are encouraged to want things *and* the fulfillment of some of these inner desires which things can provide. If we hold them to the rigid criterion of "It will still operate, so why throw it away?" they are bound tight by a purely materialistic view of life, denying the other kinds of satisfactions that goods can provide.

Now just what nonmaterial and nonfunctional values *things* can offer is another question. I think that the art of marketing itself is raising the level of these nonmaterial satisfactions, though I suspect that the job is really that of education, and that you have to blame education for false values, not marketing.

It is apropos to point out here that education very rarely practices forced obsolescence—and that it could use a little of our marketing philosophy in this regard. We keep on going through the same routines in education for a lot longer than we have any reason to. Change is so rapid in this world that the idea of spending 18 years teaching people the knowledge of 10, 25, or 50 years ago is ridiculous. It makes a lot more sense to go all the way back and talk about something really ancient—like the classics I used to teach—that is beyond the possibility of effectiveness, than to spend so much time talking about how to do a job today or tomorrow. So I would urge educators who criticize marketing's forced obsolescence to take a look at what they are doing themselves.

From the floor: You cannot say that we businessmen sell for nothing but profit, because we are part of the community. If we expect any progress, somebody must try to make it. The businessman is a part of that problem, and he has to ask himself whether his product is sufficiently constructive and valuable to survive in the long run.

Mr. Bursk: I would submit that if every man here honestly and thoroughly did that, he would get out of the business he is in. The point here is that we don't—and shouldn't undertake to do so. But when we recognize that those human beings we are trying to sell our goods to mean something as human beings, without being soft about it, we are simply acknowledging a fact. In so doing, we will be more successful marketers, and we will be well protected against launching some deleterious program.

From the floor: Isn't the relationship between business and marketing and ethics simply the fact that you have to live with your own conscience? If what you do is consistent with your beliefs as a thinking person, you are all right.

Mr. Bursk: Let me conclude this chapter by saying that I don't think the "twin dangers" we have been talking about really exist at all. We have raised them here as issues that deserve to be brought out into the open, and having looked at them we should realize that we had better go ahead and do some real selling and stop worrying.

But by "hard selling" I do not mean "high pressure" in the traditional sense. Rational selling is more effective, despite all the increased attention to and concern with the "hidden persuaders," subliminal advertising, and gimmicks. People buy more intelligently today than they used to. Tomorrow, and 25 years from now, the way our youngsters are being brought up, they will buy even more intelligently than we do.

Let me call your attention to a very specific view of selling, which I think will lead to stronger, more confident selling:

> Most people have healthy minds; they like to buy. There is no need to dig into their subconscious to free them from blocks and tensions before they buy. (Indeed, such an effort may be dangerous —may stir up conflict without enough time or skill to remove it— something even psychiatrists worry about.) Irrational resistances, even if in the subconscious, can be handled by the healthy prospect himself—and *will* be, if he is provided with a sufficient *rational* motive as incentive.

> But selling is not just satisfying present wants or playing up to old desires. Selling is a process of increasing wants or, even better, creating new wants. This is what keeps our economy dynamic. Further, the more business gets consumers to consider the pursuit of noneconomic values as approved and rational, the more it is building people's potential for a higher, less materialistic way of life. And it is up to education to see to it that consumers say *no* to the more meretricious forms of satisfaction.

> The danger of consumer motivation research is that business may rely on "scientific" techniques and forget to go out and sell. As far as getting buying action is concerned, the actual psychological subtleties may just be too tenuous for the hit-and-run of daily life. But we can use our understanding of how people buy to build a lot of little strategies for persuading people to want specific products and services, and one grand strategy of giving people continually bigger and better goals for themselves.

> In either case, there is one big, uncomplex psychology at work— the interaction of enthusiastic seller and eager buyer, out in the

open where they belong. And whatever irrational forces there are will be released if they are in your favor, contained if they are against you. Such selling is not manipulating people behind their backs; it is giving them rational motives for doing what is in their own best interests as individuals and as society-at-large.*

* Edward C. Bursk, "Opportunities for Persuasion," *Harvard Business Review*, September–October 1958, p. 119.

CREATIVITY: WHAT LESSONS
CAN WE LEARN
FROM THE SCIENTISTS?

Abram T. Collier and James Hillier

IN A RECENT MAGAZINE DRAWING, a vacation-bound driver was shown leaning out of an automobile piled high with luggage. Calling back to a woman shutting the door of a house behind him, the man was saying, "Oh, don't bother to lock the door, we didn't leave anything behind!"

Nowadays we cannot even take short trips, it seems, without carrying with us the material trappings of a highly complicated society. And the practice of traveling heavily seems to be particularly prevalent in business organizations. Like tournaments of medieval knights, business management is filled with people and functions

Note: Mr. Collier, who makes the introductory observations, is Vice President and General Counsel of John Hancock Mutual Life Insurance Company; and Dr. Hillier is Vice President, RCA Laboratories, Radio Corporation of America.

unheard of a generation ago. Hardly a decision of consequence can be taken without calling in experts from every field. Once occasional advice from the company's lawyer or accountant was all that was necessary; today management has experts to advise it on its relations with its stockholders and bankers, its employees and labor unions, its customers and suppliers, its regulatory and taxing authorities, and even community enterprises, which include not only trade associations but also hospitals, social agencies, schools and colleges, and groups almost without end. Surrounded by so many specialists, it is no wonder that business travels slowly—the wonder is that it travels at all.

It is partly because of the increased complexity which has gripped modern business that we turn to the sciences—particularly the methods of the physical scientists—to see what we can learn to help us simplify our tasks. The scientists have dealt with complexity by maintaining their faith in the understandableness and symmetry of the universe, and by constantly relating their discoveries and inventions to simplified basic concepts. They have created the most important new industry of this country—the industry of discovery. They have developed attitudes, viewpoints, and values which have proved to be strikingly effective in pushing the frontiers of knowledge out into the distant heavens. In the face of such accomplishments, it may not be idle to inquire what those attitudes, viewpoints, and values are, how they are related to each other, and how they may be related to the basic problems confronting business management.

As a man who is directly concerned with the creative process in the sciences, Dr. Hillier will discuss, in his section of this chapter, the essential elements in scientific discovery and how they came about. I will then make some comments on their application to a business enterprise.

THE CREATIVE MIND AND ITS ENVIRONMENT*

Though creative thinking is the most essential element in the scientific progress that we have been able to make in the world, we really understand very little about it. We know that creative thinking is not a simple act, but a very complex interaction of the human

* By Dr. Hillier.

mind with its total environment. We know it is necessary for the successful execution of any important development in a research laboratory. Subjectively, we scientists know what creativity is, and we seem to have no difficulty in making at least a qualitative evaluation of the degree of creativity possessed and already demonstrated by those contemporaries whom we know well. As a matter of fact, we do this with a remarkable degree of consistency.

But when industrial psychologists try to establish criteria by which they can measure, in advance, the inherent creativity of an untried research worker, they seem to have very little success. Thus, in creativity we appear to have a characteristic which is poorly defined and not yet susceptible to objective measurement, and yet is understood by those involved. Those of us who are responsible for developing and utilizing creativity in an industrial research organization find ourselves with a complex and diffuse problem. In spite of this, the success of technological developments would seem to indicate that the problem is being solved, if only by intuitive means.

It is difficult, if not impossible, to define creativity, because it includes a number of somewhat different phenomena. On the other hand, it does seem possible to describe it. I have chosen three examples for this purpose, which I believe represent three different aspects of the process. They are not meant to be exclusive, but they are illustrative.

Creativity in Action

The first relates to the imaginative association of apparently unrelated concepts. It concerns the solution of one of the basic problems in color television.

> The black and white television channels are arranged to carry a certain amount of information that determines the fineness of detail you finally get in the picture on your set. When we wanted to go to color, all the prevalent theories indicated that we would have to transmit three pictures in three colors or the equivalent amount of information. To achieve the same definition as black and white television, we would have to use the equivalent of three channels for just one picture. This was considered intolerable, and it meant, therefore, that some of the information in the picture would have to be sacrificed.

One of our engineers was very much concerned about this problem and solved it in a most interesting way. One day he was looking out the window and, essentially, daydreaming. For some reason, an experience he had had as a youngster passed through his mind. His mother had asked him to go to the store to buy a spool of specially colored thread. She gave him a small piece of cloth with which to match the color. In the course of doing this, she warned him not to try matching a single strand of the thread with the cloth, but to make sure that he used the thread wound on the whole spool. He did not understand why she wanted him to do this, nor did she explain. While he was daydreaming in the laboratory, the explanation for this request suddenly became clear to him, and the important thing is that simultaneously he struck on a solution to the color television problem, which has stood the test of time and a great deal of careful scrutiny.

He realized that the comparison between the color of a large sample and that of a fine thread was unreliable because the eye lacked the ability to distinguish the colors of extremely small objects. He correctly reasoned that in the color television system it might not be necessary to transmit fine detail in the color information. Since the fine detail in the three color pictures was using up the channel space, this would constitute a real saving.

It is interesting to note that the rather aimless answering of a dormant question triggered the solution to an important current problem. One strongly suspects that the subconscious activity of this engineer's mind had discovered this relationship and somehow thrust it into his conscious thinking.

The second example I take from my own experience to illustrate a slightly different situation. Here the understanding of a recognized problem came to me as a flash, and was accompanied by the complete solution.

In the development of the electron microscope, as in any microscope, the critical problem was the perfection of the objective lens. Over several years we had removed defects one by one, usually by the technique of applying ordinary optical theories to the electron optical case. Eventually we arrived at the point where we had one remaining defect that stayed in the picture, and the solution refused to come on the basis of comparison with light optics. In fact, we began to suspect very seriously that the analogy between electron optics and ordinary light optics was going to break down. After about six months of struggling with this problem I was mulling it over one night as I was trying to go to sleep. Suddenly, out of a confusion of ideas running through my mind, it occurred to me that one of the assumptions that had been implicit in all our work might not be valid. We had assumed that if the lenses were made with the greatest possible mechanical precision, there would be equal precision in the magnetic field produced by them. (The magnetic field is actually the lens for the electrons.) The thought I had was simply that this might not be so.

Simple as the thought was, it released a flood of ideas which, in fractions of a second, provided many reasons why the assumption would not be valid, and led to a complete solution to the problem. The next day it took only a matter of a few hours to introduce some simple correcting devices into one of our lenses, then adjust them, and get some of the best pictures that had been taken with the electron microscope up to that time. Again we have an example of the sudden formation of a whole idea, triggered off by something which we do not yet understand.

My third example illustrates still another aspect of creative thinking, or, as I like to call it, imaginative association. In this case a spark of ingenuity led to the conversion of a minor liability into a major asset.

Just prior to the war, one of our engineers was working on the problem of eliminating "ghosts," or secondary images from the television picture. These "ghosts" were caused by the reflection of transmitted broadcast signals from buildings and other objects on either side of the path between transmitter and receiver, causing more than one set of picture signals to appear on the picture tube. Observing these secondary images and analyzing them, our engineer deduced that the distance between the main image and the "ghost" image on the picture screen could provide a means of measuring the extra distance traveled by the secondary signal on its longer journey from the transmitter. Moreover, since the position of the transmitter was precisely known, the distance measurement could be used to indicate the source of the reflection.

To the engineer, these thoughts held the germ of a useful high-speed system for measuring distances with great accuracy, and he set to work turning this into a practical device. As a result, after some months of experimentation he developed the Shoran system —perhaps the most accurate navigational technique ever devised.

Perfected in time to perform valuable service during the latter stages of the war, it is used today as an extremely accurate means for mapping large and previously uncharted, or inaccurately charted, areas of the world.

Usually this would be a case of the ordinary engineering mind going ahead to solve a problem. But in this instance, a more creative man added something: he turned the problem around and got a good and useful end product from it.

Elements of Creativity

I have presented three isolated and, I believe, quite different examples of what most technical people would call *creativity*. Despite the dissimilarities between them, however, I think it is possible at this point to look at the over-all situation and find some elements that are common to all of them. It is these common factors that interest the management of a research organization.

A more complete analysis of each case of demonstrated creativity reveals the existence of two key factors: a particular type of individual and an appropriate working environment. It is my thesis that creativity in the technical sense can be nurtured only by the proper combination of these two, and the spark of creativity cannot kindle a flame if either of the two is missing or insufficient.

Let us look first at the characteristics of the individual. What should we look for in selecting a member of a research organization? I have a few traits to mention, though I am not going to try to list all of them. Here are five that seem especially important to me:

(1) The man must have a high level of native intelligence. Surveys indicate that most of the scientific personnel we find in research activities are so endowed. But while intelligence is necessary, it is not sufficient in itself to assure creativity. A man may be smart and still not be creative, but he has to be smart to be creative.

(2) The man must have a complete dedication to, and complete absorption in, his field of interest. He needs an objective recognition of the needs of his speciality, and these continue to present him with a challenge.

(3) He must be completely immersed in the field and be supported by appropriate educational background and experience, regardless

of how they are obtained. I do not mean that he must have a formal education, but he does need true education and experience, supplemented by broader interests. He never ceases to learn, but is obviously not a "professional" or perpetual student.

(4) He needs to have a temperament that keeps him continually dissatisfied with the status quo. His dissatisfaction is constructive in that he always believes there are opportunities for further improvement, even though he would find it very difficult to state these explicitly.

(5) He ought to be very sensitive to slight departures from the established pattern of his speciality. This is perhaps really a summation of a number of the previously stated characteristics. I assume that he has so thorough a knowledge of his specialty that he has been able to establish its basic principles in their simplest form. This provides a quick reference for all the varied observations he makes in the course of his work. The slightest discrepancy between his observations and his understanding of the basic principles then becomes a clue which may lead him to a new discovery or a fresh advance in his field.

We can now examine what appear to be the central aspects of a favorable environment for the creative individual. Again, I will list some of the factors that I consider important, and that form the basis for many of the management policies within our own laboratories. I do not claim that this list is an exhaustive one, though these ten seem essential to us:

(1) We believe that the creative individual must have freedom of action within his field of interest. By our original selection we ensure that the field of interest of the individual is also of major concern to the company. We do not try to change him after we take him on.

(2) We think that the establishment and maintenance of understood objectives is beneficial to creative thinking. The objectives may be set up by the individual or by the company, but in any case they must be reasonable goals with which the individual agrees and which he understands.

(3) Inherent in the environment there needs to be a certain amount of pressure toward accomplishment. The pressure should be a natural one. While it may be applied by management, it must be recognized as valid by the individual. It seems to be extremely important not to carry pressure to the point where the individual

has no time for constructive daydreaming. Perhaps this is a concept that needs more thought and cultivation in the management area.

(4) A high level of activity is important. A continued stream of accomplishments in the environment appears to be highly stimulating to an individual.

(5) A company has to be organized to recognize any valuable contributions a man makes and to be certain that his professional associates both within the company and within the professional societies of which he is a member know of his work. In our laboratory we provide this recognition by a policy of early publication.

(6) The environment should obviously include stimulating associates, both in the company and in the other professional contacts of the individual. To this should be added the cross-fertilization provided by coupling experimental and theoretical approaches.

(7) There ought to be special emphasis on the basic assumption that opportunities for technical advances are plentiful.

(8) Research management must recognize that nonconformity often accompanies creative ability, and must be willing to accept and work with personnel problems that may arise.

(9) It is important in these times that good facilities be provided along with adequate technical assistance. On the other hand, one must not carry this to the point where the creative individual no longer has an opportunity to profit from the clues which nature often provides during the execution of the more mundane tasks.

(10) Implicit in several of these is the assumption of available information. It is necessary to maintain a continued flow of information to the creative individual through good libraries, reports, contacts in professional societies, and contacts within the company.

These, I believe, are the essential elements of an environment that is favorable to creative activity in the technical sense. Though I do not have the space to do so, I could provide examples that show how each of the points I have just raised work out in practice. They provide the basic philosophy on which we have built the management organization for creative activity in our own laboratories. Though they may not resemble the principles of management as described in business school language, on closer examination I believe that all these elements will prove to be part of, or compatible with, conventional management principles.

MANAGEMENT AND CREATIVITY*

In his section, Dr. Hillier made several points I would like to emphasize. First, he stressed the element of individual imagination and the associative aspects of the creative mind. Secondly—and this is particularly true of the work in which he has been engaged—he pointed out that the scientist is concerned with the extension of his own perceptions and with ways in which he can correct what seems to be true but may be wrong. Thirdly, he referred to the obvious, but perhaps neglected, fact that men doing creative work are immersed in their subjects; they are necessarily well acquainted with nearly all that has become known in their particular field. And lastly, he indicated that scientists lose themselves in their work; they are guided by what P. W. Bridgman has called "the discipline of the fact." They are guided not by their interests, desires, beliefs, or biases, but by the objective facts.

Let us see, now, if we can find a relationship between these elements and some human relationships. It seems to me that if we distinguish the subjective and objective viewpoints, if we separate the observer from what he observes and look at both subjectively and objectively, then we get four possible points of view. In this scheme, the imagination of a man is clearly an internal or subjective matter. It is obviously a process that goes on in the individual's own mind, as he seeks to accomplish some purpose and to make choices toward some end.

If we turn to the second element we have noted in the process of discovery, we find we are concerned with the way in which external facts are perceived and transmitted to the mind. Here we are looking at the observer viewed objectively. The scientific observer, for example, in addition to a keen imagination, needs to know when using a microscope whether he has 20/20 vision and whether the microscope itself is in good working order.

When we look at the third element in the creative process, we focus on knowledge of external relationships. Here the emphasis is on what is observed, as seen from an objective or external point of view. If the scientist can place something in time and space and knows what energy and matter are involved, then, according to the

* By Mr. Collier.

well-known astronomer, Harlow Shapley, he is accounting for all four dimensions in the physical universe, and may be able to make accurate predictions of what will happen under given conditions.

Lastly, when we speak of a scientist submerging himself in his work, we are placing emphasis on his ability to see problems internally, from the point of view of the thing observed. As has been indicated, this point of view seems to require not only the submission of the individual's own interests and beliefs but also a willingness to follow facts wherever they may lead.

Four-dimensional Approach

This analysis suggests that all the elements in the creative process are logically related. Though they are different points of view, all seem to be essential. Now if, in place of the things with which the physical scientist is concerned, we substitute the people with whom administrators are concerned, we will perhaps be able to see how the elements of scientific investigation may be applied to problems in human relations.

It is possible for each of us to look at himself both from an internal and an external point of view, and we can likewise look at other individuals from both such points of view. If we do so, we may look at ourselves in terms of our own conscious awareness and our capacity to imagine and to choose. This is the world of ideas and value judgments, where a key element is our concern for making right choices. But we may also view ourselves from an external point of view and note that our body, from such a point of view, is subject to laws of cause and effect. Here our concern basically is to adopt a detached interest in learning how accurate our perceptions are and to note how responsive our resulting behavior is. Likewise, we may look at other people from an external point of view and observe with the same feeling of detached interest how they behave in relation to various stimuli and environments. And we may also look at others from their own internal points of view, with a concern for the choices they must make. Here our own value judgments will be submerged in an attempt to understand those of others.

Perhaps these basic dimensions or viewpoints can be more readily visualized if we think of ourselves as driving an automobile. In the first dimension we take the position of the driver and ask, "Where do we want to go? Shall we go fast or slowly? Shall we take the highway or the byway?" In the second dimension we ask about the car itself, "Does it have plenty of gasoline? Are the spark plugs clean? Do we realize and adjust for the car's tendency to veer to the left when braking?" In the third dimension we ask about the behavior of other cars under various circumstances. We try to learn enough so that we can make tolerably accurate predictions of their behavior, even though we do so at our peril. Lastly, though we can see out of our car, we cannot see into any others; nevertheless, by the way we drive and by the crude tappings on our windows or on our horns, we try to communicate with other drivers and to put ourselves in their positions in order to understand where they want to go, and why.

A Look at Organization

These general viewpoints seem to have been important in unlocking new frontiers in science, and it may be that they will prove to be helpful in dealing with business problems as well.

The modern business manager must (1) look at his organization's capacity to imagine and to decide, to determine its purposes and objectives, to make conscious, willing, and intelligent choices; (2) look at the perceptual apparatus of his organization and the methods by which it accomplishes the objectives it has set; (3) look at the environment of the organization and predict how it will change in the future; and (4) look at its capacity to understand the needs of other organizations and the needs of society at large. If we are right in suggesting that each of these frames of reference can be applied to the operations of the business corporation as well as to an individual, we should briefly examine them.

The capacity of the corporate organization to decide is a power that may be compared with imagination and will in the human mind. Every organization is confronted daily with choices between different goods. It must make value judgments. Should it pay high wages or low, buy expensive materials or cheap, sell at high prices or low? The character of the decision is often less important than the fact that it must be made. It is impossible to overemphasize an organization's need for confidence in its management's capacity to choose effective, everyday courses of action. Disaster closely attends any organization that cannot make prompt and adequate decisions. If a conflict in management lies unresolved for a long period of time—as it sometimes does where two key executives have different views but equal power—not only do the executives themselves become frustrated, but even more important, the sense of frustration spreads to all parts of the organization.

Probably the most important decisions that a management must make are those that relate to the determination of the purposes and objectives of the organization. The importance of these decisions may be seen in the communications industry, where neither the telephone, the telegraph, nor the electrical manufacturers defined their objectives to include wireless messages. An officer of the Postal Telegraph Company once said, "In 1900 we were telegraph men and did not think about alternative methods of communication." That company, as well as many others, might have had a quite different history if it had conceived of itself as being in the communications business generally. If the analogy to scientific creativity holds, such decisions should be made in an atmosphere of freedom in which all elements of the corporate mind fully and freely participate.

Now, our second general viewpoint as applied to business management has to do with the means by which the organization accomplishes its purposes. Like the physicist's instruments that extend his perceptions and perform his tasks, like the function of the body as the observing instrument of the mind, the organization as a whole seeks to carry out the chosen corporate objective. In fact, its internal structure follows closely the basic systems of physiology. It must have, of course, established methods for digesting fuel and raw materials to produce goods and services. A large part of the energy of the business organization thus goes into productive work that is sold to the public to satisfy public needs. But a portion of the production is used to satisfy the needs of the members of the organization, much in the same manner that the circulatory system distributes food energy to the cells in the human body.

An organization also requires highly developed nervous systems to transmit to the point of decision information obtained from within the organization and from the outside, and to transmit the decision to the point of action. Such systems are formally called authority and communication systems, and unless they work with reasonable accuracy, decisions are bound to be inadequate. A workman is no better than his tools, and an organization can be no more effective than the means it has to carry out its functions. Here the emphasis is not on freedom of choice and participation but on the training and discipline that enable each member of the organization to carry out his assignment quickly and accurately.

From our third general perspective, the organization looks at the world outside itself and seeks to learn enough about it to predict what will happen. A business organization may be required to buy or sell in one of the many impersonal markets. If so, it is imperative that it study that market objectively and predict future prices as precisely as possible. Similarly, a business organization must know its competition and predict what it will do. In addition to the actions of competitors, a business organization must forecast the probable actions of labor unions, regulatory bodies, and tax gatherers, to say nothing of the movements of national and international politics. Like the scientist who is endeavoring to find the relationship between certain objective phenomena, these questions are to be examined in a wholly detached manner, for the question is not what the market competition or government *ought to do,* but what they *are doing* now and *will do* in the future.

We come now to the last of these general frames of reference, where the organization is concerned with what other organizations believe ought to be done—with questions, again, of value rather than fact. Each individual and each organization is always part of a larger organization, and what is in the interest of one may not always be in the interest of the other. In recognition of this viewpoint, it is no longer unusual for the managements of many business organizations to look at many questions from viewpoints other than their own. Like the scientist who submerges his own interests in the discipline of the fact, business organizations have found that they can also submerge their own interests in those of the wider community, in peace as in war. In more than a few instances, although managements regard increased sales as a source of necessary profits, to be sure, they consider them primarily a record of improved service to the consuming public. Similarly, businesses which have encouraged customer-centered selling and employee-centered supervision have subordinated in a wholly legitimate way their interests to those of the purchaser or worker.

Corporations are also going far to assume new responsibilities for community needs, medical research, expanding education, and many other worthy enterprises. As Clarence Randall has said, the terrifying phrase *ultra vires* no longer stands as a bulwark for cupidity that prevents boards of directors from doing things which, as human beings, they know they ought to do. And this, of course, is the basic theme of this book.

"So What?"

At this point, someone might well ask, "So what? Possibly there are parallels between the basic viewpoints of science and the viewpoints of business organizations, but what are their practical implications?"

One important implication, I suppose, would be that if there are these four major aspects of an organization's life, sole emphasis on any one of them is misleading and dangerous. A business that pays too much attention to its internal structure (its work procedures, its incentives, its authority and communication systems) may fail to re-examine its real business objectives. A business that pays too much attention to the forces of competition, government, or labor unions may fail to fulfill its civic responsibilities and so help to bring about the taxation or regulation which it so generally fears. Equally evident, a business that becomes too much concerned with deciding what it ought to do, without sufficient regard for what is likely to happen anyway, is usually in for a rude jolt.

If such overemphasis is to be avoided, business management could regard the four viewpoints as a kind of check list:

(1) Where does it mean to go?
(2) How does it expect to get there?
(3) What will help or hinder along the way?
(4) Who else must be considered?

The second implication of the discussion, I believe, is that the age-old debate over the relative merits of an authoritarian versus a democratic form of management is a debate over a spurious issue. The lesson of scientific innovation certainly suggests that the mind can be most creative and most imaginative when it feels free. Likewise, troublesome questions in business can be solved creatively if the organization feels free to express itself on all the issues of the day. Matters of purpose and policy are governed ultimately by value judgments and should be decided by many minds. On such matters, the democratic approach is preferable. On matters, however, that have to do with productive work—the carrying out of policy— it seems plain that old-fashioned authority along with the well-trained, well-disciplined team is indispensable. The scientist must have accurate and reliable instruments, or he cannot proceed with his work. The executive in a business organization must also have a reliable organization to provide him with accurate reports and to carry out his instructions in the manner intended.

QUESTIONS AND ANSWERS*

From the floor: As a man whose job is in research and invention, I sincerely hope that the businessman will not make the mistake of feeling that to be creative he must be purely scientific. I feel very strongly that a scientist, to make progress and to create, must move beyond science and become an artist. Dr. Hillier has emphasized the individual rather than scientific law, freedom to be dissatisfied with things as they are rather than predetermined rules.

I sincerely hope that business people will give up their present undue worship of science, which has been carried so far that some even call themselves social scientists. They should realize that although what people do is in part controlled by natural laws, it involves a great deal of freedom of the will. Progress can be achieved only by recognizing this fact.

From the floor: It seems to me that the environment of the scientist is basically that of simplicity, more or less of a straight pattern, while the manager deals essentially with complexities. He can achieve only a degree of simplicity; he has no simple path or formula to discover as the scientist does.

Dr. Hillier: In commenting on that, may I suggest that another practical aspect of Mr. Collier's analysis comes from the way re-

* Businessmen present at the panel session on which this chapter is based raised certain questions which brought about the interplay of ideas reported more or less verbatim in this section.

search is applied to business problems. Apparently because scientific research has been effective, business is placing an excessive emphasis on research in all kinds of problems relating to the behavior of people, whether they are customers or workers. As I see it, much of this fails to discriminate between hard facts and values. Research on many kinds of business problems can and does make a good deal of sense, especially if the factors in the problem can be quantified in some way. It is often very productive to look at the organization objectively and to describe how it works inside and out. But research is limited to description and prediction. It cannot deal with the contingent questions of value, with questions of purpose, with whether what we are doing has any creative result. You can do research on questions of fact: what is and what will be. But you can only ponder and debate questions of value: what we think ought to be and what we hope will be.

This leads to two important points, which concern differences between research and creative thinking in the scientific world and in human relations and management problems. There is another element to be added to description and prediction: experimentation for purposes of verification. Obviously there is experimentation in the management field, but with a difference. In science the experiment that gives a negative answer has the same stature as one that does not. I do not believe this is, or can be, true in human relations and management. In business you cannot afford to fail in a major experiment with people, so you aren't as likely to try one.

The second point concerns an implicit assumption which is basic to scientific creativity. This assumption provides a powerful stimulus to the creative worker and at the same time greatly simplifies many of his problems. It is not yet at all clear that this assumption can be carried over to the management field. I am, of course, referring to the fact that the creative worker is manipulating basic natural laws which are essentially simple and which he assumes to be unchanging.

In this sense scientific creativity is very much akin to a chess game. The rules of the game are simple and unchanging. The challenge in the game comes from the great many variations which can be developed in the course of play. Interest in the game remains high as long as skill can be continually developed. But this would not

CREATIVITY: LESSONS TO BE LEARNED

be so if the rules of play changed without the knowledge of the player. In scientific research the rules of play are considerably more complex and very much more numerous, but the principle of constancy still exists. Thus, the research worker knows that if he is sufficiently clever to utilize these rules in the understanding of a new phenomenon or a new development, the knowledge he achieves will become a permanent part of the total structure of his knowledge, and will be available as a firm foundation on which to build his next step.

I believe it is here that you find a crucial difference between creativity in the research activity and creativity in management. I am not at all sure that the basic laws of management are constant, in which case the structure of our knowledge in the management field is not necessarily sufficiently stable to enable us to build on it indefinitely. Perhaps research is needed to establish unchanging laws which can be used as the basis for the development of management principles.

Maybe, then, creativity in management requires a more complex form of the scientific method than the scientist has devised. The exercise of this method is limited at present because, in dealing with people, we are unable to perform experiments on the same scientific basis available to the biologist or the physicist.

From the floor: One difference between a businessman and a scientist is that the scientist likes to know more and more about less and less until he knows almost everything about nothing, while the businessman is attracted by the opposite situation. He knows less and less about more and more until he knows nothing about everything!

This complexity that you mention presents a real difficulty. The situation is so complicated that the manager has, finally, to resort to intuition.

From the floor: Facing up to the issue, it seems to me that there is a tremendous and basic difference in the opportunity and atmosphere for the creative approach in the ordinary management situation and in the laboratory. You have pointed out that in laboratories there must be a permissive atmosphere for noncomformist behavior, and there must be freedom so each man can operate as an individual. But in the ordinary industrial situation this type of behavior carries a very real danger, particularly if it deviates markedly from the accepted standards. Social scientists have pointed out that we are becoming increasingly an other-directed group of people, instead of inner-directed, because of the morass of management structure in which we must move in this kind of society. In short, if an individual operates independently and gets out of step with his associates or his bosses, even if he is very creative it may interfere seriously with his career.

Dr. Hillier: Maybe this puts another level of requirement on his creativity. How can he do both things? The most successful managers and innovators in the management field have learned how to balance these two.

Mr. Collier: I think a distinction should be made regarding conformity. My experience in the MIT Radiation Laboratory during the war brought me close to quite a few scientists. My observation— though Dr. Hillier is, of course, much more of an authority—was this: the top-grade scientists are not basically nonconformists in outlandish personal behavior. Second- or third-rate scientists may try to be nonconformists, but the Nobel Prize winners in the lab during the war and other top men who were nonconformist in their scientific thinking were quite conformist in their general attitudes and behavior. So it seems to me that the discussion of conformity or nonconformity may often miss the point.

Dr. Hillier: Nonconformity is not really a good word to describe the problem I had in mind. The creative scientist bases his career on the critical appraisal of his understanding of the rules of nature, which he assumes are part of a completely logical pattern. Similar scrutiny of management rules, which frequently must have intuitive origins can lead to personnel problems.

From the floor: Do you gentlemen feel that the need for creativity in business is truly more significant today than it was ten or twenty years ago?

Mr. Collier: It is no different today, only we talk a lot more about it!

From the floor: How can you tell who is creative and who isn't before you hire him?

Dr. Hillier: A number of industrial concerns are trying to measure the inherent or latent creative ability in an individual before he has actually done any work, but to date they have failed dismally in this attempt.

Mr. Collier: In concluding our discussion, I should like to emphasize a similarity in the problem of the scientist and the manager. Science places supreme value on those steps that lead toward new knowledge—toward pushing out new frontiers. Science alway chooses in favor of new adventures rather than the "tried and the true." In this sense it is always radical, but in another sense it is always conservative, for it conserves past knowledge and embraces new knowledge fully only when it has been objectively verified. These are values that are equally pertinent to business and society.

When science refuses to tolerate the biases, the special interests, the unverifiable beliefs of individuals, whoever they are, it is sometimes accused of impertinence or a lack of mercy and human understanding. We suggest, however, that when within its sphere it gives its loyalty to facts over persons, it is adhering to those values on which its continued existence depends. Business likewise should—as Mary Follett urged years ago—be guided not by persons but by situations.

Before science can engage in the creative process and discover new facts about the external world, it must worship at the altar of the free individual mind, for it is only from an intimate and intricate relation between mind and matter that significant new learning comes. More than anything else, science respects the mature intelligent being—the being who rises above the limitations of his training and experience, and in perceiving things that are new fulfills a potentiality open to the human race. Business management, if it is to achieve its mission in a new society, must pay a similar respect to the free mind and the mature being.

FEEDBACK: PUTTING
PUBLIC RELATIONS IN REVERSE

Earl Newsom, Robert O. Carlson, and
Leonard L. Knott

PUBLIC OPINION: ITS NATURE AND SIGNIFICANCE*

WE KNOW THAT SOMETHING called public opinion has seemed important to generations of men, and seems today to be of increasing importance—and yet no one has been able successfully to define it.

Note: Mr. Newsom is Senior Partner of Earl Newsom & Company; Mr. Carlson is Research Analyst in the Public Relations Department, Standard Oil Company (New Jersey); and Mr. Knott is President, Editorial Associates Limited. Raymond W. Miller, who acted as moderator for the panel session on which this chapter is based, is Visiting Lecturer, Harvard Business School, and President, Public Relations Research Associates, Inc. Ralph W. Hidy, who assisted in the preparation of this panel and participated in the discussion session, is Isidor Straus Professor of Business History, Harvard Business School.
  * By Mr. Newsom.

Hermann Oncken, the German historian, commented on our failure in this regard:

> ...When all is said and done, everyone knows, if put to it, what public opinion means. But if it must be set in words, then it can only appear hedged around by many restricting clauses; public opinion is a complex of similar utterances of larger or smaller segments of society concerning public affairs; at times spontaneous, at times artfully manipulated; expressed in a multitude of ways, in clubs, assemblies, above all in the press and in journals, or perhaps only in unspoken feelings of each one of us; of the common man in the street or of a small circle of the cultured; here a true power factor, which statesmen must take into account, or something of no political significance; something again to be evaluated differently in every country; sometimes united, rising up like a tidal wave against the government and the experts, sometimes divided, concealing conflicting tendencies; at one time bringing out the simple and natural sentiments of the people, at another time being the rowdy thoughtless manifestations of wild instincts; always leading and always being led; looked down upon by the sophisticated, yet forcing the hands of men; contagious like an epidemic; capricious, treacherous and power mad (resembling man himself); and then again only a word by which those in power are bewitched.*

Today we hear on all sides that the attitudes of large numbers of people—their ideas, the pictures they have in their heads—can have a powerful impact, for good or ill, on the ability of the management of any human enterprise to do what it is supposed to do. We are told that public understanding of the actions and policies of a business management and public confidence in the enterprise itself can be a priceless asset. Conversely, it is generally assumed that public distrust of an enterprise can become so active and volatile in its harassment that it inhibits action, numbs the policy-making process, vitiates morale—in some instances even results in a boycott of the company's products.

We are reminded that the ownership of American business has undergone radical change, so that in many concerns it is spread among hundreds of thousands of shareholders. Any group of 100,000 is a political entity and a fertile ground for political ad-

* *Historisch-politische Aufsätze und Reden* (München-Berlin, R. Oldenbourg, 1914), Vol. I, p. 236.

venturers. The proxy fights since World War II have, for example, had all the characteristics of election campaigns.

Business historians have pointed out that as technology improves the burden of management shifts from the contriving of production techniques to the handling of people—labor, consumers, suppliers, and shareholders—whose interests are often in conflict and must be reconciled by management. Opinions held within these groups can be of great importance.

Furthermore, we are told that no enterprise exists in complete isolation from all other enterprises. Indeed, every enterprise tends to be symbolic of all others of its type. Thus, aroused and widespread distrust of one tends to destroy confidence in all. In a democratic society this can result in restrictive legislation that limits the elbowroom management must have to do its job in a highly competitive economy.

Business is increasingly involved with government, which both feeds on and is fed by public opinion. Government automatically commands the stage and has the first sympathy of most people. It is important, therefore, for businesses to have public confidence and understanding so that they can obtain a fair verdict in times of difference with government.

This whole complex of ideas about the force and importance of public opinion invites cross-questioning and interchange of views, skepticism and probing. Is public opinion as important to modern management as has been stated? Is this statement equally true for all corporate enterprises, or does whatever truth may be involved apply in varying degrees, depending on the size and nature of the enterprise or the scope of its market? That is, to what extent are human attitudes toward the ideas of authority and power involved in this concept?

If the thesis is generally true, why has it become true? And what is the nature of this thing we call public opinion? Is it the sum total of the logical conclusions of millions of informed individuals after critical examination of all the evidence? Or is it largely emotional in content and more accurately described as a merging of attitudes? Is there such a phenomenon as a crowd, a psychological entity in itself, which leads human beings to feel and do things as part of a group that they would not feel and do as sober individuals? And just what influences lead us as human beings to identify ourselves with groups?

A considerable library of scholarly theory, in the classical tradition, has been developed on the subject of public opinion throughout the period of Western civilization. During the past two centuries this flow of comment by historians, political scientists, and sociologists has steadily mounted. As Paul F. Lazarsfeld has reminded us, it is only within the past 50 years or so that "this classical tradition was confronted by the empiricists," * a new breed of sociologists, psychometricians, psychologists, anthropologists, and public opinion pollsters. As some of us have observed and tried to understand the work of these earnest and gifted people, it has sometimes been difficult to note areas of agreement among them—either in findings or in methodology. But the dust is settling, and there is today a conviction among them that the study of public opinion has now become an empirical social science.

At the same time—and I think social scientists themselves will agree—those of us who have somehow to deal with public opinion in a fast-changing world do not yet have access to well-organized and definitive knowledge of this complex problem. We have been aided by the rapid development in the science of opinion polls, but we still must chart our courses and make prompt decisions by rules drawn from traditional a priori assumptions, available empirical data, and large chunks of pragmatism.

We cannot proceed with anything approaching scientific certainty. Indeed, it may be optimistic to believe that the time will ever come when dealing with problems and opportunities in the field of public opinion will have become a science. With all his intelligence, there are things that man can never fully understand, particularly in that most baffling area of all—the emotional make-up of man himself.

Perhaps we can come to terms with what we call "public opinion" only to the extent that we develop insight into ourselves, into that peculiar complex we call "human nature." For example, somewhat late in the long history of life on this earth, one of our ancestors developed a larger brain than his fellows, and with it the knack for reasoning. To this we owe civilization. But so intent have

* "Public Opinion and the Classical Tradition," *The Public Opinion Quarterly*, Spring 1957, p. 39.

we been on our conscious selves that we have little awareness of what C. G. Jung calls "our undiscovered self." This is the self il-logical—the self of our whole emotional life—the source of our in-stincts, desires, hopes, fears, feelings of love and hate; the source of our sense of awe and wonder toward the mystery of the uni-verse which gives color and depth to living; the inner fire which sparks the genius of men and mankind. This undiscovered self, Jung says, is our heritage from hundreds of thousands of years.

We may decide that those who call the major issue of our time "the battle for men's minds" are misstating the problem. Perhaps it is a battle for human feelings, for men's hearts and loyalties.

Practical Approaches

There is a second area within our general topic which also in-vites our discussion. If we assume that public opinion is a factor requiring the constant consideration of business management, how can management best deal with this problem? What should be its policies in this regard? What kind of effort is called for?

It is generally recognized, for example, that no enterprise can hope to achieve public confidence unless it acts in the public interest; that is, no amount of propaganda, however clever, can make any enterprise look much better over a period of time than it really is.

But what kind of actions do we mean? Every human being is far from perfect, and every enterprise even less so, if only because it includes the activities of large numbers of human beings. And who is able to discern the true public interest in every situation in a contradictory and constantly changing world? As far as that goes, what do we mean by the phrase "the public interest"? Is the task of human leadership simply that of rushing to carry out the whims of the crowd it leads? On this question current empirical data seem to support traditional theory that the actions of leaders influence public opinion quite as much as public opinion influences the actions of leaders.

One general answer given to such questions is that the enterprise should do the best it can as it tries to make a profit in a highly complex and competitive world and tell the story to the people. And yet the best that a company can do has been known to appear to others as ruthless disregard for the economy as a whole. And there is evidence that when a company tells its story, millions of people ignore the tale—perhaps because they are preoccupied with their own stories.

Or, again, we are told that an enterprise can create a favorable climate of public opinion for itself by carrying on a continuing program of education that will persuade people to share the point of view of management in matters affecting the general interest. We are reminded that there lies at our disposal for such educational projects the whole complex of modern mass communication. Expensive though such educational campaigns can be, the simple logic behind them often seems reasonable when considered at management desks. And yet, as you know, they often do not produce what is expected.

Public Opinion Abroad

There is a third area which we cannot ignore in our discussion: the effect of public opinion in foreign countries on the decisions of managers of American enterprises. The simplest statistical summary reveals how dependent the economic health of our own economy is on the economic health and progressive stability of nations all over the world.

The United States has less than 7% of the world's population and 8% of the total land area. Yet it consumes almost half of the free world's entire volume of materials. And the rate of that consumption is constantly rising. In natural resources the United States has shifted from a have to a have-not country. Imports of iron ore and petroleum have greatly increased, and the United States today is the world's largest importer of copper, lead, and zinc. The nation is now completely self-sufficient in only two metals—magnesium and molybdenum.

Of course the opinions of people of other nations are important to American businessmen for even more fundamental reasons. American enterprises are, first of all, industrial citizens—operated and manned by millions of Americans who want to live in peace with a chance for happiness under representative government. And all Americans are becoming soberly aware that in the world of today their own destinies are inextricably involved with the destinies of hundreds of millions of human beings in far-off places—people whose languages, customs, and beliefs are strange and incomprehensible, and who seldom seem to think and act the way we think they should.

It seems to me that a clearly discernible turning point in the importance of public opinion—not only in America but throughout the world—was the declaration largely authored by Thomas Jefferson and adopted by our Revolutionary forefathers as the justification for their attempt to gain independence from England in 1776. This manifesto, the Declaration of Independence, startled the whole world of men with its proposition that all men are created free and equal and have certain inalienable rights. This proposition, a goal never wholly attainable in the world of hard reality, has stirred, continues to stir, and will continue to stir the dreams and hopes of all human beings who feel downtrodden, frustrated, and robbed of their just deserts.

In our own country, we have seen the proposition of popular rights expanded to include the right of the people to know how the institutions that cater to our needs are managed and operated— private as well as public. It is idle to question whether people have, in fact, any such legal right. The important fact is that nobody questions the right, and that it is being exercised whether we like it or not.

We have seen the banner of this manifesto held aloft in all parts of the world. Why, for example, should we be surprised at the phenomenon of nationalism? From Indonesia to India, Africa, and the Middle East, the people are alive and militantly bent on exercising their right to be free from outside domination, to run their affairs in their own way, to prove that they, too, were born free and equal with the right to achieve their own share in what life has to offer.

And yet the pressing world problem of the moment centers on the kind of leadership this movement is going to follow. Will it be commanded by power-hungry demagogues, or can it be led to fulfillment under law and order?

HEARING AND USING FEEDBACK*

Mr. Newsom has sketched the background of our concern with public attitudes—with what is already in the heads of men—and he

* By Mr. Carlson.

has pointed out that business can get into difficulty if it does not have some sense of what these attitudes are. How, he asks, can management keep abreast of trends in public opinion, some of which may eventually be translated into legislation by government, or specific action by customers?

The quickest answer is, of course, "research." At Standard Oil Company (New Jersey) we do public opinion research to help us appraise the moods of our several publics. These surveys tell us whether the man in the street knows our company and whether he likes us, dislikes us, or is indifferent to us. Frequently we follow up such studies to uncover the sources of people's knowledge and feelings about Jersey. We use a variety of research techniques; some of them probably would be classified as motivation research by Madison Avenue. In addition, we examine the extent to which people read our advertisements and react to our company publications. We encourage our affiliated companies, both in this country and overseas, to conduct similar studies and stress to them the importance of adapting research methods to their local problems and publics.

But in all honesty I must report that the use of public relations research by large companies is limited. Some managers feel these studies are valuable, but others entertain grave reservations about their worth. These doubts may, of course, be well founded: research can be done on the wrong subject at the wrong time in the wrong way. But, happily, this does not happen too often, and I do not believe that these technical failures are the real cause of the trouble.

It is more likely that the misgivings about social science research stem from a feeling that these studies are a kind of report card which passes judgment on the decisions of management. Executives are sometimes afraid that research may somehow be trying to usurp the prerogatives of management. To my way of thinking, this is an unfounded concern. Opinion research in a large corporation is designed to provide additional facts so that management can make better informed decisions with respect to the publics it serves—not to take over or check up on those decisions.

Then there is another problem. Even though businessmen may generally recognize that the social sciences have some contribution to make in helping them to better understand the point of view of the people—customers, employees, and the general public—with whom they must deal, they are often unclear about the kinds of situations which lend themselves most effectively to this sort of investigation. Sometimes they overestimate what we social scientists can do for them; on other occasions they tell us that we only elaborate the obvious and pass on to them in fancier words the information they already have. In the latter case, I am often tempted to suggest that they write down what they "already know" about the problem before the study begins and then be invited to compare these earlier estimates with the subsequent findings.

There are times, too, when research is used simply as a kind of window dressing to provide support for a decision that has already been made. Deep down in his heart many a senior executive is convinced that he has his finger on the public pulse and that he knows perfectly well what people think about his company without any outsiders telling him. I have a friend who tells this story:

> A businessman in the West Indies was under heavy attack in his community because of his labor policies. It looked as though he faced some kind of an island-wide boycott of his goods, and he was unsure what course of action he should follow. In talking to him, my friend asked, "Do you really know what they think about you on the island?"
>
> He said, "Yes. The right-thinking people know my firm brought in millions of dollars in plant and equipment, that we pay substantial taxes and have created numerous jobs where they never existed before."
>
> "Who are the right-thinking people?" my friend wanted to know.
>
> The businessman stopped for a minute and then said, "Why, they are the people who understand what I'm trying to do."

Clearly it would be meaningless to speak about the feedback process in public relations to that businessman. He had turned off his earphones to messages from the several publics which differed from him. Worse yet, he may not have realized that these publics even existed.

Even if we understand and use research to its best advantage, it may not help us very much. It is perfectly possible that we are getting no feedback because our public has nothing to feed back to us. They have no feelings toward us at all; they could not care less! Enthusiastic public relations men notwithstanding, not everyone in the world is interested in the statements made by our company officers, or in our business problems. The plain fact is that a lot of people do not concern themselves one way or another about us. As an example, I cite an article in a recent *Yale Review* reporting on a study of anti-American feeling in England.* Apparently the results of this study alarmed some people in this country because they revealed that many Englishmen had no strong feelings about the United States, either positive or negative. They simply were not interested in us.

As the writer of that article pointed out, the "I don't give a damn" attitude is a perfectly legitimate one for certain people to have on certain occasions:

> There is nothing "anti-American" in this, for they don't give a damn about Frenchmen, either. The full, horrible truth is that they hardly give a damn about Englishmen; only about themselves. They are ordinary, pleasant folk who spend their lives not giving a damn about most things; they are the despair of ideologues, politicians, and enthusiasts of adult education. They are passive; they are dull; they like being entertained; and they confine their opinions to their football coupons.†

When we encounter a situation like this, we might profit from the question asked by an old New England statesman when he was invited to comment on the opening of a new telephone link between Maine and California: "Well, do the people of Maine have anything to *say* to the people of California?" We might take a look at *what* we are communicating and see if it has any relevance to the people who are supposed to be listening.

Finally, in all our concern with telling our story and finding out what people think of it, we must be prepared to have our audience take action on the basis of what we say. Winning the interest and attention of our public may turn out to be a double-edged sword unless we are truly willing to respond to their interest in us and, in a sense, live our corporate lives under a glass. It is difficult to ask your public to tone down its curiosity and interest in your corporate actions once this concern has been aroused. The management which loudly proclaims that it wants the public to understand it must be

* Irving Kristol, "Letter to An American," *Yale Review,* Summer 1958, p. 634.
† *Ibid.*

ready to allow that same public to ask some very personal and searching questions.

Let me conclude this section, then, by agreeing with Mr. Newsom about the importance of feedback in a company's information and public relations program, but at the same time reminding you that this is a concept which is far easier to discuss in the abstract than it is to put into effect.

FEEDBACK FROM FOREIGN COUNTRIES *

As a Canadian, I join Mr. Carlson in his concern with how meaningful feedback actually is. Our experience with American corporations doing business in Canada indicates that the theory is not followed by the practice. Let me cite some examples of feedback—or lack of it.

When I read Donald David's suggestion that American business might undertake to operate some kind of foreign aid program through the government, it caused me some alarm.† We have had unhappy experiences with some United States companies in Canada which are not helping the country, but instead are creating very bad public relations for business in general, American business in particular, and for the United States as well. I would be very distressed to find this situation duplicated in other parts of the world.

It is true, of course, that many times these unhappy results come about unintentionally, or are perhaps caused by activities undertaken with the best of intentions. But when the big corporations from another country move in they seem to want to educate the native. They bring know-how, but it is often the wrong know-how for the particular situation:

> One big corporation which came into the north country in Quebec several years ago created a model community for its employees with the best of motives. The managers hired a leading firm of small-home architects and designed perfect model dwellings. Then they brought in their employees, gave them these homes at very low rents, and started their plant in production. But they found almost immediately that the labor turnover was enormous. Not

* By Mr. Knott.

† See the chapter entitled "The New Relationship of Business to Sociey," p. 66.

until they asked some local Quebec people to investigate for them did they find out the reason.

It seems that the people they employed were from French Canadian families. They were quartered in beautiful homes with picture windows, lovely grounds, and small compact modern kitchens. But here was the catch: the French Canadian lives in the kitchen. While mother cooks the dinner, father sits in the rocker and reads the paper and the kids lie on the floor and do their lessons. Everything revolves about the kitchen. The families did not like the small and compact kitchens, so they went back to the farm.

At the cost of hundreds of thousands of dollars, the firm remodeled all the houses and put in large kitchens. Here a negative public opinion reaction could have been avoided if the firm had done the necessary research at the beginning.

By way of a second example, an incident took place in Calgary recently which created intense antagonism in that area toward the United States. There is an exclusive organization called the "Petroleum Club" in Alberta, where we have a very heavy concentration of oil interests. Made up mainly of people in that industry, a great percentage of its membership is drawn from people who are United States citizens.

One of the Canadians in the oil business in the area is an outspoken and forceful critic of American foreign policy. Not long ago he applied for membership in the Petroleum Club and was turned down by the vote of the Americans, who said they did not wish to admit anyone who did not agree with them. So here we have a group of American industrialists who can deny membership in a Canadian club to a Canadian because he does not agree with the United States.

Of course, the story is not all dark. The Imperial Oil Company, for example, has gone out of its way to integrate with the community and, in fact, is completely managed by Canadians right up to the position of president. In terms of aid to education, research, and all of the technical and nontechnical fields, it has been most helpful. There are other good examples, too. But according to a survey of public opinion in Canada made in 1958, the average Canadian, nine to one, thinks that United States business is trying to dominate the country. This unfortunate figure shows up despite efforts to educate people to more positive attitudes—or maybe, because of these efforts. Perhaps Canadians feel that United States business is trying to seduce them!

My hope is that managers on your side of the border will develop both the techniques to receive this feedback and the sensitivity to hear and act on it in Canada and throughout the world.

QUESTIONS AND ANSWERS*

From the floor: I am a United States citizen, but a resident of Canada for the past eleven years, and I have traveled about 100,000 miles in every continent of the world.

The irritation that Mr. Knott expresses about American companies is so minor compared to the way the Greeks feel about the Turks and the Turks about the Russians, or the Japanese about the Chinese, that it is almost a love affair.

We are in danger of exaggerating this problem. There are stupid American companies operating in Canada, and, on the other hand, some extremely fine examples of good corporate citizenship. Just recently a group of us spent three solid days talking about all this, and finally came to the conclusion that both the Americans and Canadians alike feel that this problem exists because the unimportant 1% is given all the publicity, and the very important 99% gets very little.

Mr. Miller: Your remarks remind me of the political forecasters in the last days of the Hoover administration. They took polls in the Pullman cars, and came out sure that Hoover was going to be reelected. Personally I am afraid that American business too often bases its opinions on the men we meet in our fancy clubs. We forget the mass of the people.

Mr. Hidy: The point is: how is management going to avoid that situation? What should management do in order to assess this better? One thing that impresses me is that businessmen have not been using all the techniques of the social sciences. I am quite sure economists, historians, sociologists, or statisticians could help them foresee these developments. Shouldn't every company operating on a world-wide scale have men on its staff who can assess these trends

---

* Businessmen present at the panel session on which this chapter is based raised certain questions which brought about the interplay of ideas reported more or less verbatim in this section.

and then present them, or have alternatives ready, so that when management has a problem, they can say, "Here are all the possible courses of action"?

On the basis of historical knowledge, you can always anticipate that in any country which is rising from a low standard of living a man on horseback will appear. It has happened every time, from the French Revolution to Cuba. Businessmen should have anticipated that a Nasser would appear either in Egypt, Indonesia, or somewhere else.

From the floor: My experience indicates that we should stay out of politics completely. Sure, we can anticipate a Nassar coming up, but what are we going to do about it? What alternatives are there? That is an area where we need help.

Mr. Newsom: You are right, of course, in your conclusion that American concerns doing business abroad must meticulously avoid getting involved in any way in the internal politics of the host country. Indeed, there are some countries where governments change with such frequency that identification with one faction would result in the quick expulsion of the company when revolution puts other elements in power.

All of this means that any American company wants to identify itself as a responsible industrial citizen whatever local element may have the political upper hand. It is for this reason that many American firms operating abroad do their best to identify themselves with the people of the country and their desire to get on with economic and social progress.

Unfortunately, what the people of a foreign country may feel toward an American corporation operating in their midst is not completely dependent on what the management of the company does. For one thing, it is importantly affected by the actions and statements of our own political leaders in Washington.

In this situation, the managements of many good American corporations doing a business abroad avoid attempts to persuade the nationals of those companies to American beliefs and customs. Instead, they try their best to understand the beliefs and customs of the host country and do their best to accommodate their actions to what often seems a strange way of going about things.

I do not think it is possible to hope that all the people in a foreign country where we do business can come to love us unreservedly. There, as in our own country, there are marked differences of opinions. Indeed, there are times when one senses a gathering animosity toward everything American. It is particularly at these times that good American citizens living abroad are especially careful and patient, very much aware that some small incident can crystallize attitudes of animosity and do great harm not only to their own enterprise but to the United States.

From the floor: It seems to me that we are really trying to rationalize the maintainance of the status quo by all this. We always take our readings in terms of where we have been, instead of where the world is going. In the past we have been in the role of a father to all these peoples; now the "children" are growing up. How does the son-father relationship reconcile itself to a dynamic situation? It doesn't, and we had better realize it. Instead of vainly attempting to keep everything as it was, or is, we should anticipate what is coming and work out patterns and relationships which fit the kind of age that is soon to be upon us.

MANAGING THE EDUCATED

Peter F. Drucker

FOR THE FIRST TIME in our history—or indeed in the history of any country—managerial, professional, and technical employees have become the largest group in our work force. They not only outnumber all other white-collar groups, but they have even overtaken manual working groups, especially the machine workers.

Equally significant, for the first time in our history, and again for the first time in the history of any country, people with a high degree of education—that is, people who have finished high school—constitute more than half of our total labor force, including those employed in agriculture.

This trend is certain to accelerate sharply. The number of managerial, professional, and technical employees is growing at the rate of 10% each year—three times as fast as the total population. The

Note: Mr. Drucker is a consultant on business policy and management organization. He is also Professor of Management at the Graduate School of Business, New York University, and author of many well-known books and articles on American society and business management.

number of machine workers, on the other hand, has not grown at all since the end of World War II and is indeed beginning to shrink not only in its proportionate importance but even in absolute numbers. Today managerial, professional, and technical people are one fifth of the American population at work. Fifteen or twenty years hence they are likely to constitute two fifths, perhaps even one half. This would mean that every other American gainfully employed would work as a manager, professional, or technician.

The development of an "educated society" is going to come even faster, for the people who do not have a high school education are to be found predominantly among the older population. Among those under 50, high school graduates already account for something like three quarters of the total. College-educated people, who 30 years ago were still so insignificant in number as almost to escape statistical notice, are a full third of all the newcomers to the labor force, so that 20 years hence 1 out of every 3 people gainfully employed in this country is likely to have attended college, if not graduated.

Here is a basic change in the structure of this country and of our economy. In times of economic swings and of international crisis little attention has been paid to it, for other events seize the headlines. Yet it is so important in the long run, and perhaps even in the short run, that it may prove to be more significant than any other single change. Surely its impact on us in business and management will be both profound and long-lasting. It challenges basic axioms of business management and business economics. It creates new opportunities and new problems for management. And it will force us into basic new thinking about organizational structure, authority and responsibility, and the relation of people working together in an organization.

A good many managers today are familiar with the management of highly educated people in special organizations like research laboratories or design-engineering departments. All of us know that these groups pose a good many new problems. Indeed, our meetings and our magazines are full of discussions on how one manages research people, how one makes a human being out of a Ph.D. in mathematics, and how one goes about managing the professional in an organization.

Yet very little of this, I am afraid, is really relevant to the basic problems we face, or is really concerned with them. For the essence of the big change—and we are well past the mid-point in it—is not that we have to learn how to organize highly educated people for special work outside or next to the traditional business organization. The essential point is that tomorrow, if not today, more and more of the people in the normal traditional organization, in the day-to-day operations of a business, are going to be people with very high education; people who work with their minds rather than their hands; people who do everyday "line" work rather than special "long-hair" work and yet who are different in their background, their expectations, and the way they work from the people who did these line jobs yesterday.

Specifically, we face major new situations in three areas: (1) the economics of business enterprise, (2) the personnel management and the personnel behavior of the great bulk of our employees, and (3) basic organization. I shall try to outline some of the directions we can already see in each of these three areas.

New Economic Outlook

Economists will undoubtedly be busy for many years trying to analyze the causes, lessons, and characteristics of the recession of 1957–1958. One of the most important lessons we can already define:

> In the industries that were hard-hit—especially the manufacturers of durable consumer goods and their main supplier, the steel industry—production dropped faster between the summer of 1957 and the spring of 1958 than it ever has in any major industry during a comparable period in our history (faster even than during the 1937–1938 slump). In some companies it dropped 50% or so. Yet employment fell only 20%. Actually, while we headlined the unemployment news, the real story should have been the tremendous crisis resistance of our employment. And, much more important, personnel costs hardly fell at all. They too showed almost complete recession resistance, which, of course, explains why profits in these industries tended to disappear altogether. This is simply a manifestation of the great structural change in our labor force, the structural change which has made the "production worker," that is, the machine operator, increasingly secondary, and those employees more important whom the accountants call "nonproduction work-

ers," that is, the white-collar employees and especially the managerial, professional, and technical employees.

The industries that were particularly hard-hit by the recession are among the ones that have changed the least in their employment structure during the last ten years. They are essentially old-fashioned in the composition of their labor force, compared, for instance, with the chemical industry, the petroleum industry, or the paper industry. Yet even their manufacturing employment dropped much more slowly than production, and total employment fell even more slowly—as evidenced by the personnel costs. Also, employment fell the most in respect to low-income labor; it barely moved in respect to high-income labor. In other words, even in these industries labor costs have ceased to be elastic; they have become more or less fixed.

It is important to stress that this happened in industries which in their production concepts are industries of yesterday rather than industries of tomorrow. They also rank with those firms that have the highest average age in the work force. Thus, they are still much closer to yesterday's labor structure, both in respect to job and educational background, than the growth industries in our economy like electronics, chemistry, and so on. Yet even in these industries, which could have been expected to behave pretty much in the traditional pattern—could have been expected to decrease employment at least as fast as production and labor costs at the same rate as production—employment proved highly inelastic and total personnel costs even more so.

I submit that this is the "normal" in an economy in which managerial, professional, and technical employees are the largest single group. If you add to this group the foremen, craftsmen, and highly skilled workers, you have 22 million employed people, out of a total of 64 or 65 million, whose employment is of necessity highly stable. Or to put it more accurately: the need for these people does not fluctuate directly with the volume of production, and to a very large extent their employment is tied more to the expectation of future production than to current orders. These are, in other words, people who are employed not according to the number of pieces or the number of hours worked but rather according to the expected capacity. And in the majority of cases they have to be on the payroll regardless of the present volume of business—partly because they are needed as long as the business operates at all, partly because they represent too much of an investment, too much of a "capital resource," to be discharged.

This is in sharp, indeed irreconcilable, contrast to the axioms of the economists. Every economist still assumes that business adjusts to short-term fluctuations in the economy by laying off or hiring people. They disagree whether this adjustment is the way out of a recession or whether it is the cause of recessions and depressions, but they all still believe in the phenomenon itself. It is quite clear, however, that this is no longer true. Though this would have been clear even without the lesson of the recession, since it follows from the structure of our labor force, the economic dip served to dramatize the change. So the economists—and let me add the accountants too—would be well advised to assume that business cannot adjust at all by varying labor costs; that labor costs, for any short-term period, can be considered fixed, determined by future expectations rather than by present volume of business. In many industries—a conspicuous example would be retailing—this is indeed already an established fact. Yet we lack economic theory for such a situation. As a result, we do not really understand it.

We also lack business policy for it. It is obvious that what I have just said spells out great fluctuation of profit, since it is the only factor left that can give. This is one of the functions of profit in a free enterprise economy. If we cannot adjust easily to short-term fluctuation by adjusting labor costs, the leverage on profits must become conspicuously greater, as indeed it proved to be during the recent recession. We need, therefore, a financial policy which starts out with the assumption of high year-to-year fluctuations in actual profits, and which therefore focuses on a rate of return over a cyclical period—over a wide range of fluctuations—rather than on annual profits. We need instruments of financial analysis and control for such a new situation. And we need to think through our capital investments with much greater sophistication, instead of simply basing them on the idea that today's expected rate of return will actually be realized in any one year during the life of the new investment.

But there is another and perhaps even more important implication in this new economic situation. The rise of our economy was based on the steady increase in the productivity of the direct, manual producer, the farmer, and the machine operator. Incidentally, most of us in business are not sufficiently aware of the tremendous contribution the increase in farm productivity has made to our economic growth. During the last 30 years the annual step-up in productivity on the farm was at least of the order of 6% per year—twice that of manufacturing industry. In very large measure our economic growth and our capacity to produce can be credited to this progress.

There is reason to believe that the main increase in agricultural productivity is over. There is still a very substantial number of farmers with substandard productivity, farmers who are indeed marginal in every sense of the word. They may account for almost one third of our farm population. But even if all of them left farming—and over the next 20 years most of them will—it would not materially decrease our farm production or farm productivity, since these marginal farmers contribute almost nothing to the supply of foods and industrial raw materials for our economy. All the flight from the farm will contribute is additional workers for industry, and workers who unfortunately are precisely the kind we need the least: unskilled and very largely uneducated people.

We can expect, by contrast, very sharp productivity increases in the manufacturing industries, simply as a result of increased mechanization and automation. But these increases may be largely an illusion. We will indeed have dramatic upswings in output per manhour of production worker. But the very fact that our managerial, professional, and technical groups have been growing so much faster than the total economy indicates that we can obtain these productivity increases of the machine operator only by adding nonmanual workers. In other words, I would submit that all evidence today, both that derived from an analysis of the over-all figures and that derived from any study of an individual company's shift to automation, indicates that increased automation only shifts the demand for labor from the machine operator and his manual work to the highly educated man and his mind work, but does not result in actual increase in the over-all productivity of the business or of the economy.

What I am saying is simply that from now on our increases in productivity in this country will depend above all on our ability to increase the productivity of the nonmanual worker. Two thirds of our total labor force in 1956 were not working with their hands—

the managerial, professional, and technical workers; the clerical and sales people; the workers in service work; and finally the supervisors. Yet no one even knows how one measures the productivity of people in this kind of work. All we can measure today is the productivity of people who work with their hands to produce a physical output. No one, I am afraid, would claim that the productivity of these mind workers has gone up appreciably. Certainly such data as we have do not indicate that there has been a great increase. Since their numbers have gone up at least as fast as total production of goods and services, one must deduce that the productivity has at best remained the same.

This I submit is the primary challenge to American management. First, here is our major inflationary factor. The wages of these people go up, or are pushed up by the union contracts of industries in Detroit and Schenectady. You may or may not agree that the manufacturing worker should have received the full benefit of higher productivity; but whatever you would like to believe, over a long period of time manufacturing productivity has risen roughly parallel to manufacturing wages. The major inflationary factor is the nonmanufacturing workers' income, which goes up along with manufacturing workers' incomes but without any noticeable increase in productivity. Because of its impact, this is a bigger responsibility than the cost control of a business, for we are talking here about the cost control of the American economy.

The productivity of these people can, to a substantial extent, be increased in the way that we have increased the productivity of the manual worker: by the investment of capital in machinery. This is certainly true in clerical and other office work, where automation will undoubtedly have a major impact and where it may be more important and have greater results than in the factory. This may also be true for the very substantial number of people who are engaged in selling—where automation may not mean so much in terms of use of machinery but certainly will bring great changes because of the planning and systematizing of work that it demands.

But for the managerial, professional, and technical people, and they are the real core of the problem and the real opportunity, capital investment in machinery—in physical tools—is not going to mean much. Their work is not physical; it is work of the mind.

The only way to increase their productivity is to increase the output and the effectiveness of the mind. This can be accomplished only if we succeed both in making each of these men more productive in his own right and then in making his contribution more effective throughout the entire company.

Future Personnel Problems

This leads me to my second major topic: the management of highly educated people at work. Let me say again that I am not talking about the management of highly educated people in special programs such as research. I am talking about highly educated people in the ordinary, everyday, line organization.

Our concepts of personnel management were largely formed around World War I or shortly thereafter. They grew essentially out of experience in working with machine operators of very limited education. The famous Hawthorne experiments, for instance, were conducted with people who had, on the average, barely finished grade school. I think there is serious reason to doubt that tomorrow's employee will conform to the image upon which our current personnel management practices depend.

What are the expectations of people who have sat on school benches for at least 12, if not for 16 years, and, however little they may have learned otherwise, have learned to expect to work with their minds and to apply thinking, concept, system, and theories to their jobs? What are the expectations of people who have, as a matter of course, been given an education which only a short generation ago was reserved for a very small, essentially upper-class group? What work, opportunities, and treatment do they expect?

Is "scientific management," as the term is commonly understood, at all applicable to them, let alone "scientific" for them? Is it right to try to make the job as simple, repetitive, or highly organized as we possibly can? I doubt it.

Let me say that we have evidence that people who now come out of school expect something different from what we offer them. I do not want to attempt to define "automation." I do not want to argue whether we mean by this the substitution of machine for manual labor or a new concept of the organization of work by system and process. It is already fairly clear that the major driving force in the development is neither machines nor concepts but the changed educational structure of our work population.

People who have spent 12 or 16 years in formal education are not attracted to the job of a preautomated factory, least of all to the assembly line, which socially, if not technologically, is already obsolete. They are looking for jobs in which they can exercise what they have learned—that is, jobs in which they can work by using their minds—and they are looking for jobs in which they have the opportunities of educated people for better pay, advancement, and chances to make a contribution. The assembly line as we have known it cannot survive in this country—there is plenty of evidence that the young people in Detroit, Flint, or Schenectady simply do not want assembly-line jobs and will take them only as a last resort and with a deep consciousness of frustration and defeat.

Another new problem turns around the mobility of this kind of worker. To the old laborer, who at best had a manual skill but no education, mobility was a threat. Even in this, the most mobile country in the world, he was much more afraid of losing a job than he was attracted by better opportunities elsewhere. Stability of employment and job security ranked highest in his priorities.

Is this still likely to be true of today's and tomorrow's worker with his high degree of education and his conceptual training and skill? I doubt this very much. We see today in the electronics industry, for instance, a revival of the itinerant specialist in the tradition of the exceedingly highly skilled trades of old, like the printing business of 50 or 100 years ago. We see young men with a specialty who simply look on a job as an opportunity to ply their craft, who could not care less for job security, and who are almost unbelievably mobile. This is very much more characteristic of tomorrow's most important employees than fear of job loss, attachment to a job, and the resulting very low mobility of today's or yesterday's worker. This poses a very real problem for us in management, and it is a problem which we are not attacking by trying to keep down turnover rates. We have to think through how we can best make use of such workers, who are inherently mobile, who know a good deal of the world and are at home everywhere, and whose contribution to us very largely consists of their mobile and easily transported knowledge and skill.

The real problem of managing people at work, however, is not to satisfy their expectations. It is to think through the demands on them. What should we expect from people who are highly educated and who work as managers, professionals, and technicians? We have, during the last 30 or 50 years, increasingly tended to talk about "average jobs." "Scientific management" is focused on finding the "standard job," or the amount of work that can reasonably be expected of everyone. This, I am afraid, is the wrong way to make demands on tomorrow's worker. There we shall have to make demands for extraordinary performance, for performance that contributes not the minimum but the optimum, for performance that steadily pushes the limitations outward and reaches for new contributions and new excellence. Otherwise we can never expect to obtain the benefit of the great, almost revolutionary, change in the structure of our work force and of our work. And this in turn quite obviously means very real changes in the way we structure and define jobs.

Above all, however, we must recognize that this new worker cannot be supervised and that his performance cannot be easily measured. He can only be motivated. He must reach for excellence. He must want to contribute. He must try to develop himself, his capacity, and his contribution. All we can do is pay him. The supervision that we could give to the manual worker simply cannot be applied effectively to people who have to contribute their knowledge, conceptual skill, imagination, and judgment.

While we have been talking a great deal about motivation these last 20 or 30 years, we know very little about it—and I do not believe that many of us would claim that we even apply the little we know. The comments made in Mr. Zaleznik's chapter are most interesting in this regard.*

The New Organization

The greatest challenge, however, may well come to our concept of organization. Let me give you an illustration—intentionally taken from the armed forces rather than from business. If you look at a modern air base, you will find on it, in addition to a fairly small number of flying personnel, a very large complement of highly trained professional and technical people who exercise judgment.

* See the chapter entitled "New Directions in Human Relations," p. 253.

In rank they may be quite low. The crew chief in charge of the maintenance of a group of planes, for instance, is a master sergeant —and will never be more than that. Yet who "commands" the crew chief? Who can give him orders? The commanding general of the base can remove the crew chief, demote him in rank, or overrule him. But he cannot "command" him. The crew chief decides whether a plane is airworthy, what has to be done to put it in shape, and how long it will take. In other words, he exercises judgment, and he has a high degree of final authority within his field.

Or take the meteorologist. Again there is a ceiling on his rank— he is rarely more than a captain or a major, and will not rise higher. Yet while he works within a highly specialized area, his sphere of concern is the entire base rather than a part of it. He is a "specialist" with a "general" sphere of authority and responsibility. Again, who can "command" him? It is his professional judgment and knowledge to which he is really responsible rather than a superior officer. He can be removed, and he can be overruled, but he cannot be commanded.

You could go through the entire base and pick out one technical or professional function after the other and say exactly the same thing about it. Yet the commanding general has a final decision and a final responsibility. He does "command"—and the difference in performance between a mediocre and an outstanding commanding general is still the most important and the one truly decisive "variable" in the performance of the whole base. The general is not just a "coordinator," nor does he just listen to his functional people and synthesize their judgment and advice. He has real, final authority. And yet, except in a merely formal sense, he can hardly be said to be over all these people. He has a *different* job to do rather than a higher job.

On the chart, of course, none of this is shown. The chart shows the line of command from the general on down as it has always existed. And, in polite fiction, every one of these men exercises delegated authority—though the Air Force, smarter in this than most businesses, realizes that these people do not do part of the general's work but do their own work. The reality of organization we can muddle through, though no one is very happy with the way we do it. But we do not really understand what we are doing, nor do we really understand how to organize such a system.

This is the new organization, in which highly educated people contribute theoretical and conceptual knowledge, through responsible judgment, for a joint effort. This is the organization of an educated society, the organization in which the bulk of the people are managerial, professional, or technical. And this organization does not answer to our traditional organization concept and indeed cannot be organized on this basis.

Our organization concepts, no matter how refined, are all really variations on the traditional organization of a fighting force as it first emerged well over 3,000 years ago—in China, in Egypt, and then, shortly after the Trojan War, in Greece. It was an organization which succeeded in bringing together fairly large numbers of people for unskilled, repetitive, drilled work. When we began to build large-scale business organizations some 75 years or so ago, we simply took the prevailing concepts of military organization and adapted them. The principle of such an organization was authority, and the basic problem was to make responsibility commensurate with authority. To this day, the relationship of authority to responsibility is central to our concept of organization.

For the new organization of highly educated people, authority and responsibility may well be the wrong principles of organization. It may well be that we will have to learn to organize not a system of authority and responsibility—a system of command—but an information and decision system—a system of judgment, knowledge, and expectations.

Let me say that this does not involve a greater emphasis on human relations. In fact, we cannot solve the organizational problems we face by an emphasis on relations between people. We cannot, for instance, solve them by emphasizing the informal organization as against a formal one. We need a formal organization that is focused on the new reality. This will have to be an objective focus on the work to be done, the risks to be taken, the decisions to be made, and the actions to follow therefrom, rather than a focus on the relations between people.

We have some tools for this—but only the beginning. Even the little we have indicates that we may well face very radical changes—changes aimed not at making the central decision-making authority less effective but at making it more effective and, at the same time, at building the organization according to the need for information, judgment, decision, and execution rather than according to the hierarchical concept of command and response. This is anything but easy or painless. We may have to learn to consider authority, responsibility, rank, and reward as four separate and distinct variables to be merged in a configuration, rather than as synonyms for the same thing. We may even have to learn to look at an organization as a process (and as one that corresponds to organic biological processes) rather than as merely a mechanism; in other words, as something in which there is no "higher" or "lower," but only a "different."

Other Problems

I could discuss a good many other things. For instance, what impact will this change in the basic structure of our work force and of our work have on the labor union? Here is a major institution of American life, a major power center, and a major element in our society and our economy. Historically, it has been able to embrace only yesterday's worker, the manual machine operator. Will it succeed in reaching tomorrow's worker? Or will it become essentially stagnant and sterile? It is perhaps not irrelevant that, in sharp contrast to 25 years ago, the age structure of the labor union is today a good deal older than that of the work population in general. In other words, labor is becoming an institution of the old rather than the cause of the young.

Another area for discussion is the way in which we direct our personnel efforts. What emphasis, for instance, do we still give to the first-line supervisor and to labor relations in our management thinking, even though these are the tasks and priorities of the past rather than of tomorrow? It is possible that tomorrow we will have two employee groups, distinguished primarily by sex. It may be that the women will provide the bulk of our unskilled labor force, both of machine tenders and unskilled service workers, whereas the men will do the new work, the managerial, professional, and technical work. Here is a change for which we are totally unprepared and which would introduce some very serious tensions and problems into American life and business.

There is also the question whether this shift in the basic structure of the American population is likely to result in basic changes in demand; whether there will be a move, for instance, from more durable consumer goods, which have a high-status importance for the low-income groups, to more community satisfactions, such as education, which have a high-status importance for the managerial, professional, and technical group.

But I think I have said enough to indicate that we face very real problems, enough to substantiate my own conviction that the shift in the structure of American society and in the jobs in American business is, in retrospect, the really fundamental event of these last years, rather than the recession on which so much of our attention has been focused. And I think I have also said enough to show why I do not believe that I am writing about something in the future; the challenges and the opportunities are already here, and they demand thinking, understanding, and action from business and management.

QUESTIONS AND ANSWERS*

From the floor: In England we have found the typical organizational structure breaking down under conditions of very rapid change, whether in growth or in rapid technological advance. A recent study of about eight or ten electronics firms in England has shown that under conditions of rapid change the old hierarchy breaks down. Then either the firm becomes chaotic and gives up working in this sphere, or people relax and say, "Well, we have got to get the job done, so the heck with the formalities."

Once the organization relaxes this way, you release a sudden and terrific enthusiasm and you are off. When you get over the stage where the line hierarchy feels uncertain, unstable, and by-passed, you begin to move. And when things clear up, the line men find that they don't have to worry about their jobs; they still are needed in the organization!

One other point on this matter of autocratic command: we have been looking into this, and we have decided that to get the job done when you have educated people in your work force, you have to give people a chance to use their brains and training. We have come around to saying that we don't command, but are aiming at a catalytic organization.

---

* Businessmen present at the panel session on which this chapter is based raised certain questions which brought about the interplay of ideas reported more or less verbatim in this section.

Mr. Drucker: Since I am so unsympathetic to this point of view, I hesitate to comment! First, I don't think I was talking of autocratic management. Very few of us in this room would believe in it. Let us forget how many practice it; we don't believe in it. Still, we do have an authority structure because of the responsibility involved—an authority not just of position but of knowledge, which is not unimportant and has its own responsibility—so this is not, I think, the problem.

The issue is not only one of methods; it is one of basic organizational structure, too. Good methods may release a tremendous enthusiasm, but they only release *real* enthusiasm if the mess was unspeakable before! What you do need is a new kind of organization to cope with rapid growth and change. This implies a very considerable degree of conceptual rigidity, though not of organizational rigidity. You cannot create it by sitting down and being nice to everyone or discussing it together. You can create it only by analyzing a very difficult society and building the machinery for that society.

It is quite conceivable that a wave of enthusiasm will carry you a considerable way. All our electronics people have been through what you are discussing, but every one of them has run out of enthusiasm within three years and been up against the hard fact of the need for organized management if they are to have a solid operation in which people can work independently and yet together. But what do they have to know to do this? What do they have to tell? Whom do they have to tell? Who makes these decisions? These are not riddles that you can solve by being enthusiastic. I love enthusiasm, but it burns out.

From the floor: Do you think this new group, in establishing its status symbols, will bring a change in the direction of production output, and thereby meet some of the shortcomings Mr. Canham pointed out? *

Mr. Drucker: Leaving aside any discussion of values and looking at the economy as an economist, I think you can anticipate some changes in detail. If you ask me what is going to be the main growth industry in the next ten years, I would say, "Obviously education is."

If you ask which industry in our country has shown the greatest

---

* See the chapter entitled "For a Revised Sense of Values," p. 75.

growth in the last ten years, I may surprise you. It happens to be paper-book publishing, not aircraft or television. On a percentage basis, that has been our most rapidly growing industry, and the record industry is second. I am not saying that these two will replace the washing machine, but I am saying that it is very likely that we are seeing a shift of priority in demand preferences.

From the floor: If the major problem in management in the years to come will be managing the educated, do you think it is possible that we could get some help on how to proceed from institutions like universities which already manage the educated?

Mr. Drucker: I think we have to learn to look for lessons wherever we can find them. The institution which has the most experience and can teach us the most things not to do is the hospital! We can learn a lot from such groups as the engineering department of a defense contractor. But a university would not teach us very much, because essentially its structure is so different. Basically, most universities consist of individual scholars working in one house but not actually working together.

From the floor: What do we do with the large group of people in the next ten years who have been forced to grow beyond their capacity, and are now being pushed by this group of experts for their jobs?

Mr. Drucker: I think this is going to be a very real problem. We have it in our first-line supervision in many places. Our first-line supervision in many industries today is the oldest age group, and the least educated. They have dead-end jobs. It isn't polite to say it, but it is true. And what about the hordes of narrow specialists who have suddenly seen their jobs expand beyond their abilities? These people are perfectly adequate to do the job of yesterday and perhaps even of today. Can we give them an understanding of the new knowledge that is hammering in on them? Obviously management development programs would not be flourishing if the problem were not acute. You can't fire them, and you can't retire them yet, not for 20 more years. We have to make them effective, somehow, or live it out. The real question is now to make their successors tomorrow, who *may* well have the education, much better.

PERSONAL VALUES AND
BUSINESS DECISIONS

Edmund P. Learned, Lee Minton, Edward
J. Hanley, and Kenneth W. Underwood

Part I—The Broad Outlines

AT THE OUTSET, I would be less than frank if I did not say that men generally seem to have difficulty in discussing the kind of topic to which this chapter is devoted. All our experience at the Harvard Business School, including the Danforth Seminars, when managers,

Note: Mr. Learned, who makes the introductory observations, is Professor of Business Administration, Harvard Business School; Mr. Minton is President, Glass Bottle Blowers Association of U.S. and Canada, AFL-CIO; Mr. Hanley is President, Allegheny Ludlum Steel Corporation; and Mr. Underwood is Associate Professor of Social Ethics and Public Affairs, Wesleyan University. Arch R. Dooley, Assistant Professor of Business Administration, Harvard Business School, Robert L. Katz, Assistant Professor of Business Administration, Harvard Business School, and Herbert R. Smith, Pastor, Needham Congregational Church, Needham, Massachusetts, also assisted in the preparation of the panel session on which this chapter is based.

professors of economics and business, and men from religion and ethics have joined in exploration of this area, indicates how difficult it is for people to talk about religious and ethical values. But the need for talk exists. In view of the increased interest in ethics and religion and the stated and unstated feelings of many businessmen, there can be little doubt that today's managers want to do the right thing and do not know for sure how to accomplish it or even define what it is. Somehow we must learn to talk consciously and intelligently about these questions that are so much on the minds of responsible men.

One reason men have difficulty holding a meaningful discussion in this area is that they are forever casting themselves and their associates in stereotyped roles of one kind or another and then battling stubbornly to batter down or defend fixed positions. The authors of this chapter are not doing so. They write not as representatives of business, labor, and religion but as whole human beings with particular interests, experiences, and backgrounds, and their views should be read with this fact in mind.

Another inhibiting factor has been a lack of concreteness in the discussion. Different people react differently to the same terms and generalizations. To try to pin down this particular examination of the topic, the chapter has been divided into two parts. In the first section each of the authors will set out his general thoughts on the relationship between personal values and business decisions. Then, in order to bring their thinking and attitudes to bear on a particular situation, they are going to comment on an actual incident, a business problem that really did arise. That incident, their comments, and my summarization will form the second part of the chapter.

Why is all this important to the business manager of today? Granted that he is troubled by the relationship between his deepest beliefs and his business decisions, is this really a significant and legitimate concern?

Perhaps we can agree that widely varying systems of values, ethics, and religious beliefs, acted on implicitly or explicitly, are inherent in the behavior of all people. Every major decision involves a conflict among the values held by some or all of the individuals, groups, or parties affected by the decision. Business administrators as well as labor leaders, government officials, and legislators find themselves continually choosing among conflicting values. The choices they make and the ultimate criteria behind these choices will inevitably influence the values that will govern our society in the future. If the business community is to meet the religious, ethical, and economic requirements of our society, its members must be able to identify the conflicts involved and determine which values or criteria they seek to serve.

We are proceeding on the assumption that many businessmen intuitively wish to do the right thing and that more conscious discussion of values will heighten their powers of discernment and understanding and help them all to fulfill the active and socially responsible role that circumstances are thrusting on them. It is wholly possible that within the next 20 years the behavior of businessmen, the choices they make, and the methods by which they work with others will determine whether or not they are to continue to have a significant place in the determination of the values that govern our society.

THE COMMON RESPONSIBILITY OF
LABOR AND BUSINESS*

Public attention today is being directed toward trade unionism and its alleged shortcomings and neglect of its responsibilities to society. Perhaps a new look is justified, for much has transpired since unions became a dynamic factor in our industrial society. Perhaps we should pause to reflect on the past and anticipate the future. But to do so accurately and fairly, we should take a good broad look and not just a peek at one side of the collective bargaining table.

No longer is labor a commodity to be sold in the industrial market place. During the last two decades, America has evolved into a classless society. The wage earner lives side by side with the white collar or professional salaried employees in beautiful communities. For the most part, the so-called "lowly worker" is no longer low. His trade union, acting as his agent, has elevated him to a social status unprecedented in the world's history. He has social status because his union, through enlightened leadership, has negotiated

* By Mr. Minton.

not just decent wages but dignity, seniority, pensions, profit sharing or stock option plans, accident and disability insurance, and paid vacations and holidays.

While we acclaim this social evolution, we often overlook the responsibilities that have been created and that affect not only labor but management and the public as well. We overlook the fact that by creating a classless society we have at the same time created a more homogeneous industrial community. It is time for us to consider what this means.

Management still derives its authority from the legal relationship between itself and its stockholders. Management, as a trustee, is still responsible for securing the stockholders' interests. Management still retains its so-called prerogatives: the right to make financial decisions, to determine production methods, and to decide what machinery or materials should be processed, where plants should be built, and how many men should be employed in what jobs.

These rights can no longer be exercised exclusively in terms of how successful they will be in paying dividends to stockholders, however. Millions of wage earners are also stockholders, and for the most part they are not interested in short-term fat dividends. Billions of dollars are invested by wage earners because of their faith in American industry. More billions of dollars are indirectly invested by wage earners through pension funds—again because of their faith in American industry. What is the cornerstone of this faith? A belief that American industry will provide full employment at decent wages so that everyone will be able to buy the things he needs, and a belief that everyone will be able to participate in building a better community in which to live.

These beliefs can be transformed into realities only if management as well as labor shares in them, sets aside its own narrow system of values, and understands the values of others. As a leading personnel executive recently stated, "We share certain basic desires and needs for good health, security on a job and at home, the love and affection of family and friends, self-esteem and the regard of others, the feeling of doing something worthwhile, and pride of achievement.... It is the whole man who becomes hungry, gets sick, grows tired, becomes emotionally upset.... It is the whole man who comes to work."

This fact is too often overlooked. More important, and going a step further, the whole community is affected by collective bargaining between labor and management. The whole community shares in increased productivity, high wages, and adequate corporate profits. The whole community is affected by a recession or a strike.

There is no room for conflicts which arise from differences in purely personal objectives. The labor leader cannot base his decisions solely on what will read well in the record when he stands for re-election. The corporate director cannot base his decisions solely on huge profits when addressing a stockholders' annual meeting. Similarly, when negotiating a contract, both must try to set aside personal prejudices and selfish objectives. Is the wage demand or offer reasonable? Are increased pensions needed? Are the health and accident insurance benefits too low in relation to hospital and medical costs? Is the seniority clause unfair to the older worker who has given his best productive days to building the business but who no longer has as much energy or vitality? This is the way these questions should be put by both sides.

Today, it is the whole worker who is employed and the whole community in which he lives that is affected by business decisions. In reaching these decisions everyone involved must consider the values and purposes of all of us.

ETHICAL VALUES AND MANAGEMENT ACTION*

I wonder how many company executives or union officials have pronounced feelings of personal value conflicts in the great majority of the decisions they make day after day. Very few, I would suspect. And yet personal values, or ethical considerations, do play an important part in everyday decisions. Consciously or subconsciously, they bear on every decision made, however routine it may be.

Let us consider a situation that could present itself to any supervisor at any time. What recommendation should be made on the continuation of sick leave pay for an employee who has had ten years of service and has now been absent for a six-month period? Involved here are the employee's personal situation and the welfare of his family, the views of the community on company policy, and the effect on other employees as to precedent, on the one hand, and employee morale, on the other. Combined with these considera-

* By Mr. Hanley.

tions is the hard fact that the continuing well-being of the whole enterprise and of those dependent on its success is involved, if not in this decision regarding one employee, then in an accumulation of such decisions.

Or take another decision, and a more important one, perhaps, because it directly and immediately affects the lives of many people: should a business enterprise invest a very large sum of money in new plant and equipment to reduce its cost of production by eliminating certain operations that have been necessary heretofore? Curiously enough, almost the same kind of problems are involved. They relate to the individuals whose jobs are immediately affected, the plant community, other employees of the company and their attitudes, and the continuing well-being of the total enterprise, its owners, and its customers.

These two are typical of the millions of business decisions made throughout the country every day. For the most part, among ethical business and union leaders, these problems are resolved on the basis of what is right in the light of all prevailing circumstances. Sometimes one factor will seem overriding in importance, sometimes another, but to the person making the decision, the right course emerges as he considers all facets of the problem in the light of his fundamental beliefs.

Business and union leaders normally face a great many decisions each hour of their working day. In many cases, the decision must be made in less time than it takes to explain the problem. Furthermore, the person making the decision may have little or no realization that he has applied moral and ethical yardsticks.

Just what are these beliefs? Our fundamental beliefs are the total result of our schooling, our religious training, and our whole life experience. Perhaps I can throw some light on this subject by reviewing briefly the objectives of the Allegheny Ludlum Steel Corporation, as we have published them. They are as follows:

> To conduct the affairs of the company in the long-term interests of its owners in order that they may receive the highest possible return on their investment.
>
> Specific objectives: To build and maintain the most effective commercial and personal relationships with present and potential customers by supplying or making available to them quality products best suited to their needs, at competitive prices.

To carry on research and development programs whereby new and better products may be marketed, changes in market requirements met, and a strong competitive position maintained as to the nature, variety, quality and price of the company's products.

To provide and maintain necessary facilities and equipment enabling production and manufacturing operations to be conducted at maximum effectiveness and economy.

To build and maintain relationships with employees based on mutual understanding and goodwill; to provide opportunity for growth and development of employees; to maintain and improve a high standard of general working conditions, with particular regard for the safety of employees.

To recognize the responsibilities of the corporation to the communities in which it operates, cooperating in activities which benefit the community and its citizens.

To keep company personnel, customers, stockholders, and the public informed concerning products, operations, finances, and other matters of mutual interest.

Of all these objectives, the first is the primary and most important one—but it must be read thoughtfully and in the light of the specific objectives which follow. Why is this the key to our operations?

I could write a long, and I hope, convincing article on the absolute necessity of profits in our free enterprise system, but O. A. Ohmann has answered the question succcinctly in these words:

No enterprise is making its maximum contribution to progress or discharging its full *moral obligation* to the society which supports it, unless it generates surplus capital to start new enterprises or to expand and improve present ones.... Profits not only are essential to technological and cultural advance, but they add stability to an enterprise and they sustain it during off-seasons, recessions, and all kinds of emergencies which may interrupt the operation of the business or make it unprofitable for a time.

In the broad sense it is this surplus of production over consumption which supports research, education, many of the finest elements in our culture, leisure for children in school and oldsters in retirement, and in effect represents the creative front or growing edge of our civilization.*

* "Search for a Managerial Philosophy," *Harvard Business Review*, September–October 1957, p. 51.

I am firmly convinced that no decision will be of benefit to the long-term interest of the company's owners if the equally long-term interests of its customers, employees, and plant communities are not given every consideration. I am likewise convinced that right decisions made in the long-term interests of the owners will always square up to Christian principles.

CHRISTIAN REALITIES AND BUSINESS DECISIONS*

Perhaps it is most relevant to begin one's comment about "personal values and business decisions" with the observation that in every human organization someone must carry the burden of living with conflicts and tensions, of listening to varied claims and understanding them well enough to articulate them, of making discriminating judgments between them when they conflict, and of finding their mutual relationship when possible. This is the terrible burden of leadership, and the great temptation is always to deny that "thou art the man" who must carry this cross.

The formulation of a position out of the complex of conflicting claims on oneself and the communication of it in a situation where criticism or bargaining is legitimate and expected is perhaps the hardest thing we are called on to do. It takes our full resources as men and tests our deepest loyalties. It is no wonder that we are always tempted to cut off negotiation, to stop the dialogue with the other side, or to idealize to the point of hallucination a world in which men work in harmony and by implication accept our view of the needs of the organization. The mark of maturity, of a personal ethic grounded in reality, is an awareness that tension and conflict between men with different perspectives and value systems is a normal and inevitable aspect of human life.

There are, of course, many perspectives on business ethics seeking to say this, but as a Christian ethicist, I am particularly impressed by the insight Christian thought gives to the experience of tension and conflict in life. The Christian faith affirms that man knows the nature of God and of ultimate reality in the unique person of Christ. The God incarnate in Christ cannot be generalized into law or principle, a point I want to develop later. God cannot be

* By Mr. Underwood.

subsumed under a person's own will. God is in tension with us, judging and transforming us, so that we work in harmony and unity with Him. He does this by love, not by generalizing our own unique individuality and personhood. In faith, we know this love to be a mutual and reciprocating experience between persons with their own wills, potentialities, and perspectives. These are, according to the Christian view of community and business organization, brought into fullest play in a give-and-take between men who are not expected to be like somebody else or to be absorbed into another's values and hopes, but are given the opportunity to make their own positive contribution to business and society.

Now one might say that what is really being pressed for here is an awareness that conflicts in business, between individuals or between groups such as labor and management, are at heart matters of personal values and moral principle, and that the good man is the man who resolves various concrete and technical claims by applying his personal values to them.

Is this what I have done in the appeal to Christian love as a guide to business behavior? Not quite. What is implied in this kind of talk is a two-level metaphysics which needs to be examined. This metaphysics is the source of much abstraction and confusion about ethics and business. Such two-level metaphysics assumes a separation between fact and value. Its chief ethical problem is that of "clarifying our personal values and moral principles," figuring out their "order of priority," so that we can face each changing situation, each issue, with what we like to call clear guidelines.

In this kind of thinking, value is located in a world or realm by itself, just as fact is. It is the world of human subjectivity, with its own structures and laws. We are to love it well, but as unreality, unsullied by facts, by the confusions and ambiguities of the real world. Indeed, we are to find in this value world the inner peace and calm that is to sustain us against the storms of competitive business life.

But in truth this kind of value world is nowhere, and the attempt somehow to "apply" or "bring" personal values to the facts of business life creates an unreal problem. Fact and value are names of identifiable aspects of experience, but they do not refer to the real elements of which the world is composed.

When we say that it is a fact that a specific proposal is being made to a company president, we mean that something has occurred about which one statement would be ostensibly more descriptive than another. When we lend our support to a planned course of action in a business and say that its results would be "good," we are saying that among its other real properties and qualities the proposal has that which promises to fulfill a desire or interest of the particular person making the judgment about it. The value judgment inevitably involves the concrete relations of persons and institutions, and concrete relations cannot be talked about in abstraction from their value. In reality only that which exists has value, and everything that exists has value.

The principle of the interrelation of fact and value would seem to be elementary metaphysics. But all around us we see business, university, and church people talking of facts and moral principle as if they could be separated in discussion and decision in the real world. We see men engaged in the astonishing mental feat of imagining nonvalued entities and nonexisting values. There is evidence of this in such familiar phrases as "management prerogatives" and "union rights."

If we try to utilize the Christian faith in facing new demands from others, it is much better to be open to all the factors and forces in the situation, to see it in its own terms and uniqueness. It is not very helpful simply to apply a favorite moral principle such as honesty, maximization of profit, service to the community, and so forth. When a relationship to another person or organization is reduced to an example or test of a personal value or principle, it is sure to be interpreted in too rigid or narrow terms and to appear as little more than an expression of self-righteousness, rather than of genuine concern for others and for what is really happening in the world.

The Christian gospel is primarily the story of great events, of great acts of God, not merely an accumulation of moral principles and values. The great all-embracing event is the Incarnate God revealed in the life, death, and resurrection of Christ. Take the resurrection itself. Can this be reduced to a principle or value or law? It must be understood in itself, in its uniqueness, in its transformation of our whole understanding of life and death. It is not fully explained by past events. It brings new meaning to the present, and it opens up new hopes for the future.

As a Christian, I try to reason, by analogy, about the events of my life, my business, and my world, knowing that the Incarnation reveals the nature of the power that truly rules this world. Thus, when confronted with a concrete situation, I seek to respond with all my resources (principles, technical knowledge, and so forth) to understand it on its own terms, to discern what is new in it, to see it as something more than the continuation of past demands and past relationships.

Men in business are never given the moral choice between personal values and the threat to these from circumstances without value or principle. Rather, they must choose between various proposals and demands by men and organizations, all of which combine principle and data, value and fact. The choice is not between some 100% "right world" known by the man of principle, in business or labor, that needs to be defended against the demands of others who could compromise this ideal. The choice is between demands of men who argue for shifts in past arrangements of power and goods in terms of mutual and differing value and factual perspectives on the present and future.

Part II—A Specific Situation

STRIKE IN TOWN*

(KNECHTEL FURNITURE COMPANY)

Cast of Characters

Narrator
Steve Gray, union leader
Howard Kennedy, plant manager
McIver (Mac), union worker

* This is an edited script of the movie, "Strike in Town," produced by the National Film Board of Canada and distributed in this country by the Mc-Graw-Hill Publishing Company.

Mrs. McIver, his wife
Joan Simmons, their daughter
Al Simmons, their son-in-law
Jim Cameron, personnel manager
George Hoffmann, company president
Carl, company treasurer
Men in plant (workers)
Chairman of union meetings
Conciliator, nominated by union and company
Mayor of the town

NARRATOR: Last September things were quiet around town, but then most towns this size are quiet. Population 4,003, and sometimes it seems half of that's kids. Twelve miles of streets; a weekly, *The Post*, circulation 2,500; two banks; 1,100 telephones; and at least a dozen churches. It was a good fall: fine crops, factories busy, and people weren't worrying about things up at the big plant. The contract was up for negotiation, but only a few people thought anything about that—McIver for one. McIver thinks union 24 hours a day.

Scene: McIver's daughter's house. All playing bridge.

MCIVER (MAC): Let's see now, that's 600.
MRS. MCIVER: Doubled.
MAC: Twelve hundred.
JOAN: Oh, that's awful! Well, anyway, we weren't playing for money.
MAC: Well, I'd better be off. It's pretty late as it is.
AL: Ah! Can't take it, huh?
JOAN: Dad, won't you have something to eat?
MRS. MCIVER: I know, I know ...
MAC: No, thanks, Joan. I have to slip over to the union office.
MRS. MCIVER: Don't tell me. Another committee meeting.
AL: At this hour?
MAC: Negotiation committee. Steve Gray had to go to town. He said he wouldn't be back till the 10th.
AL: Well, couldn't it keep?
MAC: Listen, when you're a few years in the union and get some

committee working, you know it can't keep—there's a new contract coming up...

MRS. MCIVER: Mac's just like an old firehorse come negotiation time. Just make sure you do settle, Mac. No strikes, eh?

MAC: Company talk, and from my own wife. I notice these women are very glad to get a few extra dollars from our pay envelopes, really gunning for them, eh, Alec?

AL: Maybe, but I think she's right. We're doing O.K. Don't rock the boat.

MAC: Well, a nice son-in-law you are! Two years in the union and already you're quite happy and contented about everything. That's no way to talk. We want a wage boost, and we want a new seniority system...

AL: Seniority! Doesn't mean anything to me.

JOAN: Alec, don't get him mad.

MAC: It doesn't mean anything to you now, but it will someday. You wait until you're my age.

MRS. MCIVER: Keep cool, buster, keep cool.

JOAN: Daddy, he's just trying to get your goat.

MRS. MCIVER: If you're going to a meeting, you better get started, for Pete's sake. Don't make your speeches here. You know, I get so fed up...

MAC: All right, all right. That's all the thanks I get. Don't bother to wait up for me; I'll probably be late.

AL: I'll take her home. Bye, Dad.

MRS. MCIVER: Bye, now.

MAC (*muttering*): Don't rock the boat, huh?

Scene: The mill, with men assembling for a meeting.

NARRATOR: September 28th. The negotiation committee of the union was working on changes in the new contract. This year most of the talk was wages and a new seniority system. Wages, that's simple. Seniority, that's not. Say they have to lay off someone here in the finishing department—then it affects only finishing, the man with the lowest seniority is dropped, but some men thought they should go for plant-wide seniority. That means if there's a layoff in finishing, it's the man with the lowest seniority in the whole plant who goes off, no matter what department.

MAN: ... I remember last year when the firm had to shut down in here. O.K., I get 15 years' seniority, but I was laid off.

MAN: Some kids in other departments had only 8 months, but they were kept on.

MAN: I could do that work too; it's not fair. I go for seniority.

MAN: Seniority's not in my pay envelope; I say go for wages.

MAN: I hear they are not going for more wages, they're going for seniority.

(*All men talk at once.*)

MAN: ... 15 cents. What do you say, Mac? You're on the committee.

MAC: Oh, I'm not talking. Take it easy; here comes Kennedy.

NARRATOR: Howard Kennedy's plant manager, so naturally the men don't want to tip him off to what they're after in the new contract. As it says, the contract is supposed to secure the full benefits of orderly, collective bargaining and safety and physical welfare of the employee, the economy of operation, quality and quantity of output. The contract runs one year at the plant. They've signed six of them now, and no trouble yet; nothing that couldn't be settled through the regular grievance procedure. For the company, this sort of thing is handled mostly by Cameron, the personnel manager.

Scene: Office of Company President George Hoffmann.

CAMERON: Oh, Howard. Just the man I want to see. Come into Mr. Hoffmann's office for a minute, will you?

HOFFMANN (*on telephone*): Yes, that's right. Sure. Of course we want the Cartwright order. It will keep the plant busy for three months. We don't want to give a firm price right now because we're starting negotiations with the union. We don't know how it will affect our prices. (*Pause.*) Well, see if you can stall Cartwright for a while and let me know. O.K. (*Hangs up.*) Well, Jim?

CAMERON: Don't know any more than I did yesterday.

KENNEDY: There's talk that they are not going after an increase.

CAMERON: Huh! Well, I don't think they're shooting the moon. They'll probably ask for a small boost.

HOFFMANN: How small?

CAMERON: Oh, 8 to 10 cents.

HOFFMANN: Small!! 10 cents would add $10.00 to the cost of a bedroom suite—in the better grades, maybe $15.00. Ten cents an hour is not small, Jim.

CAMERON: Well, it's small for a start. We'll bargain from there.

HOFFMANN: 10 cents an hour is not small whichever way you look at it. It's not just our cost, but by the time it gets to the retailer, what with sales tax and all, it pyramids. The bedroom suite would go up $30.00 more in the long run. The public would not take a price jump like that.

CAMERON: Well, I think the union would come down on wages. What they're really after is plant-wide seniority. Isn't that right, Howard?

KENNEDY: That's what I hear.

HOFFMANN: No! They've been nibbling away at management's prerogative all along, but that's going too far. The first thing you know they'll be running the place and we'll be just ... just office boys. (*Points to picture on wall of old plant.*) Do you see that plant? My grandfather ran that plant his way, and I'm going to do the same. And there'll be no talk about seniority changes, Jim. Remember that!

CAMERON: Don't forget, Mr. Hoffmann, that this seniority system would help us, too. Of course the problem is, how to work out a good one. Anyway, the union is having a meeting tonight. We'll soon find out what they are after. (*They exit.*)

Scene: Union meeting in local town hall.

STEVE: ... had long talks about this, and I think you all know that we're trying to serve in the interest of every man in this local. Anyway, the contract's up for negotiation. Now if any of you men don't like what we're recommending, well, all you have to do is say so, but we think we're a little closer to the situation. Now, we've put a lot of time and a lot of thought into this and we got our recommendations ready. (*Much talk.*) Now—on pay. There's been talk going around that we're not recommending a wage boost. Now I don't know how this talk got started. It isn't true. We are ... (*Much talk.*) ... but not as high as some of you may want. We're recommending 9 cents an hour for everybody across the board. (*Much talk.*) All right, all right. You don't have to buy it, but your committee recommends this, and I so move.

CHAIRMAN: You've heard the motion. Any discussion? Brother Kreuger.

KREUGER: Brother Chairman, what I would like to know is, how'd the committee get this 9 cents?

STEVE: One, on productivity. Our output's going up each year, and two, on the company's ability to pay.

MAC: We're one of the biggest companies in this business, and all we're asking is 9 cents.

STEVE: Now, we didn't just pick this figure out of thin air. We got advice from our research department. We studied the company's figures. We think we can get 9 cents.

MAN: What about seniority?

STEVE: Now, I was just coming to that. Now, we think we can get 9 cents, but we're tying this to plant-wide seniority. Now, we think this plant-wide seniority is just as important, maybe more important. Now say they won't go for it; say they come up past 6, maybe 7 cents. Well, we can bargain a few cents to get that seniority.

MAN: I don't like this tying business. I say go for wages separately. If we get seniority too, O.K. But I don't care that much.

STEVE: There's some of you seem to forget this is a union. Now maybe some of you younger guys want wages most, but some of the older brothers need more seniority protection. Anyway, that's what your committee thinks. So we're going after both, and we're going to get both, if we stick together. (*Much talk.*)

CHAIRMAN: Brother Simmons.

AL: Well, maybe this isn't the time to say this, but well, sure I go along with the demands. But what I say is, I don't think we ought to get too tough. We all know what it is like in the furniture business right now. This town's still O.K., but in other places ... well, we all know one company where they went out three months ago, and they're still out. I can't afford anything like that these days.

CHAIRMAN: Thanks, Brother Simmons. Any other opinions? Are you ready for the question? You've heard the motion. All in favor signify by raising their right hand. Against? All right, carried. Do I hear a motion to adjourn?

MEN: Move we adjourn.

CHAIRMAN: Adjourn.

Scene: Al Simmons' home. Mrs. McIver and Joan talking.

JOAN: What about that other time—you know, the time Dad was on strike. Was it pretty bad?

MRS. MCIVER: I guess you were too young to remember. It was bad enough. I hope we don't have to go through that again.

JOAN: Dad's so hotheaded; he's always looking for a fight. Al's more easygoing. I don't think he wants this any more than... (*Door bangs.*) That must be them now.

MRS. MCIVER: It's about time. (*They enter from the meeting.*)

MAC: ...and what's more, just you remember, without the union, you'd be a punk making 60 cents an hour, and without a whole lot of other benefits the union got you before you ever joined, but...

AL: All I'm trying to say...

MAC: Ah, you make me turn. Talkin' at the meeting like that, I never heard...

MRS. MCIVER: Now what?

MAC: Are you ready?

JOAN: Well, Pa, aren't you going to sit down and have a cup of coffee?

MAC: No, no. I want to go home. Come on, Flo.

MRS. MCIVER: Well, we seem to be in an awful hurry. Could you spare me five seconds to get my coat on? (*Puts on coat.*)

JOAN (*to Al*): What happened? What's the matter, Alec?

AL: At the meeting, I just got up and said what I thought. That's all.

MRS. MCIVER: 'Night, children. 'Night, Alec.

NARRATOR: October 10th, when negotiations started, and they started well, the company wanted an extension of the trial period for all new employees to three months. The union agreed to recommend it to their membership. The union asked for two weeks' vacation with pay after four years, instead of after five. The company agreed. They compromised on changes in shift bonus; hours of work remained the same, 45. So it set well enough to start. Then they got on wages and seniority. That was different.

Scene: Negotiating room. Company and union.

CAMERON: So we'll go up to 3 cents and that's all. That's final. And that's the best we can do.

WORKER: It's not good enough, and you know it. Three cents! What's 3 cents in a pay envelope? A buck thirty-five!

WORKER: Big deal!

MAC: How do you think our families can keep up any sort of a decent standard of living on a measly 3-cent raise?

CARL: The company cannot pay out in wages money it doesn't have.

MAC: Doesn't have! Doesn't have! You've got it all right and more! We want 9 cents, and 9 cents is a drop in the bucket compared to the money you're making.

KENNEDY: Look, Gray, you tell the boys they're getting 3 cents this year. They'll eat it up.

GRAY: We told them. It gave them indigestion. Look, you don't think we're picking figures out of the air, do you? You can afford 10 cents easy, probably 11 cents, but we'll settle for 9. Prove you can't pay 9, and we'll buy. The figures say you can pay, and you haven't proved you can't.

KENNEDY: Your figures are all . . .

STEVE: *Your* figures!! Right from your own annual report. They show you can pay.

CAMERON: Now look, Steve. We've beaten all over that before. Those figures are for the year ending last April. Things are different now. They're tighter all around. You can't set next year's wages on last year's profits. Take a look at our position now.

STEVE: It's not just your position. It's our work too. Our output's been going up. We're entitled to a share of the extras.

HOFFMANN: Your output's been going up because we spent a quarter of a million mechanizing the plant, and we can't pay that off if we meet your demands.

CAMERON: He's right, Steve. We just can't go to 9.

MAC: We'd be after 15, if 'twas only wages. But we want the plant-wide seniority too.

CAMERON: Here we go again.

HOFFMANN: You'll not get plant-wide seniority while I'm running this company. You've got departmental seniority, and that's fair.

STEVE: What's so fair about it? Things get slack in the machine shop, so Jimmy Bain with 20 years gets his slip and some two-month kid in veneer stays on. What's so fair?

CAMERON: What do you want us to do? Switch Jimmy to veneer and bump the kid? Jimmy doesn't know that job.

HOFFMANN: We can't afford a ring-around-the-rosy with everybody learning a new job every time there's a layoff.

CAMERON: Now look, Steve, we know it's tough. But what's your answer? Most of our jobs are skilled. A man can't learn a dozen new trades just to start a new seniority system.

MAC: Baloney! Most of the jobs could be learned in this plant in a day. Blindfolded. Easy.

HOFFMANN: That's not what you say when you're talking wage rates.

STEVE: McIver's a little optimistic there, but basically he's right. A lot of jobs in this plant can be learned in a few days. What about those guys with 20, 25 years? Don't you figure you owe them the investment of a couple days' training?

KENNEDY: I'm running a plant, not a training school.

CAMERON: If it were just a few men, O.K., we could see that, but if layoffs increase, and the way things are they may—why, why it would be like musical chairs around here. No, gentlemen, until you can answer that, we have to stick to the present system.

WORKER: We'd like a recess. O.K.?

CAMERON: Well, boys, I think it's your turn to leave, eh?

NARRATOR: Recess is a time for each side to re-examine its position. Is the other side solid or weakening? Is this really their final offer? Is it time for a change in tactics, perhaps even to make a concession?

HOFFMANN: Have you got those figures, Carl?

CARL: Yes, right here.

HOFFMANN: Well, Carl's figures here show that to continue our usual dividends and pay off the bonds for mechanization, we can go to 6 cents safely, but only just; anything over that and we may have to raise our prices. Now we can't do that the way the market is.

CAMERON: How would the plant-wide seniority system affect these figures?

HOFFMANN: Oh, well, you can skip that.

CAMERON: Oh, no. Let's hear it.

CARL: Can't say. Too many imponderables.

HOFFMANN: I won't go for plant-wide seniority. It doesn't make sense. You know it cuts down our efficiency, upsets every department, and slows down our output when times are rough, right when we need efficiency the most.

CAMERON: If we get the Cartwright order, what then?

HOFFMANN: Cartwright. That might be different. A firm price and three months' work in one month. What's the matter, Cameron, do you want to see plant-wide seniority?

CAMERON: I want to see this thing settled without a strike, and the union feels pretty strongly about seniority. Even if you went up to 6 cents I don't think they would drop the seniority demands.

HOFFMANN: I'm not so sure the whole union's that strong on seniority. Can Gray hold them together?

KENNEDY: Yes, I think he can.

CARL: And they've got a good-sized strike fund.

CAMERON: Yes, I think you can hold them all right, but they'll probably offer to drop a couple of cents in exchange for the seniority.

HOFFMANN: All right, we'll come up a bit, but no seniority talk. Now, if we... (*Knock on the door.*) ...oh, here they are now. Come in, gentlemen. (*They enter.*)

NARRATOR: Cameron was right. The union said they would come down to 7 cents in exchange for the plant-wide seniority system. The company came up to 4 cents, but wouldn't hear of seniority changes. They met again the next day and the next week. It was no good. Two weeks later, in November, they took their case to conciliation. A conciliation board usually is made up of a company nominee, a union nominee, and a chairman agreed on by both sides. It's set up by government and represents the interests of all citizens.

Scene: Hearing room of the conciliation board.

CHAIRMAN: Our recommendations aren't binding, of course, but I hope they'll be acceptable. It's the public interest that counts.

STEVE: Any idea how long it will take to bring down the report?

CHAIRMAN: We'll try to have it down by Christmas. (*Men all talk.*) No one else has anything to say. I guess we may adjourn.

NARRATOR: December 6th, waiting for the board's report was tough for the company. The Cartright order, the one they wanted so badly. They'd taken a chance and made a firm price, but could they deliver the goods, or would the plant be closed—stuck tight?

Scene: Restaurant. Hoffmann, Kennedy, and Cartwright (who has left the table.)

HOFFMANN: Before Cartwright comes back, how'd it go?

KENNEDY: I think fairly well.

HOFFMANN: What do you think of our chances on the board's report, I mean?

KENNEDY: Well, I figure they'll support us on the seniority issue, but about wages, I don't know.

HOFFMANN: That could be worse. Even if we do take a bit of a beating on the price of the piece, we'll be able to make delivery.

KENNEDY: But suppose the union doesn't accept the report?

HOFFMANN: Do you think they'll actually strike on seniority?

KENNEDY: They're dead serious, George.

HOFFMANN: We gotta get this order, Jim. Our backlog's only one month. Surely if we go for a wage hike ...

KENNEDY: Don't forget that if the conciliation report recommends a raise, our board of directors may not accept it.

HOFFMANN: That's my baby. They're tough, but I think I can sell. Here comes Cartwright.

CARTWRIGHT: Sorry, gentlemen.

HOFFMANN: That's all right, Charlie. I was just talking to Jim about this union thing. He says he thinks everything will be playing safe.

CARTWRIGHT: Well, if you can guarantee delivery.

HOFFMANN: You'll get your delivery date. Don't you worry. All we need now is your order. We'll get you delivery.

Scene: Union Christmas party. Stage of hall with Steve as Santa.

SANTA: And now we're going to have a Christmas carol. We have a choir of boys and girls whom you all know, and they are going to sing for you under the direction of Mr. Miller. (*Crowd cheers and Santa ushers children on stage.*) Well, they're all here now ...

MAC: Pssst! Steve, Steve. (*Mac is whispering to Steve from door off stage. He gets Steve's attention and beckons to him.*)

SANTA: I'll be back. In the meantime, you all enjoy the singing.

MAC (*whispers*): The report just came in. I've got it in the room across the hall. (*They go into room across hall.*)

STEVE: Hi, boys.

MAC: I knew you'd want to see it straight away. (*Steve reads report.*)

MAC: Well...

STEVE (*pauses*): The board recommends 7 cents an hour, but they don't support us on seniority.

MAC: The boys won't buy that.

STEVE (*picks up telephone*): Four-seven-nine. (*Pause.*) I'll talk to Cameron.

MAC: So they won't support us on seniority, eh?

STEVE: Hello, Jim. Steve Gray. Well, did you get your copy in the mail? (*Pause.*) Yeah. Well, we've got a general meeting for the 3rd; maybe you and I ought to get together before then. Well, I thought we might talk about it. (*Pause.*) No, I don't think the boys will buy. (*Pause.*) You don't, eh? Mmmm. You'll call me, then? Fine. O.K. Goodbye. (*Hangs up.*) Cameron doesn't think the company will buy the report, either.

MAN: The company won't buy? Why not?

MAC: If the report doesn't even back us on the seniority...

STEVE: He doesn't think they'll go for the 7 cents. Now we probably want to cut the seniority decision.

MAN: So what happens?

STEVE: Strike vote, I guess. Well, I gotta get back up there.

NARRATOR: On January 3rd, the union called a general meeting and voted 163 to 38 to strike. Immediately following the meeting...

Scene: Men coming down stairs of union hall.

AL: H'lo Steve.

STEVE: Hi, Al. How about a cup of coffee?

AL: Oh, O.K. (*They go to lunchroom.*)

STEVE (*talking to Al*): So there it is, Al. You think we're striking for a 3-cent raise and a change in the seniority system. You're wrong. It's for a lot more than that.

AL: More? How come?

STEVE: It's for things that maybe we'll get years from now, things that you may not even see.

AL: For instance...

STEVE: Well, in this plant, a 40-hour week, a guaranteed annual wage.

AL: Who knows? I can't see where this strike is going to get ...

STEVE: You can't get everything at once, Al. These things take time. We're a lot better off today than our grandfathers were—better working conditions, better pay, more security. But what we got didn't come easy. A lot of union men worked for these things; they didn't come all at once.

AL: If we're gonna strike, why don't we wait for something that's really big?

STEVE: This is big enough for now. You see, Al, every gain we make we've got to take in bits. Like this is one bit—a small one maybe— but just as important as the others.

AL: Do you have to strike every time you want something?

STEVE: Not always, no. Management is learning to negotiate, and so are we. But when a showdown comes, and it means bite or no bite, well, then you may have to strike. It's the only weapon. Every once in a while we'll have to sacrifice to keep it working.

AL: Yeah.

STEVE: Say, look, Al, you may take a ribbing from some of the boys over the way you spoke out tonight, even from Mac.

AL: I just said what I thought.

STEVE: Sure, why not? But look, if Mac and some of the others, well, get a little bitter, don't take it too hard. Sometimes we're just as prejudiced as management. Let's get going; a strike means work for me. (*They leave counter.*)

Scene: Hoffmann's office. Hoffmann is reading a letter aloud.

HOFFMANN: As you know, the union has not accepted the report of the conciliator, and in accordance with the majority vote of the membership, the plant will be struck on January 10th, midnight, upon the completion of the night shift. Signed: Gorman. Can't we beat it, Jim?

CAMERON: You mean break it? Scabs and all? Nope, not while I'm on the payroll. Mind you, you'd probably beat them, but it would ruin your labor relations for 10 years. The first place that would show up would be in your costs.

HOFFMANN: Yes, but the Cartwright order. We've just got them as customers, and if we don't deliver, we'll lose them for good.

Scene: A street in town.

NARRATOR: The town heard about the strike call, and fast. Most people hear about labor relations only when they're bad, when some racketeer gets hold of a union, or some company locks out its workers, or there's a strike. They don't hear about the thousands of agreements signed and honored by both sides. They don't hear about labor relations until they're in the headlines.

WOMAN'S VOICE: Humph! These labor bosses! They just tell them to go on strike and they have to. The government should step in and show these strikers who's boss!

2ND WOMAN'S VOICE: If they do go on strike, I'll have to close down.

3RD WOMAN'S VOICE: You don't need to tell me. I know what happens, and I'm not going through that again. You put that coat on and go down to the employment office and get yourself another job before everybody else thinks of it.

4TH WOMAN'S VOICE: The ring isn't paid for—we might as well quit looking for an apartment.

1ST MAN'S VOICE: Three cents an hour, 24 cents a day. Why, if they're out for two months it will take 'em years to make it back.

2ND MAN'S VOICE: That makes nearly $6.00 on the books, and we can forget about trying to collect a lot of that for a while.

MRS. MC IVER: Strike welfare adds to $21.00 a week. And if there's anything real urgent like the mortgage, the union will try to help.

Scene: Mayor's office.

MAYOR: You can say that I will do everything I can. No. Change that. Make it "the town." Say, "The town will do everything it can to prevent this tragedy." I don't think that's too strong a word. And you can also say that I have called a meeting for tonight in this office with representatives of the union and the company to see if we can't work out some sort of an agreement.

COMMENTARY

Failure of Management *

It is unfortunate that management is so poorly portrayed in this incident. The president appears to be prejudiced, impetuous, and perhaps not even intellectually honest. His broad, general state-

* By Mr. Hanley.

ments about management prerogatives simply reflect views he has inherited from his forebears.

His acceptance of the Cartwright order with his fingers crossed, for example, indicates that he had very serious doubts that he would be able to carry out his delivery promise, solemnly given. In short, this incident is not typical of business today, and so does not illustrate my basic thesis: right decisions will generally be made by successful business managers because they are moral and ethical men with built-in scales of justice.

As for the company itself, the kind of orderly industrial relations procedures which provide a foundation for justice to all employees seem to be nonexistent. Negotiations are carried on in a catch-as-catch-can manner, with each management representative putting in his two cents' worth. No one appears to be willing to examine the real facts in dispute, and there is no evidence that anyone has considered any alternative which would prevent real injustice.

The value issue presented, the question of seniority, is fraught with problems and bears the seeds of misunderstanding and controversy. But there are so many ramifications to the problem that the sketchy presentation of the issue here does not help anyone understand how involved and contentious it can be.

Basically, the seniority problem is a company and union problem. It is a well-established principle of industrial relations that length of service is a major factor for consideration in promotions and lay-offs. If two workers in a department are each qualified to fill a particular opening, the one with the most seniority gets first call on the new job. If one of the two workers must be laid off in a reduction in work force, the one with the least seniority is the first to go.

Carefully defined in union-management employment contracts, thoroughly understood by the workers themselves, and fairly and properly administered, a good system of seniority, on a job and departmental basis, is indispensable to the orderly functioning of a large plant. This was recognized by Mr. Cameron, the personnel manager, when he said, "Don't forget, Mr. Hoffmann, that a good seniority system would help us, too."

An improperly drawn seniority plan, or one that is badly administered, can reduce a plant to shambles. Unless the plan recognizes job requirements and employee qualifications as well as seniority, it is worthless. A plant janitor, regardless of long tenure, is not likely to be qualified to replace the first melter on an open hearth, the skilled operator of a multi-million dollar continuous rolling mill, or the electronics maintenance man.

These are facts generally recognized by unions, by management, and by the employees themselves. This being true, it is the clear duty of a company's management to keep its eye on the main ball—the over-all job of keeping the business alive, its production lines rolling, and its sales and earnings on a healthy and growing level.

While it may seem unfair, purely from a seniority standpoint, to lay off a janitor with 25 years' service and keep a bright young electronics repairman on the job, the manager of today's plants has no other choice. If the electronic gadgets break down, the plant will not operate. And if it does not operate—and operate profitably— eventually nobody will have a job.

I have posed an extreme case for purposes of illustration. Actually, the inequities that arise and the disputes that grow out of seniority are usually much more subtle and complicated, and much less visibly soluble.

But, one important factor to keep in mind is that seniority is relative. You do not improve the seniority of one man without relatively lessening the seniority security of one of his coworkers. Thus, while it is easy for an individual worker to make an excellent case for what is right and just for himself, it is much more difficult to ensure that seniority decisions—and most business decisions, in fact—are right and just not only for a single employee but for the company and all its employees, owners, customers, and plant communities as well.

Incidentally, I might also point out that the dialogue has a union slant, and conveys the distinct impression that all gains for employees have been wrung by the union from a reluctant management. Perhaps this is so for this company, because it seems to me that management's actions indicate an immature approach to labor relations which is hard to reconcile with a union history going back at least six years. But from my experience I can testify that such advances are usually the result of actions taken by both the union and management.

I would like to comment, now, on the position of the union. Steve, who is business agent, indicates his philosophy in his statement that strikes are sometimes necessary to gain benefits. I would agree that they may be at times, but, by and large, reasonable people can correct difficulties over a period of time by other means, usually by negotiation and bargaining in good faith between employee representatives and management. In this particular case, I deplore the adamant and inflexible stand taken by both union leaders and management. I believe progress might have been made without a strike being called.

If I were a lawyer fortunate enough to be invited by both sides to enter the case, I must confess that my inclination would be to join the union's side. This inclination arises not so much from the merits of the union case as from the faults of the management as depicted in the story.

Mr. Hoffmann's position at the end is very difficult to understand. He has an obligation to his board and stockholders to make a profit on a continuing basis. Furthermore, he has obligations to his customers and employees. If there is no strike, he improves his standing with the customers, including Cartwright, from whom he has just received his first order. The reputation of the company is of importance to the employees, too, because their continuing employment is dependent on good customer relations. Mr. Hoffmann also has an obligation to his community, its merchants, and its citizens, who will suffer from a strike.

In the light of these elements and particularly in view of the additional fact that the company was willing to go to 6 cents per hour prior to receipt of the Cartwright order, which seemed to change things materially, it is very difficult to see why the company did not immediately resume negotiations with a view to exploring the mediation board's recommendations as a basis of settlement. Had management taken such a course, there is no doubt that the union would have been under considerable pressure to accept the recommendations also. Had the union finally refused, the onus of the strike would have been on it.

In any event, Knechtel Furniture Company should give more attention to its employee relations. It is my opinion that the seniority problem might have been settled on a mutually satisfactory basis other than the plant-wide seniority demand, perhaps to the advantage of all. Regardless of this one contract settlement, as long as seniority is so seriously in dispute it is bound to be a recurring problem, because something seems to be basically wrong.

One other general observation: human nature is presented in an unflattering light in the flashes of comment by townspeople as the strike breaks out. Each individual complains in a self-centered way about how the strike will damage his own personal interests. Perhaps the shrewdest one is the woman who orders her husband to get down to the employment office and get another job, "before everyone else thinks of it."

Without suggesting the repeal of the first law of nature, which is self-preservation, I would like to suggest that all our problems might be a little less worrisome if somehow people could be made to think less of their own selfish interests and more about what is right and just and good for the community in which they live. Perhaps this is an impossible expectation, but I think it is a good sign that this chapter weighs such matters.

More Honesty Is Needed

With real earnestness, I have to say that management of this type does exist in America and in Canada today, believe it or not. Immature it may be, but this kind of thing does go on. I know of a recent strike, for example, that was called over the issue of a 12 cents per hour raise for men whom everyone agrees are being paid 50 cents per hour below the industry rate. The manager resists it because, he insists, he has cut prices so low that he cannot afford to raise wages.

More important, however, in the Knechtel case is the lack of confidence which has developed between the management representative and the union officer. Each is trying to outmaneuver or outguess the other in order to maintain a position which is unsound in the first place. As a consequence, an entire community is threatened. Such a breakdown should be prevented at all costs.

This breakdown has developed partly because of a lack of honesty and integrity on the part of management. True, the personnel director informs the president—directly and honestly—that as long as

* By Mr. Minton.

he is on the payroll, he will not become a strike breaker and will not go out and hire scabs to run the plant. For that I commend him. But he is not honest in his dealings with the labor union official. Seniority is important and becomes even more significant as a man gets older. But in this instance, it is blown up out of proportion because it is tied to a proposition which becomes not only a bargaining matter but an emotional issue as well.

If the company were honest in explaining that it has a new contract which will supply three months' continuous work to the plant, the seniority issue might be removed, because in time the workers would realize that to take the strike would mean loss of that new business.

In other words, if the employer were honest in his own personal values, maintained real integrity, and brought his people closer to his company, he would not have the strike vote, because the employees would know that there is a real reason to continue working. They would be willing to resolve the issue by trial and error, if by no other way.

Thus, emotion must be kept out of these issues wherever possible. Truth and integrity have to be built in, so these problems do not become the kind of explosive issues that cause strikes. I am not saying that strikes are never necessary, of course. In this instance, after six years of complacent bargaining it might well be necessary to shock somebody into realizing that there are two sides to this problem. But often they can be avoided.

Personally, I would not take a strike on a simple seniority issue. It would have to be a pretty vicious matter for me to consider it. I have made public speeches to our industry, and we bargain industry-wide for our skilled people, saying that I hate strikes. I think you will find most labor leaders do, at least the people who have to participate in them.

That is why I am opposed to compulsory government arbitration. To me, it is an admission of weakness in men, because there is no conflict of value that cannot be resolved if men want to be reasonable with one another and recognize their own weaknesses or the weakness of their own position.

Were I Gray, I would have done exactly what the conciliator's report urged, as I have done with conciliators' reports in other instances, even though I know full well that they are nothing more than political documents which give you maybe 50% of what you are entitled to. I would not have said, "Well, boys, let's go on strike and blame it on the government." At that point, then, the responsibility of leadership enters in. In the Knechtel case, there was a lack of forceful leadership on both sides.

With true leadership combined with integrity, crises like the one disclosed here can be avoided.

What Is Really Going on Here? *

In this incident one feels the tremendous complexity of the levels on which tensions and conflicts occur. It is necessary for us to understand these because we need to appreciate the limits on the main actors in this situation and, more importantly, the possibilities of breaking out of a stalemate.

In the first place, the story shows us the tremendous private conflicts taking place in the homes of the union people involved and how they affect the relations between husband and wife, father and son. The incident does not disclose the tensions in the families in the business community, and the omission might be significant as the sign of a kind of prevailing cultural attitude which assumes that the worker's wife is more immediately and deeply involved in labor controversies than the businessman's family because her family income is much more seriously affected. But this assumption is based on a purely economic interpretation of the relationships between people in a family. It ignores the variety of psychological and social concerns of a businessman's wife, which certainly may affect her attitude toward her husband's role and no doubt have some possible influence on how he conceives of his task in this situation. These tensions are private in the sense that they are lived with outside the business office and outside the union hall. They certainly have powerful claims on the major figures in the controversy.

Secondly, there are conflicts over the official role that the leaders are to carry out and the values for which they fight. The primary responsibilities of the presidents of the labor union and of the company are not resolved in their own minds. They are somewhat defensive or edgy about their roles, shifting them with the changing circumstances. The wife of the union leader says, for example, that

* By Mr. Underwood.

when it comes time for negotiations, he becomes a "firehorse." Thus, he puts on a stern face, pressing his claims hard, exaggerating them for emphasis. His role in that situation must be understood in terms of what he thinks one does in negotiation, and also in the framework of a hope for a happier situation when events settle back to routine again.

The third level of conflict is over personal loyalty within one's own organization. The story reveals what all of us know from our personal experience in organizations: in our official capacity, there are some facts which we can tell some men in our organizations but not others, because of the need for range in organization and the necessity to evaluate people within it. Note that the company president tests the personal loyalty and probes the basis of judgment of his subordinates by asking about their attitudes toward the negotiations.

One has to ask here whether personal loyalty to the president means in this case accepting his position on the issues without genuine and full discussion of alternative views. One senses that the president feels his position so strongly as a defense of his whole family tradition that the subordinates make only very guarded comments about their own different ways of looking at the labor-management conflict.

Fourth, there are conflicts over the interpretation of one's corporate responsibilities as a union or business leader. Businessmen, as we all know, have management responsibilities to many groups— workers, stockholders, customers, personnel, the community—and they are certainly not easily treated as additive or separate. In the union, there is no single, all-encompassing responsibility to the "workers" as a whole. We see in the union meeting that there is a conflict over the importance of the seniority issue between the younger generation of workers and the older men.

Then tensions show up over the nature of the claims of the community on both business and labor as expressed through the mayor, whose professional role as a politician inescapably involves him in the reconciliation of the broad and varied interests of the community. The reaction of the businessman and the labor leader to the mayor is not explored in the story, but may be crucial in the settlement of the controversy or continuation of discussion. Is he seen as having, and does he have by the nature of his function as a politician, a role different from that of the representatives of business and labor, and thus an important perspective to offer?

These varied roles, with their distinctive value claims and personal symbols, are objectively present in the situation, and the tensions that these roles produce are also there, subjectively, in the businessmen who must make decisions. These paradoxes are not resolved simply by institutions like a board of directors or a union meeting. The decisions of a board certainly may clarify positions and interests, but someone must make a decision as to whether a demand is to be met, opposed, further discussed, and so forth. At that point the tensions reach their height, and are involved in the choices that are made.

There is no doubt in my mind that the furniture company president is confronted by new demands which are not to be understood merely in terms of past demands. For example, the union wants company-wide seniority even in administering layoffs in connection with technological unemployment. The president is strongly tempted to deal with the union only on issues of the past, mainly the wage rate, and to hold that past institutional arrangements on seniority are so inviolate as to be beyond discussion. The union leader, on the other hand, indicates no appreciation of the value of these past arrangements in making possible the greatest use of different skills, blows up the issue out of proportion, and makes a proposal for the future which breaks radically from the past.

The defense of the past by the company president, you will recall, is of a bloc of "management prerogatives," not to be chipped away by labor. The defense—mostly implicit—of the union proposal for the future is made as if it could be deduced from the laborer's rights to control the obsolescence of his chief property, his skills. Here is the importance, you see, of man's respect for his job. From my own perspective on this situation, a stalemate seems inevitable given the tendency of both sides to convert abstractions or mental constructions of "prerogatives" and "rights" into supposedly real entities, which, if compromised or bargained away, would mean a personal moral defeat.

But if we look to the past, "management prerogatives," such as the right to deal with seniority and technological innovation, are not a bloc of inviolate forms or principles written into the universe but patterns of relationships worked out over time to meet certain situations, to get a job done, to achieve the changing purposes of a business enterprise. The "rights" of labor have been and will be redefined in the give-and-take of daily work, and no ideal way to administer seniority and protect skills and individual dignity can be deduced from them alone.

The company president should be willing to enter into some discussion of the union's proposals on seniority, and the union leaders should be willing to consider seriously proposals short of their own demand for company-wide seniority. I do not have enough concrete knowledge of a business enterprise to envision the possibilities between the two positions, but I am sure that choices or alternatives would probably open up once the parties involved seriously studied both the limits and possibilities in the concrete situation.

The concrete situation always has within it more mystery and richness of reality than envisioned in the abstract. New knowledge of the possibilities for controlling the effects of economic growth on workers and management might be expected to emerge from negotiation. New knowledge is gained not simply by an objective look at the facts but by encounters between different groups of men who value different things and see different facts. In such negotiation technical knowledge, personal values, and moral principle are not abandoned but brought into play consciously and seriously.

Aware, then, of the intimate relation of personal values to the way a man reads a conflict situation, we need to look finally at the kind of value concerns which are operative in contemporary business culture. These are the major value problems that occur in all business conflict situations, and illustrate the utter pragmaticism of much of our society, and, in particular, of the images that businessmen present of themselves to one another in their day-to-day operations, if not in their public relations pronouncements.

The larger and varied interests of life that may be or ought to be seriously and consciously considered in business decisions are often obscured or falsified when the merely technical or functional questions are made the primary or only questions in policy decisions. The businessman is likely, when pressed to discuss his ethical assumptions before his colleagues, to stress that his basic motive is to maximize his profits or to look after his self-interest and those of the company. He does not wish to appear as a Jack Do-Gooder before his business friends.

But these pragmatic phrases beg the hard and real moral questions as to how narrow or wide or deep or shallow the actual factors taken into consideration, consciously or unconsciously, in the formation of company policy are.

On the other hand, the attempts, particularly in church and university circles, to affirm the reality of the social responsibilities of the business profession often neglect the pervasive preoccupation in our society with the immediate, tangible, and quantitative factors in business, often at the expense of the long-run, intangible, and qualitative aspects of life.

Let's be more specific. Note that the discussions between the furniture company president and the buyer rightly center on the question of whether an order will be filled on time and at a price that will permit the customer to meet his competition. It is interesting to note that the furniture company president makes no effort to explain the new factors, certainly hard to qualify, which the union and the community press him to consider in his decisions as to his future operations. Why not? Does he refuse to deal with these other social factors consciously, or does he assume rightly that the other man would not understand or wish to deal with a president who had so broadened and deepened the factors he took into serious consideration in planning his business?

Obviously, we are dealing with the most serious kind of cultural and moral question. How widely accepted in our society is the image of the businessman as a member of a "socially responsible profession," and not merely the creature of the more traditional management concern for maximization of profit?

The Faculty of the Harvard Business School, the National Council of Churches, and many other forces in our culture now talk of new social ethics in business. Is this a controlling image in business decisions in our society or merely a creature of public relations?

Perhaps we can say this much about the general cultural situation: the decisions men face today in business generally require responsible consideration and reconciliation of a variety of interests. The term "social responsibility" has reality in that businessmen are exposed constantly to many demands on their resources—bargaining with unions perhaps being only the most formal and regularized. These interests cannot simply be added up, as if they existed in isolation. They must be seen from a point of view which looks at the whole operation of a business and its impact on society.

Indeed, today we must reach for a conception of justice which goes beyond a pagan *quid pro quo,* an eye for an eye, a tooth for a tooth, to some deeper Judaic-Christian awareness of a higher justice in which a variety of interests are molded and transformed by leaders into contributions to the life of the whole community.

This is a justice, a pattern of relationships, that emerges out of the serious and sensitive attention to one another's needs and dignity. It is a justice informed by love and expressed by leaders who dare to go beyond the simple, the tangible, the short run, the neatly calculable, in their business dealings in order to discover new mutual relationships in which none of the parties involved are diminished but grow in an atmosphere of common concern and continuing communication.

This is not to express abstract idealism. The "pragmatist" is right that every qualitative judgment has its quantitative side—its dollars-and-cents cost. He is right that part of the American genius is the ability to imagine the utilitarian implications of pure research. But the problem in our culture is overcommitment to this dimension of life and failure to transform and direct our pragmatic considerations by attention to larger and long-term ends.

The story leaves us reflecting on the possibility that in all of life a too direct or complete absorption in pragmatic affairs may finally be self-defeating. The president of the company has understandably been deeply troubled over the effect of the union's attitude on his ability to deliver on his biggest order. That is the most immediate and tangible of his business decisions. But the opportunity to achieve this objective depends in great part on his ability to assure the union leaders that his practical judgments about seniority are made within some larger frame of values, the main one being the right to continue existence as a growing union.

The larger ends of justice and mutuality must discipline and direct the techniques of bargaining, of proposal and counterproposal, or the techniques merely become slick and evasive, the object of suspicion and deception.

To be efficient in handling technological layoffs and restraining workers assumes some frame of values within which efficient methods of administration are carried out. If there is an error about the purposes of the administrative structure—if the dignity and worth of all parties involved is not genuinely the objective—then, it seems to me, no amount of practical know-how learned at business schools will make it possible for men to live and work together.

All this is to say that our personal values are developed within some community of faith and are never wholly separate from the attitudes of the whole culture.

Where these days do men turn for clarification of the ultimate meaning of their work? Certainly the relations of economic activity to a faithful perspective can seldom be discussed within business in the terms used here, but it may yet be possible in our society for men to gain some perspective on their daily lives out of such discussion within the university and the church.

The Open Mind *

I shall try to summarize the meaning of this discussion in a series of categorical statements.

Business decisions inevitably involve tensions and conflicts in values between the parties affected by them. Men tend to seek stable relationships in which they can find relative peace and certainty in a well-worked-out balance between economic and technical factors, personalities and groups. But both history and the behavioral sciences make it safe to predict that these stable relationships will be upset, change will come about, and new relationships and understandings will be established.

Leaders will find it hard but rewarding to discover how to release the creative talent of the individual so as to permit him to achieve a well-developed and rounded personality, while at the same time accomplishing the purposes of the organization and meeting the claims of the larger community. The job of achieving such integration among conflicting forces is not easy, but it is even more difficult to take the next step of adjusting to change and the need for new integrations.

Management has always had the opportunity to exercise social responsibility, as broadly conceived in this discussion, but in recent years circumstances have required a greater exercise of this re-

* By Mr. Learned.

sponsibility. We can safely predict that this trend will be accelerated in the next 50 years.

Many businessmen are aware that the historic religions and ethics of our civilization give more weight to human values than to property values. They seem uneasy with their social role because their life work includes the making of profits. They seem unsure of their social standing. Intuitively, businessmen, like other men, want to respect themselves and be respected. They want to serve the good. The question is what is good and whether they can serve the good in the business environment. The good is not inconsistent with the earning of profits; indeed, the factors that enter into the maximization of profits in the long run are ethical considerations.

There are many criteria, including profits, that affect the final decisions. Does not the actual behavior of many leaders of the business community demonstrate that they consider not only stockholders but also employees, customers, local communities, the nation, and even the world, as far as possible? Our actual behavior is clearly more socially responsible than the way we talk about it. Nevertheless, only when leaders do what they believe to be right will they be able to live comfortably with themselves and the difficult course of action they must follow.

Leaders might also find it easier to live with themselves and perform their social role if they wholeheartedly accepted the fact that the ultimate criteria for right decisions, known for ages and included in many religious or ethical systems, do not provide clearcut, direct answers for specific situations. Men working with others of different points of view and holding different values must find these answers through the use of all their resources in free discussion. Men need not be afraid to seek the right answers in this way because they are finite and cannot claim the wisdom of the Infinite Being. Though men's answers are imperfect, they are nearer to the ultimate answer when there is open and free airing of different points of view.

There is a spiritual significance to every man's work and especially to that of leaders of men. Quite personally, what does this mean for daily behavior? I need not fear the burden of responsibility, any situation, any conflicts, any difference in values, and the fact that I have not decided what the real problem is or what the preconceived solution might be, for down deep in my heart I know I can draw on the resources of other men's expertness, points of view, and values to reach a balanced conclusion or plan of action.

All I need to do is to reach out for these resources, have the imagination to comprehend who might have interests or points of view to offer, possess a genuine desire to listen to their contributions with an open mind, and have a capacity to articulate the other person's point of view to facilitate an exchange of ideas.

I recognize that the foregoing sets a standard of perfection. I do not expect perfection either in myself or in others, but I shall be able to live with my imperfect self and imperfect answers while endeavoring to achieve the perfect goal. I have faith in this process and in my ability to participate in it with an open mind. I do not intend to commit the sin of pride or self-righteousness. I have faith that through an exchange of ideas with men of different views we are likely to achieve better answers than I can alone. I will attempt to fill my own personal destiny and do my share of God's work in this way. For better or for worse, each of us is going to realize his spiritual destiny in connection with his work. He will not find it in some ideal world, detached from reality.

THINKING AHEAD IN
ECONOMIC GROWTH AND STABILITY

Charles A. Bliss

IN ONE OF THE SMALL TOWNS of England during World War II, so
the story goes, the townspeople were frustrated and depressed by
the disruption of their lives caused by the incessant Nazi bomb-
ings. The factories were destroyed, and they literally had nothing to
do. A good minister in the community said he thought he could
do something about it and find them some useful work, so he went
off to nearby London to see what he could locate.

On his return he brought a large assortment of buttons that were
all mixed up, and he asked his flock if they would come the next
morning at 9 o'clock and sort buttons. They agreed, and the morale,
activity, spirit, productivity, and creativity in this community rose
once again. They all dressed a little more neatly; they showed up
on time and worked hard. All went well until, unfortunately, one

Note: Mr. Bliss is Professor of Business Administration, Harvard Business
School.

of the workers returned late one night to find their leader mixing the sorted buttons to provide the next day's work!

Now, I start with this concept: the essence of economic activity is the production of goods and services, and if we have the creativity and the capacity, and if we do turn out goods and services, we have the essentials of a high standard of living. The important thing is that this standard is measured in terms of what we do, in terms of our activity. Any inactivity saps our standard of living by just that amount which might have been created. And over against it all are the satisfactions of creative work, even to the degree of humbly sorting buttons.

I recently had the privilege of spending eight weeks in a management training program in the Philippines. On this trip I passed over and through areas with far, far lower standards of living than we enjoy in this country. Now, we may have what appears to some people to be a materialistic society and a surfeit of economic goods, but believe me, economic goods rate high among the necessities of the full life, and the vigor and creativity needed to produce them are basic requirements for all men. People all around the world are vitally interested in promoting economic growth.

Stability versus Growth

Can we have both growth and stability? If we continue to have successive periods of plenty and scarcity, should we have them perhaps on a low level rather than on a high one, because the farther up one goes the more violently one suffers in the downswing? Is there any probability that we can have both economic stability *and* economic growth?

Of course, we have to decide whether or not we really want stability, how much we want, and what we are willing to sacrifice to achieve it. The surest security, as I imply, comes from not trying to climb too high. To what degree does our economy depend on a willingness to take the long chance, to avoid the easy path? It was Malcolm P. McNair who made the point some time ago that people who are tough-minded will not take the easy way, will not seek safety first, because, paradoxically, when everybody tries to play it safe, there is no safety for anyone.

Some degree of instability, then, seems to be essential to growth. The problem is how much we can stand and how much we want.

Assuming that the businessman wants the maximum of both that he can get, what are the forces with which he has to contend?

At the present time one important characteristic of our industrial economy is the relative emphasis on durable consumer goods. Any such economy, it has been argued, is necessarily unstable, for the demand for such items can and often will be postponed or speeded up far more than the demand for nondurable goods.

It is likewise true that capital goods—even more than durable consumer goods—are subject to wide postponement and extreme acceleration in our modern economy. The recent business cycles we have experienced have been largely inventory cycles. But these reductions in inventory often start a swing of capital investment and badly distort our economic growth.

Forces for Stability

At the same time, we are moving increasingly to an emphasis on services of all kinds. The growth of this area of activity in a high-level economy tends to improve stability, for one thing, because inventories are not involved to any large extent. Accordingly, I think we can look forward to greater stability to the degree that services increase in our economy. Another factor leading to stability is the increase which all of us recognize in government activity. Though government expenditures do swing widely as the cold war occasionally gets hot, the activity of government in the economy basically makes for—or can be manipulated to make for—stability.

Looking ahead, then, we must ask ourselves what the relative proportions are going to be between the unstable area—which might itself be stabilized by general activity and deliberate management action—and the stable sector based on our emphasis on services and government activity. Personally, I reach the conclusion that we will have more rather than less stability in the future.

Relating Capacity to Consumers

One of the interesting aspects of the period that lies ahead involves the surge in our population. People are now talking about the 1960's being the golden years because, they say, then we will have a larger population, and more will be in the buying ages. But do more people in the 1960's necessarily mean greater economic growth and stability? In terms of standards of living, does it not mean a reduction rather than an increase? If we have more mouths to feed, then the per capita share of any national product is less. Furthermore, if you know your population figures, you know that this ground swell involves a lag in the number of men and women in the productive age groups—the 30's to the late 50's. Therefore, there are going to be relatively fewer producers, more old people and children, and more mouths to feed. More people, alone, do not make for either economic growth or stability.

Why then do the optimists see increased population as an opportunity for economic growth? The reason, I think, is this: we now have the capacity, even an excess capacity; we have the factories and the machinery; we can work longer hours if need be to turn out an increased flow of goods and services. The new buyers will increase the demand on our capacity, and accordingly increase our national output. If so, then it seems to me that we are currently in a situation where the real problem is the existence of a capacity to consume rather than a capacity to produce. And to return to my theme, it is important that we produce.

The creation of goods and services in a given period of time is the very essence of our standard of living. What we produce in a particular year is the exact equivalent of our standard of living in that year. We do not live on the expectations of another year; we live on goods and services. I suppose it is true that if we fail to maintain our seed corn, to this extent we are living on the future, but basically the extent to which we produce, and consume, determines our national standard of living. If we can create a full flow of capital goods, if we can match rising consumer credits with rising production, then by so doing we will have created our own rising standard of living.

Now, you ask, where does all this come out in prices? H. J. Davenport wrote 45 years ago, "The price of pig is something big; because its corn, you'll understand, is high-priced, too; because it grew upon the high-priced farming land. If you'd know why that land is high, consider this: its price is big because it pays thereon to raise the costly corn, the high-priced pig!" Clearly our price mechanism is composed of many intermingled factors. Wages are not the sole influence in rising prices, for if we do not like high prices, we will refuse to pay them. If management does not like the high prices of material, it will refuse to pay. If we do not like the high-priced corn, we will not pay for it, or for the high-priced pig.

Looking ahead, it would seem to me, as it does to others, that the factors leading to price increases are stronger than those pushing them down. A price structure is something like a swarm of bees, in which individual bees change their relative positions but the swarm as a whole moves together. So specific products may go up or down in price, but the average itself is likely to move up, but not necessarily by a great amount.

Prospects for Growth

What then are the prospects for high future economic activity? If the cold war grows hotter or colder, a new situation is obviously set up, but it is common practice in forecasting not to try to divine these possibilities. The important question is the degree to which we will continue, assuming no outbreak of war, along the lines of our current high activity in the areas of goods and services. As I see the years ahead, these varied activities of consumers, business-men, and government are likely to increase and push our national output ever higher. I see no reason for any cutbacks that would make serious, long-sustained corrections necessary.

There are several specific areas in which managers can influence the direction of the economy:

- Inventory adjustment is one area where the businessman will have to be more careful than he has been in the past. He will need a combination of caution and alertness; his skill in this area over the long run is going to have a major influence on economic stability.
- The degree to which pessimism or optimism seizes us will help determine our future development, and the businessman has a major responsibility for setting and maintaining the public mood.
- We have by no means exhausted the full productivity of the equipment which is available to us. As we move ahead both here and abroad, we will be able to produce more abundantly.
- We will achieve greater growth if we aspire to the kind of risk taking that makes for high economic growth rather than try to play it safe.
- We have to see to it that we use our capacity for production wisely and successfully. We are dealing with a management

problem, not a production problem. We have to make sure we are producing the goods that people want; in large part, our problem is distribution, not production.

Our past experience suggests that our capacity to create goods and services in the years ahead is far beyond what we presently contemplate. Opportunity is great, if we can only capitalize on it. It is up to alert business management to see that we do, intelligently and with an eye for reasonable stability, in the next 50 years of growth.

QUESTIONS AND ANSWERS*

From the floor: Do you believe that our resistance to price increases is lessening over the years?

Mr. Bliss: I don't think so. Essentially, price is only the relationship between our means or capacity to purchase goods and services and the supply of these goods and services. And, therefore, it does not follow that we necessarily are going to have a price rise.

I wonder whether businessmen realize the character of the price changes that have taken place in recent years. For each sector of the national economy we have price measures available. Take durable consumer goods—that would be automobiles, appliances, and so forth—the capital goods sector, the consumer nondurable goods sector, construction, government, and so on; in which of these areas has price inflation been most serious? In which one has it been least?

Now the man who supports the doctrine that the recent inflation is wage-induced would have to say it's probably most serious in steel and automobiles—the durable goods areas. As a matter of fact, it has been least in these areas. It's highest in the services, in construction, and in the government—many of these being the nonmonopolistic labor situation areas. Wages have gone up in durable goods, matched in part by production. Perhaps, though, this higher wage yield has had its influence on the wage structure outside its own area, and, therefore, the increase has spread to areas where productivity increases are restrained.

From the floor: What disturbs me, and I consider this an economic issue, is that we may rock along for a few more years buying more

---

* Businessmen present at the panel session on which this chapter is based raised certain questions which brought about the interplay of ideas reported more or less verbatim in this section.

than we can pay for, piling up a great debt. What are we going to do about it?

Mr. Bliss: What was the cost of the last war, or the war of 1914? Was that a cost borne by the then current generation or subsequent generations? My thesis is that in each instance it was borne by the current generation—and it was a cost measured in goods and sweat and tears, yes, and lives too. These physical costs had to be borne in that period of time. For the later years it was a reassessment of who would have what share of what.

Now the point that I have been stressing is that it is the production of goods and services that counts, and if we can produce them, why then of course we can buy them, and looked at in the over-all, we can pay for them. I would like to observe that basically, and from this point of view, there is no difference between government debt, business debt, and personal debt, though government debt and personal debt are most often criticized. It is important and essential that we have a matching amount of savings, but note that it is not the dollar amounts of debt that are critical.

As I suggested earlier, consumer debt is not a bad thing. I think most individuals buying on time and counting on our growing economy are not exceeding the risks that we like to think are the very essence of our way of life. The majority of the people with consumer debt are not on the verge of bankruptcy but are the young, the newly married, who are, for the most part, moving along in their economic careers. They are just as eager to have the present use of the goods we can readily produce as I am to have them purchase them.

From the floor: We hear talk that taxes have to be high. What's going to happen when the taxes finally get to the point where somebody is in real trouble?

Mr. Bliss: Well, in a sense our tax payments are payments for service. Of course, we do our best to see that we get our money's worth, and in my experience I think that in most instances we do. In general I think that among the trends we shall see in the future will be an increasing activity of government, because we want things which we can only accomplish collectively. It follows, therefore, that our payment for these collective purchases will be to our collective purchasing agent, the government, and will be in the form of taxes.

CONVERTING FARM PROBLEMS INTO BUSINESS OPPORTUNITIES

John H. Davis, Earl Coke, and William T. Brady

TODAY THE AGRIBUSINESS SECTOR of our economy stands on the threshold of what can be a new golden era in consumer products, business potential, and farming opportunities. Since it constitutes between 35% and 40% of the total economy and represents over 50% of the total business and industrial assets of the nation, its fate is highly important to the rest of us.

But to enter the golden era, American business and American agriculture must meet some tough conditions and face up to some realities being imposed on us by research and technology. Those who cannot adapt to progress or who deliberately choose to fight it are finding themselves in trouble to the point of real hardship, while

Note: Mr. Davis, who makes the introductory observations, was, until recently, Director, Program in Agriculture and Business, Harvard Business School; Mr. Coke is Vice President, Bank of America; and Mr. Brady is President, Corn Products Company.

new opportunities are being opened up for those who can utilize and take advantage of scientific advances.

Unfortunately, most farmers and many businessmen in enterprises associated with agriculture fall in the former group. Out of their troubles arises what we call the "farm problem." Let us take a closer look at this all-too-familiar phenomenon and see, specifically, how closely it is tied to the great forward strides of technology.

The principal weaknesses of the food-fiber sector are its spotty progress, brought about by serious lags in certain phases of its development, and the piecemeal and segmented manner in which policy decisions are being made. The result is that we have:

- Production outrunning demand.
- Low incentives for quality products—particularly at the farm level.
- Irregular movement of commodities to markets.
- Economic instability.

On the whole, the market operations of individual firms—particularly the dominant firms—are efficient and well performed, but the total market structure of which they are a part is weak, disjointed, and unstable. The range between the most efficient and the least efficient units is relatively wide—particularly in the farming segment.

In general, the agribusiness sector is highly competitive, paying lower than average wages to workers, lower than average salaries to management, and lower than average returns on investment. The allocation of funds to research is but a fraction—roughly one fifth—of the average of all American industry.

All this means that somewhere around 3 million of the 4 million farm units in the United States are uneconomic to operate. They are simply too small to make efficient use of technology. Put in another way, roughly 1 million farms produce about 80% of all that goes to market, leaving a mere 20% for all the rest. In addition, we are plagued by a more unstable market situation in agribusiness than in almost any other sector of the economy.

Why have we not recognized these basic facts in formulating national policies? Primarily because food-fiber problems have been looked on as farm problems, when they are not. They are agribusiness problems, and their solution depends on balanced progress taking place simultaneously in production, processing, and distribution. This means that businessmen engaged in the manufacture of farm supplies and in the processing and distribution of farm products have an important role to play in solving farm problems. And to succeed they must work in harmony and unison with producers. This, in turn, places on both business leadership and on farm leadership new responsibilities—responsibilities which today they are not prepared to carry.

Because business and farm leadership have not seen clearly the nature of the agribusiness era which technology has ushered in and because they have not moved in harmony with the forces of change, farmers have turned to Washington for help. Yet, despite our many farm programs—which involve us in an expenditure of some $4 billion each year on various projects—the food-fiber sector of our economy continues to be in trouble. To make this all the more ironic, I suspect that 25 years from now we will look back and decide that what happened in Washington in the way of farm programs was relatively unimportant in determining the ultimate trend of events. The point is that action by the federal government, either good or bad, cannot alter the general basic course along which the forces of science and technology are carrying us. At most, it can merely alter the rate at which change and progress actually take place.

Today those farmers and businessmen working on the frontier of agribusiness who accept and take advantage of the underlying forces that are operating in our economy are finding challenging opportunities in the development and perfection of new products, new methods, and new markets made possible by science and technology. They are characterized by a closer interlocking of decision-making processes with respect to distribution, processing, and production. This interlocking of decisions is being accomplished in a number of ways, including the common ownership, either by farmers or businessmen, of the successive steps in developing end products and by so-called contract farming—often referred to as vertical integration. Already this trend of interlocked decisions has progressed to a marked degree in broiler, fruit and vegetable, and dairy operations. Recently vertical structuring also has begun to penetrate egg, pork, and beef production and shows signs of moving into other commodities. Of necessity, the type of vertical structuring that is evolving differs greatly from one commodity to another.

There is every evidence that technological change will continue at a fast pace—probably at an accelerating pace. Also, there is every evidence that the trend toward coordinated decision making will continue. This is essential if we are to take advantage of new developments as they come along. In addition, it seems certain that policy making at all levels—production, processing, and distribution—will be more and more market-oriented.

In this fast-changing picture each firm and each farm will have to wrestle with problems peculiar to itself, with problems common to all units performing the same functions, and with problems relating to other functions with which it is interdependent. All in all, the decision-making processes in the agribusiness sector are highly intricate and complex and are growing more so.

Furthermore, decisions are becoming more and more conditioned by the requirements of the market, which in turn reflects consumer demand. The quick freezing of food, for example, imposes stricter requirements on varieties, planting dates, cultural practices, maturity at harvest, harvest methods, and the scheduling of deliveries to the plant. In brief, the functions of production, processing, and distribution have to be geared together for a common objective—the development of products for specific markets in the quantities needed and with deliveries properly timed.

The successful businessmen and farmers of the future will be those who move in harmony with the forces of technology and progress—taking advantage of new advances and even helping in their discovery and development. For those who do this well, the future offers great opportunities.

COORDINATING PRODUCTION AND MARKETING DECISIONS*

In discussing the conversion of farm problems into business opportunities, you have to start off by deciding what the farm problem is. At the risk of oversimplification, I would conclude that it is this: the lack of coordination between production decisions and marketing decisions.

* By Mr. Coke.

Over the years, production has become increasingly out of gear with markets. We have seen goods turned out in quantities and in kinds for which there simply have been no buyers. At this point we run to the government for help. But instead of being of assistance, by and large government action has created problems. It did not get the various factors into adjustment; in fact, in my opinion, they are more out of adjustment than ever.

But practical solutions to the problem are in the works, and they are coming about more rapidly than many of us realize. They are sneaking up on us in various ways, not from government but from the combination of talents and skills of production, processing, and merchandising organized to meet the sweeping changes taking place in the nation's production and marketing methods. Production for a market that demands more uniformity of product, quality, availability, and consumer convenience and appeal is the order of the day. In the past there was always a market for agricultural products somewhere at some price. If the product was off-color, off-flavor, or substandard in any way it sold on the market for a lower price.

Today, however, new and efficient methods of merchandising are being rapidly adopted, and they require that products be standardized and of a uniformly high quality. More and more, products that do not meet the specifications of these merchandisers do not even enter the market at any price. These changes are due, primarily, to:

(1) A rising standard of living. Consumers demand quality products.

(2) The rising value of human labor relative to other factors of production. Standardization through specification saves labor and decreases the cost of marketing.

(3) The mobility of the American housewife, giving rise to shopping centers and supermarkets.

Adjusting to New Forces

Examples of organizations and individuals who have coordinated and are coordinating production and marketing decisions are numerous and increasing every day. Let us look at some of these approaches, starting with cooperatives because there has been so much publicity and talk about that device as the only possible solution.

In my opinion, this is not so. I think the cooperatives can help, and in some places they are doing a good job, but they are too often limited because of size and a philosophy which decrees that everyone in a particular industry should belong. They make no discrimination between high-cost and low-cost producers, for example.

There is a real opportunity for organizations of cooperatives, industry, and private concerns who work together. For example:

> In California 700 grape growers and a winery have combined their production, processing, and marketing activities into a coordinated unit through contractual agreement. The growers' cooperative, Allied Grape Growers, provides an assured supply of grapes, which they process into wine. They purchased the processing plants (wineries) from the corporation that became the sales, promotion, and distribution organization, the United Vintners. Thus the growers, through their cooperative, produce the grapes and the wine under the specifications of the United Vintners, and this corporation distributes, promotes, and sells the products.
>
> The contract between the two organizations provides for a fixed charge per case of wine for selling and for profit sharing. Incentives for efficiency in both groups are a part of the scheme. For example, United Vintners determined that bulk shipments of wine from California to the East coast would be to their advantage and have constructed a tanker that is now in use for this purpose. Allied Grape Growers and United Vintners now produce and sell 23% of the wine marketed in the United States.

Individuals as well as organizations can coordinate production and marketing decisions:

> An ex-newspaper editor, whose net worth 10 years ago was very modest, today has a herd of more than 500 cows and distributes milk directly to the consumer. He also has a broiler enterprise which includes producing eggs and hatching and growing broilers at the rate of 50,000 per week. Contracts for the killing and marketing of the meat complete the enterprise. He grinds and mixes the feed used for the dairy and the chickens at his own mill. Good management, sufficient size to permit efficiency, marketing and production coordination, and proper use of adequate capital are the keys to his successful operation.

Coordination of production and marketing decisions is not limited to any one type of organization. There are many different approaches. Consolidated Foods Corporation is now a "grower of food, processor, distributor, and sponsor of voluntary chains," as its president recently described his company. He went on to say, "We have sought to build the company through the addition of growing, processing and distribution operations, each representing constructive, successful activities in their own fields and constituting a profitable, diversified corporate whole."

The American food system is gearing itself to meet the demands of food retailers. Today 9% of the food retail stores are doing 65% of the business. This has sparked many changes in the food system. The livestock and meat industry is a good example:

> Most of the fresh meat in many market areas today is sold by packers to retailers through a few clerks who sit in a central office and sell large lots of carcasses on retailers' specifications as to government grade, weight, age, cure, trim, and time of delivery. The small butcher shop is rapidly passing into history, and with its passing the packer no longer delivers his brand-name product in small quantities to many separate, independent shops. Fresh meat, brand promotion and advertising, and a large sales force have been replaced by specification buying and an order taker.

> The packer who meets the new market demand must be assured of a stable supply of animals that will slaughter to specifications. To do this, some have entered into the feed-lot business, while others are purchasing cattle which are finished on a custom basis in large commercial feed lots—another relatively new institution which has emerged to meet the needs of modern merchandising. To some extent, the process of integration of beef production has moved back to the breeding ranch and range either through contract or joint ownership.

> Under this situation, competition still exists. It is not large competition, to be sure, but the five or six buyers and the several packers battle each other. It is not a closed market by any means, though it certainly is not the kind of market that we used to have.

These illustrations indicate the various ways in which individuals and organizations have attempted to make the adjustments necessary to meet the changing forces in our food system. These forces are compelling, but the profit opportunities are many for those who are able and willing to adjust. The success of any attempt to fit an enterprise into the modern food system will depend on the manager's ability to provide a stable supply of the commodity, control its quality, rapidly adopt technical improvements, and benefit from economies of size and freer exchange of technical information. Proper management and the availability of adequate capital are also essential.

I should point out here that the shortage of capital has proved to be one of the greatest handicaps in accomplishing this kind of integration. As a matter of fact, I am inclined to think that the key factor in determining the amount of progress that we will make in combining production and marketing decisions will be the amount of capital available. If you survey the possibilities in almost any industry, you can see ways to get groups together in an organization large enough to give efficiency and coordinated action—if you can get the capital. One reason we have made such progress in the West is that we have people who are not afraid to use money in ventures like these, and the dollars are there for them to use.

Moving toward the Future

Many people are afraid of this whole trend toward integration because, they feel, it is going to take away the farmer's prized and age-old independence. But I do not think that a farmer has much independence if he lives on $1,000 a year as a lone operator when he could have $4,000 as a part of a system. If he calls that "independence," he can have it! So I cannot shed too many tears, although I do recognize that there is a social problem involved in all the changes that are taking place that cannot be disregarded— and, I might say, a political problem also.

In short, then, I do not think we are spelling the doom of the individual farmer, but rather moving into a time when the individual farmer will be able to operate on a sounder basis than before. He will be able to count on some stability in the market, tied in with his ability to produce.

As I look ahead, the possibilities for everyone—businessman, farmer, and consumer alike—are promising indeed. For those who can coordinate production decisions with marketing decisions and for those who benefit from such coordination, the future will surely be a golden era.

TECHNOLOGY: PROBLEM AND PROMISE*

The forecasters seem to be telling us that these are particularly significant times. The country is heading, certainly, into a new glorious age of technology. And we have made an economic recovery that has restored confidence bruised by the recent recession. Once again, we are hearing positive talk about a growing population and the great new demands it will place on farm and industry. Combine the developing situation of a growing populace and its new demands with a public attitude which not only accepts change but often is impatient for it, and add to this the ability of our technology to achieve stunning changes—these are the forces which will shape a new and different America.

All this promises splendid opportunities for agribusiness and the industries it supplies. They, along with all industry, should benefit from an increase in population; more mouths to feed may help bring the equation of supply and demand into balance once again. But infinitely more exciting is what technology may be able to do to transform the wonderful raw materials produced by agribusiness into still more wonderful food and nonfood products. Here the potential is a multiplication of demand rather than a mere addition to that which exists.

But this will take a lot of doing. There are real challenges ahead, particularly for the manufacturer, whose technical brains must create useful new products and whose sales forces must market them successfully. And unless business succeeds, agribusiness cannot prosper.

The technical progress of our own industry, corn refining, has been outstanding. A food processor—like our firm—is startlingly different today from its predecessor a half century ago. My company turns out more than 450 products, many of them derived from corn. The corn kernel has become the basis of hundreds of items which serve such various industries as food, textiles, paper, foundries, pharmaceutical, mining, tanning, brewing, and so on.

The hard distinctions between farm-grown and man-made products are fast being broken down. So important a part is played by starch chemistry in our processes that it is often impossible to say

* By Mr. Brady.

whether more credit is due Mother Nature or the laboratory. And then, sometimes, the two collaborate, as they do in breeding new strains of grain, either sorghum or corn, endowed with the unique qualities that are required for the manufacture of highly specialized products.

The Threat of Synthetics

If our own industry is helping to expand and diversify the markets for farm products, other industries are ingenious, too. I need mention only fibers and industrial alcohol as examples of man-made products which are now well entrenched in markets once dominated by agricultural products. Obviously, the invasion has only just begun, and it will spread to a much wider front. For agribusiness and for processors of farm products, including corn products, advances in technology can increase our vulnerability.

It might be said that the threat lies most heavily over agriculture. Probably the buyers could not care less. Our customers, whether they are housewives filling their grocery larders or purchasing agents for the companies to which we sell, are far more concerned with price and performance than with how the product is made. Theoretically, at least, the manufacturer can adapt his processes, even his entire business, to meet changing conditions or the demands of his customers.

But the theory looks frivolous alongside the facts. The facts are that we, as processors, have today (and probably will continue to have) a tremendous stake in American agriculture. We depend on the farm for the great quantity and high quality of our raw material needs. For the most part, our complex plants and equipment are designed for the processing of grain, and only grain. A good part of our internal organization and our external relationships are a reflection of our identity with agriculture.

At the same time, the farmer depends on us to an extraordinary degree. We are the sales agents for his products: the more we can sell, the more corn we are going to buy. Furthermore, it is important to realize that while our industry does not purchase a big percentage of the total agricultural crop, we do take up a large part of the cash crop. For a farmer, cash flow is extremely significant today in contrast to the situation in which I lived as a boy on a farm

50 years ago. We did not need much money, then; we borrowed everything, and we had horses and equipment, so our cash requirements were low. But today a farmer needs a lot of money to fund his enterprise. He has become a businessman, a capitalist. To get that capital he needs markets for his cash products.

Outlets for Products

To return to my main theme, there are two kinds of outlets for the processor today: the food line and the industrial. The food business has been quite good, because there are more people eating, and this happy trend is likely to continue for years to come. In addition, the quality of the food consumed has improved. When there is full employment people are going to eat more, and they are going to eat better. Today we know more about proper foods, about nutrition—even though none of us knows too much about it! Even in bad times the food business is stabler because of the supports being put under our economy. Pensions, unemployment benefits, insurance, and so on provide some cash for people even in a recession. And the first item that money goes for is food.

The industrial business has also been good, thanks to the abundance of farm products, which has kept prices favorable, the intrinsic quality of farm products as raw materials for industrial goods, and the genius of the chemist and the engineer. But competition, as I said before, is gathering strength, too.

Fight for Survival

As a matter of self-interest, then, we are committed to a course which will serve to broaden and diversify farm markets. In general, our aim is to maintain leadership in this one area, which will grow increasingly important and more competitive. I am referring to technology, and I speak of it in its broadest sense.

We are using research, as most industries do, to extend the prime of market life of each of our products. But we are more active than most other industries in the field of basic research. Here we hope to attain the knowledge that later may lead to entirely new products made from grain and other farm products.

In my own company we spend more than $5 million a year on research and related technical work. One of the subjects we are

studying is nutrition, for I believe that some of the greatest advances
in health and medicine in the future will be made in this field. As
an example, let us consider the field of essential unsaturated fats,
currently so interesting to the medical profession. Research through
the past several years has proved the great importance of the type of
fat ingested. Corn oil and other vegetable oils, used in moderate
quantity, definitely reduce blood serum cholesterol levels. The
positive relationship between blood serum cholesterol and coronary
disorders has not yet been completely established, but the modern
physician is more than satisfied with the proof to date and recommends changes in dietary habits for improved health and longevity.

The principal raw materials for the chemical industry today are
petroleum, natural gas, and coal—in short, hydrocarbons. The price
of oil and natural gas has been going upward steadily: the quick
reserves are being depleted, so the producers are having to go
deeper and further out to get their supplies at the same time that
labor and equipment costs are rising.

This is why I believe eventually hydrocarbons will be replaced by
carbohydrates as basic raw materials. They have the same atoms as
hydrocarbons, but the arrangement is different. The research we are
doing will ultimately make it possible to use carbohydrates and
other agricultural products as the basis for a tremendous chemical
and fertilizer industry. Grain, particularly corn, can be raised in
any quantity desired if we have a market for it; the current problem,
then, is overproduction. Cost of production of the final product will
be a major factor in this field.

Technology and research have already brought us the greatest
advances in corn milling since the birth of the industry. One after
another, the traditional manufacturing methods are giving way to
more compact, more efficient processes that improve yield and
quality and help offset rising costs. The full impact of these dramatic
changes has not yet been felt, but there can be no more protective
sales insurance today than holding down costs—and, therefore,
prices—and maintaining product quality. Those who are really successful in this respect will most likely see their efforts result in a
tidy growth of business and a consequent increase in demand for
raw materials.

Although the home ground for technology is usually considered to be the laboratory, at Corn Products it is also to be found in the general offices. The most obvious example is a newly installed computer system. But the whole science of management—the technology, if you will—is rapidly being refined by experts. Here we may not be innovators as often as borrowers, but we are doing our best to keep up with the most modern techniques in this increasingly complex area, because we are convinced that better management, better decisions, and more capable people are the most telling factors in the company's aim of growth and security.

Even in the sales area, the need today is for great utilization of technology. This is particularly true in the introduction of new, tailor-made, highly specialized products to industrial customers. We have to know their manufacturing problems. Our sales efforts have to be directed to their technical people. And after the sale we have to provide service to assure full customer satisfaction.

Of course, there are many other programs intended to gain or hold an advantage over our widespread and powerful competition. But the technical activities I have just described, which might be labeled "a program," are the platform on which we hope to build a broader business for ourselves and thus for the products of agriculture.

This is an agribusiness era, all right. It is also an era of unprecedented demands, of technology capable of effecting swift and sweeping changes, and of industry in transition. As long as we have some vision of what is ahead, and the physical vigor and the intellectual discipline to face up to it, we can look with confidence to the future and to the great needs which are to be satisfied.

QUESTIONS AND ANSWERS*

From the floor: "Vertical integration" seems to be the popular phrase these days. Perhaps ten or twenty years from now, after a few legal difficulties have been taken care of, we might visualize Swift & Company in the retail business and A & P in the meatpacking business. But what have you gained? In other words, there are certain periods when vertical integration seems to be the popular

---

* Businessmen present at the panel session on which this chapter is based raised certain questions which brought about the interplay of ideas reported more or less verbatim in this section.

project. Then there are other periods when horizontal integration seems to be the fad. There are arguments for and against both of them.

Mr. Davis: What do you think is bringing about this vertical integration? Do you think it is just the desire of the supermarkets and the chain stores to get back into processing and the processors to move the other way?

From the floor: I don't think the chain stores have much desire to go back, because they have a good thing already. But I think the packers have a desire to go forward.

Mr. Davis: Are you saying that maybe this is just a passing fancy, and will disappear in time?

From the floor: I am just throwing that out as a possibility. Just like supermarkets: the whole trend is against them, despite their tremendous growth, and I am not at all sure that ten years from now they may not be dwindling. We may see more specialized stores springing up.

Mr. Coke: I am sure the trend is going in the direction of efficiency first, though it will certainly be slowed down because of the fear of government action. No doubt there have been people who have considered how they might integrate, but who have decided not to because they don't want to get in trouble with government. But I think integration is good for the consuming public as well as the economy. Anything we can do to get food or fiber to the consuming public at a cheaper price through economy of operation seems to me beneficial, and the forces are all moving in this direction.

HOW EFFECTIVELY ARE MANAGEMENT AND UNIONS LIVING TOGETHER?

E. Robert Livernash

AS WE LOOK BACK over the last 25 years or so, the history of labor-management relations separates itself into three overlapping stages: organization, contract development, and accommodation. Surveying these three from the vantage point of today, it is evident that we have attained a very significant degree of accommodation in the day-to-day dealings between companies and unions—though a quick glance at the day's newspaper headlines might leave you with just the opposite opinion. As a matter of fact, I would say that this increasing accommodation, this developing skill at working effectively together, has become one of the key characteristics of our new society.

These views are, of course, my own, though they are drawn from an intensive study which Professor Sumner H. Slichter, Professor James J. Healy, and I have been making under the auspices of the

Note: Mr. Livernash is Professor of Business Administration, Harvard Business School.

238

Brookings Institution. This research, which has provided me with the richest background on the subject that I have ever had, has focused on the union-management relations of 250 or 300 companies over the years since 1940.

Let me hasten to say that the comments in this chapter are not the conclusions of that study, but rather impressions I personally have formed during the two years we have worked on the project. Let me also point out that because so many companies were involved we could not possibly hope to make a detailed examination of each one. Some companies were studied quite intensively, others more superficially. Furthermore, our sample is not a precise, representative one, though it did cover different industries and different sections of the country. But a study of the relations between management and labor in this fairly large number of selected firms has yielded a great deal of highly useful and important material as well as considerable perspective with respect to the changing climate of relationships.

Our study and this discussion have as primary background the spectacular increase in the strength of the labor movement. Growth began in 1932 and was, of course, greatly encouraged by the New Deal. In the ten years from 1935 to 1945, union membership expanded from roughly three and one-half to fifteen million as part and parcel of the great political, social, and economic change created by the 1929–1932 depression.

From Violence to Harmony

I have indicated that the historical growth of union power during these years can be divided into three overlapping periods dominated respectively by, first, organization and recognition; then, contract development; and, finally, by accommodation. Borrowing heavily from Professor Benjamin M. Selekman, union-management relations evolved during these periods from the violence and conflict which took place during the organizing stage to the containment-aggression associated with the development and elaboration of contract provisions, and then gradually to the relative stability and mutual understanding associated with accommodation.

During the organizing stage we witnessed significant violence. The sit-down strikes are the best-remembered symbols of that period when the major segments of American industry were converted from nonunion status to the focal point of union power in our economy.

The struggle for union recognition did not end with the passage of the Wagner Act in 1935 nor with the subsequent declaration of its constitutionality. Considerable violence associated with recognition continued during the prewar period, but progressively declined during the war and postwar years. Legal recognition of unions was in fact a partial and limited recognition. Managements resented unions, looked on them as transient institutions, and were not ready to make serious attempts to work constructively with them. Union leaders, on the other hand, tended to feel that force was the only argument management could understand. They were suspicious of employers and automatically opposed most of the proposals put forward by company representatives. These attitudes on both sides reflected the union aggression and management containment associated with the years of contract development.

Our earliest contracts were little more than recognition documents in many instances. For example, the 1937 contract between the United States Steel Company and the Steelworkers Union was a simple document of two typed pages. These early simple agreements have grown over the years into comprehensive basic agreements with various supplements to cover such topics as pensions and insurance. The elaboration of contracts with respect to discipline, seniority, internal wage structure, method of wage payment, production standards, hours and overtime, grievance procedure, arbitration, and other subjects did not take place without a struggle. Unions aggressively sought new and more inclusive restrictions on management, and managements attempted to contain the union.

Looking back on this evolution of union-management relations from the vantage point of 1958, it is clear that a great deal of accommodation has now been achieved. Noneconomic clauses in the contract have increasingly attained stability and permanence both in wording and in interpretation. This has produced, and been produced by, a true meeting of minds between unions and managements in an ever-larger proportion of cases. This is the most significant development of recent labor-company history and is worthy of a little more elaboration.

I should make clear at the outset that the accommodation about which I am speaking concerns the noneconomic areas such as discipline, seniority, internal wage structure, and other similar topics. Of course, these matters are in no sense strictly noneconomic since costs and profits can be significantly affected by them, as will subsequently be discussed. Day-to-day administrative matters can, however, be distinguished from wage levels and employee benefits. Permanence and stability are not implied with respect to wage and benefit increases. Unions continue to seek "more and more." While there has been modest improvement in wage negotiation, there is no intent to imply that real differences in points of view do not remain as a basic consideration in the functioning of our economy.

But let us now look briefly at some areas in which a significant degree of accommodation has been achieved. Prior to and during World War II seniority was an area of significant conflict. The trials and tribulations of the War Labor Board in attempting to secure agreement on such clauses amply testifies to this fact, as do the number and seriousness of the grievances which were brought under the early seniority clauses. It is not too much to say, as of today, that the application of seniority to layoff is almost mechanical in its character in many union-management relationships. There are a minority of instances where seniority with respect to layoff continues to be a serious issue between the parties, but for every such case, there are many where management and union have arrived at true agreement on the layoff clause and its administration.

While in good part accommodation in the application of seniority to layoff has been achieved through management acceptance of the principle of seniority, some extremely statesmanlike seniority clauses have been written during the postwar period. Management training costs have been minimized by the grouping of jobs and by the displacement of workers from the bottom up rather than chain bumping down through the group. Certain jobs have also been protected from bumping. At the same time, plant-wide protection has been given to workers through such devices as a labor pool or float line. Such clauses satisfactorily integrate the objectives of both management and union.

There are a larger number of instances where management and unions are not in agreement on the application of seniority to pro-

motion, but, again, on the whole, a high degree of accommodation
has been achieved.

Seniority in general is an area in which management has made
very real concessions in the accommodation process. In a few
instances the concessions have been extreme and developed into a
competitive handicap. In most instances management has adequately
protected its interests, and early fears have not been realized.

In contrast with the seniority area, unions have perhaps made
the more major concessions in reaching accommodation in the
areas of discipline and internal wage structure. Managements have,
of course, given up the right to discipline except for just cause.
Unions at first protested almost all discipline. Today managements
operate systems of progressive discipline without major protests
from unions. Again, a few instances should be noted in which
managements have been weak and have not maintained adequate
discipline in their companies.

As to the internal wage structure, unions initially did not discriminate in their claims of job rate inequities and brought grievances
on a wholesale basis. Today unions in fact accept a stable internal
wage structure, typically based on a formal or informal job evaluation plan; and job rate grievances, both as to their number and as
to their seriousness, present a picture which shows marked improvement over the war and early postwar years.

All these comments about accommodation are illustrative and in
no sense complete. The implication is not that accommodation has
been achieved to the same degree by all companies and unions nor
that all areas of contract administration show the same degree of accommodation. For example, there is less accommodation in the
area of production standards, both with and without wage incentive
plans, than in the areas of contract administration previously mentioned. Some wage incentive plans have become quite demoralized,
largely as a result of union pressures. Also, some companies and
plants continue to have disorderly day-to-day relations with unions.
But in spite of differences and qualifications, there is great improvement today and a healthy contrast with the hectic contract administration of earlier years.

Cost of Poor Relations

I want now to look at some of the considerations which seem to have influenced the relative success which different companies have had in dealing with unions. Let us first examine the negative side of the picture—companies which have lost competitive standing by the way in which they have dealt with unions—and, subsequently, some management policies and characteristics which have been accompanied by relative success.

The term success is used in a twofold sense: first, developing and maintaining relatively good union-management and employee relations, and, second, maintaining labor efficiency and competitive labor costs. Interestingly, these two aspects of successful union-management relations appear to go together. This is an opinion and might be debated. Temporarily a policy bordering on appeasement may produce improved union-management relations by a sacrifice of competitive position. In the long run, however, companies and plants in a weakened competitive position are likely to have deteriorating union-management and employee relations. On the other hand, companies which have firmly maintained their competitive position, particularly with respect to labor efficiency, seem to obtain a more lasting and superior degree of union-management accommodation.

It is unquestionably true that a significant number of companies have lost ground competitively by the cumulative effect of continued grievance concessions to unions. This does not appear to be a matter of large companies as compared with small companies, nor of one industry as compared with another, nor, finally, of dealing with one union as compared with another. The key point relates to differences in management policy and administration. For example, in almost any major industry it is not difficult to single out one or more companies whose competitive position has been seriously weakened.

Managements weaken their competitive position primarily by the cumulative effect of day-to-day concessions in grievance settlements, particularly by giving in to union pressure. There is a whole variety of union pressure tactics: wildcat strikes, slowdowns, threats of strikes and slowdowns, refusals to work overtime, refusals to accept temporary job assignments, and so forth. Some work practices which are used as pressure tactics are based on a contract clause. One contract was discovered which had 43 mutual consent clauses. Other work practices which are utilized as pressure devices in securing favorable grievance decisions involve a silent or ambiguous contract.

The use of pressure tactics by unions has declined as part of the process of evolution in union-management relations. Such tactics are much more logically associated with the organizing stage and the contract development stage than with the accommodation stage. They have declined also, and more specifically, as managements have learned to refuse to yield to such tactics and to discipline employees for engaging in them.

The historical importance of pressure tactics may be illustrated by a rough judgment with respect to wildcat strikes. Consider as an illustration the major companies in the following industries: automobile manufacture, automotive parts, basic steel, agricultural machinery, meatpacking, rubber tires, plate glass, and electrical manufacturing. The major companies in these industries have been selected not because of any particular characteristics of the companies or the industries but only because our interviewing in these companies has been extensive enough to develop an informed opinion on the subject.

Hardly a company in the group has not had difficulty with wildcat strikes. A small minority of companies established policies which substantially eliminated the problem prior to World War II. At the end of World War II a large proportion of the companies had had and were having quite hectic plant relationships. Some companies and unions began to work out these problems at the end of the war and shortly thereafter. It is probably correct to say that by about 1952 wholesale pressure tactics were a thing of the past for a good majority of the companies. By 1958 only a small minority of companies were having major problems with wildcats, though elements of pressure tactic problems existed in a larger number. It is also true that in 1958 a significant number of companies, though they had solved the direct problem of wildcats, still carried a heritage of inefficient practices and conditions which they had not been able to eliminate.

The importance and significance of yielding to pressure tactics can only be seen over a period of years. Production standards and manning requirements are undoubtedly the most important area to be considered, although discipline and inflexibility in the utilization of manpower are also significant.

The temptation to yield to pressure on a particular production standard can be very great. For example, in one plant a wildcat developed over taking one man off a job which, prior to technological change, had been a two-man job. The loss to the company in production because of the wildcat, which came at a time when the company could sell every unit it could produce, would have paid the wages of two men for some three thousand years. From a short-run point of view, a given concession may have a totally insignificant effect on profit and labor cost, whereas a wildcat can cause considerable loss. Production and sales considerations have "kept the plant going" under such calculations and pressures. But continued over five or ten years, a policy of concessions can have a cumulative effect of great significance. One company, for example, finally reached a position in which it required almost four times as many man-hours to produce its product as its two major competitors. Other examples could be cited in which labor efficiency fell to about 50% of normal.

If management gives in to pressure tactics—in other words, if pressure tactics pay off from the workers' point of view—such tactics may well be utilized on an increasing scale. The following company record of man-hours lost by wildcat strikes illustrates both the problem and its correction:

1948	190,000 man-hours	1952	1,000,000 man-hours
1949	339,000 man-hours	1953	337,000 man-hours
1950	188,000 man-hours	1954	66,000 man-hours
1951	456,000 man-hours	1955 and after	Not significant

In late 1952 this company instituted a policy of discipline for wildcats with the approval and support of the international union officials. In 1953 the record was not particularly good because of sympathetic walkouts when the new disciplinary policy was applied. In 1953 the penalties for wildcats were made more severe. This led to considerable improvement in 1954. There has been no problem since 1954. On the other hand, this company, in plants where the wildcat problem had been severe, now finds itself with a fairly high proportion of poor production standards and a poorly operating wage incentive plan. Again, the point to be emphasized is the cumulative effect over a period of years of giving in to pressure tactics and the uphill struggle to restore worker efficiency once it has deteriorated under such pressures.

A management policy of discipline for wildcats, the common effect of which is to prevent wildcats if applied consistently, is not simply one phase of a more general disciplinary policy. It stands in a much more important position in the totality of corporate policy. It represents a clear-cut top-level decision not to yield to or to condone pressure tactics in the administration of a union contract. It necessitates that this labor relations policy take precedence over immediate production and sales requirements.

Some companies, as earlier implied, had the foresight to institute such a policy prior to World War II. Most large companies now have such a policy. Some companies, however, have still not faced up realistically to this problem.

The reasons for facing up to the problem in fact as well as in words should be made perfectly clear. One reason, which has been emphasized, is to prevent the gradual deterioration of the competitive position of the company. A second reason is that it is quite impossible to develop and apply consistent and rational interpretations of the labor agreement, of personnel policies, and of industrial engineering policies if decisions are based on expediency and pressure. Related to this second reason is the fact that constructive union-management relations cannot develop if there is a pattern of pressure tactics in prosecuting grievances. Finally, I should like to mention separately that the morale of first-line supervision is greatly improved, and its effectiveness increased, by such a policy.

It may seem peculiar for me to have spent so much time discussing the subject of union pressure tactics. The matter, however, has not been adequately recognized. Any assessment of the impact of unions on management must give recognition to the fact that a significant number of companies and plants have seriously weakened their competitive position over the years by conceding to such pressures. The assessment should also take note of the fact that the uphill battle to restore efficiency has sometimes necessitated a long strike as

well as years of gradual improvement. Some plants and companies
have simply not recovered. Top union officials are well aware of
these problems and typically appreciate the fact that they cannot
maintain respect for contracts if management gives in to pressure.
Finally, constructive employee and union relations are not com-
·patible with pressure in the grievance machinery.

Characteristics of Relative Success

As we look at companies and unions which have enjoyed relatively
successful union-management relations over the years and maintained their competitive position at the same time, we find a number
of common characteristics. The first is management by policy.

It may seem naïve to stress management by policy in 1959, but
labor relations and personnel relations have had a difficult struggle
over the years to get adequate consideration in top-level management policies. Successful companies stand out as having more
adequately thought through their long-range labor relations and
employee relations policies and developed ways and means to
implement them.

A mechanism frequently found in companies with more successful labor relations is a top-level labor relations policy committee. This is particularly desirable to assist in achieving mutual
understanding between line and staff in the formulation and implementation of policy.

Labor relations as practiced has elements of both line and staff
functions. The distinction between line and staff is not easily
stated or implemented in the area of labor relations, and, realistically,
responsibility is not exclusively vested in either line or staff. There
has been a tendency in some companies, with the development of
strong unions, to delegate too much responsibility to labor relations
executives and supervisors. In other companies labor relations has
been too weak to do an effective job and has been too much
dominated by production and sales considerations.

This question is not one of how a company is organized on
paper. On paper labor relations may be entirely advisory or may be
given various direct responsibilities. The real question is whether
or not labor relations and production executives and supervisors
are actually playing on the same ball team and not passing the buck

back and forth. In companies which have achieved good labor relations it is perfectly clear that long-range policies have been thought through and that both line and staff are in agreement on the fundamentals of these policies so that they are cooperating effectively in carrying them out. Companies with poorer labor relations frequently reflect a kind of crisis consideration of labor policies, too much dominated by short-run economic considerations and uncertainty and buck passing in administration.

A second characteristic which definitely stands out in successful companies is an important phase of the first characteristic, namely, that such companies demonstrate a high degree of management initiative in formulating and carrying out labor relations policies.

A good case can be made that many companies are demonstrating a good deal more initiative in labor relations today than in past years. This is true with respect to both negotiation and administration. Rarely today does a company blunder into a strike. Companies increasingly do not let a strike take place without negotiating to a point where they are prepared to take a long strike if a settlement is not achieved. This kind of negotiation involves thorough preparation, with company proposals and positions well worked out. It contrasts sharply with negotiating in a negative fashion on union proposals alone.

Many companies are also showing more initiative in the administration of contracts. They have thought through the functioning of the grievance procedure and have established policies and practices which tend to secure a high proportion of grievance settlements at the first and second steps of the grievance machinery. They have supplemented the contract with adequate labor relations and personnel policies. They have worked out procedures for handling different types of problems.

While managements appear in general to be doing a better job in the negotiation of contracts, in the administration of contracts, and in employee relations, particularly by demonstrating more initiative and ingenuity as well as responsibility in the way they approach these problems, some companies are more forward-looking in this respect than others. This is a qualitative type of comparison which can be demonstrated by examples but which cannot be described well in general terms. Nevertheless, relative success in labor relations appears closely associated with the degree of management initiative which has been demonstrated.

A third characteristic of relative success is a high degree of successful decentralization in the administration of labor relations policies. This is a complicated subject, as we well know. Not all labor relations decisions can or should be made by lower levels of production and labor relations personnel. In some ways central controls have been increased and strengthened. For example, corporate-level industrial engineering has typically been strengthened in recent years.

However, while recognizing that we are dealing with a complicated subject, companies achieving relative success in labor relations have a labor relations staff developed in depth and a strong foreman group. An interesting study could be made of the quantity and quality of the labor relations staff of today and of 20 years ago. There is no question as to what such a study would show. By today's standards it would show glaring deficiencies in the earlier period. Today it is a real pleasure to discuss labor relations problems with lower-level labor relations supervisors. Their sophistication is in marked contrast with the inexperienced and minimal staffs of 20 years back. But, again, some companies are better staffed in labor relations than others, both as to quantity and quality, and those achieving a higher degree of labor relations success appear to have staffs which are developed in greater depth.

A comparable improvement has taken place in first-line supervision. There has been a change in the character of first-line supervisors, and they, too, have developed experience in labor relations matters. Again, companies with good labor relations are very conscious of the importance of maintaining a strong group of first-line supervisors. Both preventing grievances and successfully handling grievances are highly dependent on developing a strong labor relations staff and a strong group of first-line supervisors who cannot be described as errand boys or the men with the flashlights in their pockets.

Finally, relatively successful companies have carried out a balanced policy of firmness and fairness. Almost all companies proclaim such a policy. The question, of course, is one of implementing both aspects of this policy, and this requires more than an empty slogan. Some companies have been deficient in implementing firmness. They have commonly lost competitive position. Some companies, on the other hand, have been deficient in implementing fairness. A management policy which is simply tough is no more successful than a weak management. The most basic art of labor relations is a judicious combination of firmness and fairness.

In conclusion, I want to re-emphasize that I think the degree of accommodation we have developed in union-management relations is quite significant. As you look over the road we have traveled, the working association of today, which covers so many topics that were subjects of such fiery controversy and bitter warfare just a handful of years ago, is encouraging and quite surprising. We have made remarkable progress in the last 20 or so years, even though it is an uneven progress in which some companies have been decidedly more successful than others.

I have not attempted an over-all appraisal. Problems remain in the labor relations area, particularly on the economic front. The accommodation achieved, however, appears to me to be meaningful social progress. Further, I am firmly convinced that the capitalism of today, just because of this adjustment of unions and management to each other, has a far stronger chance of survival than the capitalism of an earlier time.

QUESTIONS AND ANSWERS*

From the floor: It seems to me that management must deal with the growing political power of unions. In a sense, they are trying to equal the power of management. Their cry is, "We want more and more and more," regardless of economic conditions or management's ability to pay what they wish.

Mr. Livernash: I feel that the political climate has been turning against unions, and I would venture to say that this has been true since back in 1947. I cannot consider unions as strong political organizations, or in any sense as dangerous ones.

There is room for a difference of opinion here, I'll grant you. But one of the interesting features of our trade unionism in comparison

---

* Businessmen present at the panel session on which this chapter is based raised certain questions which brought about the interplay of ideas reported more or less verbatim in this section.

to similar movements abroad is its nonpolitical nature and the small degree to which unions have been successful politically. That goes for the past ten years—despite the 1958 elections. They have been singularly unable to push through the political projects they have sponsored in both state and federal legislatures.

Furthermore, their goal has been primarily always the same, and always limited: they want legislation that will enable them to be more effective in collective bargaining, and they want to defeat bills that will cripple them in their efforts to bargain. Unions crave various kinds of benefits and Social Security—protection for members' families—but they have no political aspirations as such. They are not interested in developing political strength aside from specific benefits and legislation which will help them bargain more successfully with management.

Finally, they have a narrow political base. Let us say there are 18 million organized people in the United States. Numerically, this is not high.

All in all, then, I cannot work up any great heat with respect to unions in the political arena.

From the floor: I think the proposals of labor leaders have been dealt with in an extremely lukewarm manner by the rank and file. In spite of the amazing growth of the unions which you have mentioned, the members have given only halfhearted support or consideration to many of the proposals offered by their leaders.

From the floor: It seems to me that the unions have made a very great effort to get control—or greater control than they have already—over management. They want to take over responsibilities which basically belong to management. They want to do the job of managing.

Mr. Livernash: It is true that at one time unions were pressing for more control over layoffs, promotion standards, and so on, but I think those matters have been stabilized in most industries now. In some of these fields, management has conceded; in others, the unions have given in, until we now have what I consider to be generally a sound accommodation in noneconomic matters. There have, indeed, been occasions when managers have been weak—when they have not stood up for their rights—and they have lost in some degree the prerogative to run their businesses. But this is not the general rule, and when it happens it has not come about because of any plan on the part of the unions. Rather, it comes about because of pressures that are felt by management on specific issues, to which it succumbs. Companies that have maintained worker efficiency are the ones that have profited from better union-management relations.

From the floor: Isn't the unions' wage policy the main cause of today's inflation?

Mr. Livernash: I cannot place the blame on any particular group. I think it stems from a wide variety of causes. I do believe that it was a step forward in economic understanding when General Motors proposed a wage formula that was based on the annual improvement and cost-of-living factors. In my judgment we would have had more wage-price inflation had it not been for that five-year contract and its influence in the economy. I don't wish to whitewash the unions, but any policy that doesn't reflect the true cost of living, plus modest improvement in real living standards, is not compatible with workers' views of progress and prosperity.

This formula, however, when associated with "demand-pull" inflation, creates additional secondary inflation. Monetary and fiscal policy, to be effective in this situation, may slow up our rate of growth. To date there has been no practical answer to the dilemma, but at the same time it is easy to exaggerate its significance.

NEW DIRECTIONS IN
HUMAN RELATIONS

*George F. F. Lombard, Abraham Zaleznik, and
Fritz J. Roethlisberger*

MANAGEMENT'S QUANDARY IN A
CHANGED SOCIETY*

THE QUESTION IMPLICIT IN THE THEME of this book—what is management's role in the new society?—is one that the first generation of business managers in the twentieth century seldom asked. They knew what they were about, or thought they did: the manufacture and distribution of goods and services. Their roles derived solely from these purposes. Today the role of management is not so clear. Because the question is a new one, perhaps we should examine

Note: Mr. Lombard is Professor of Human Relations, Harvard Business School; Mr. Zaleznik is Associate Professor of Business Administration, Harvard Business School; and Mr. Roethlisberger is Wallace Brett Donham Professor of Human Relations, Harvard Business School.
  * By Mr. Lombard.

253

some of the background that makes it significant for business administrators. This will not be an attempt to gaze into the future but a diagnosis of where we stand now.

What do we mean when we speak of the manager's "role"? The term is used in at least three senses. To start with, it can describe the task of working out a new ideology, a new set of ideas on what management is all about, or, at the least, a revision of our old ones. The emphasis is on the idea that what we need to make the new society a reality is a new explanation of what "ought to be," as though, given the statement of what should be, the behavior of people will change in the desired direction.

This use of the term leaves something out. I know of no society in which there is an automatic relation between beliefs about what behavior ought to be and behavior itself. A change in the one does not lead directly to a change in the other. The relation is always more complex, though many managers have been slow to learn this.

For others, the term "role" denotes the set of activities that are the visible part of a job. In this use, role is equated with job description and perhaps with time study, but is used in speaking of jobs at higher levels of an organization. You can say that you make a time study of the worker at the bench, but you must "study the role" of the middle-management executive.

This definition, too, leaves something to be desired. We speak in this way of the role of ants in a hill and of bees in a hive. There are the workers, the soldiers, the drones, and, of course, the queen. The single-mindedness with which the visible activities of these roles are carried out, almost to perfection, is impressive. Yet few of us, if asked, would say in defining "role" that this is what we have in mind. No one of us wants for himself or others the experience of living and working in this way. We have no impression that the ant's work, his role, is meaningful to him. This seems to be outside his concern. Yet it is the *meaningfulness* of our roles that is important to us. I wish to call attention to this in our discussion of roles in business organizations.

Search for Meaning

I am not talking about what a worker should do or does, but about what his job means and means *differently* to him. For all men it is not simply what they do but the meaning of what they do that causes the furor. Whether the gift is a case of whiskey, a bolt of cloth, or a hotel room is not important, but what the gift means to the giver, to his customer, to Congress and the newspapers, to you and me, is of sufficient concern to attract a nation's interest at the dawn of the age of Sputniks.

So when I speak of the business manager's role, I am referring not only to his visible activities and to the creed he uses to explain and defend them but also to the underlying values which sanction and make legitimate what he says and does. We must look not at the audible statement and the visible activity alone but at that which makes the shouted and the seen seem worthwhile.

Most of us would agree on the major source of worthwhileness for activities in business. The job of people in business organizations has long been thought of as providing the goods and services which society needs. In other words, we have valued the purpose and the product. The test of "right" behavior for the business manager has not been kindness, helpfulness, or charity, though these have not been forgotten. The overriding test for business enterprises has been the production of better or more efficiently made goods.

This value made legitimate the jungles that assembly lines became in some older factories. It accounted for the endless and dreary repetitiveness built into jobs that could have been made interesting with a little imagination. It led to the specialization of middle-management tasks to the extent that people working on one aspect of a product did not know how their work affected other steps in the process of production. At one extreme, not much more than a generation ago, profit for the individual was an unquestioned social good. Laws now curb some of the extremes that many once thought fit and proper and indicative of the skilled business operator.

The questions implicit in these ideas about productivity and profitability as the sources of the businessman's self-esteem and of the esteem in which others held him seemed to pass quickly. As I said, government regulated some of the excesses. The rise of labor unions restored a balance. Then the fear of defeat in World War II, which business and business leaders had an important part in forestalling, once again made the product and its efficient production a matter of immediate importance. Productivity, not for profits in the sense of the 1920's, but for war and then for the very different (but for many millions of people long-delayed) postwar demands of peace, still sanctioned such behavior in many organizations.

Today there are other differences. The traditional purposes and goals of business are being widely reconceived. The product is no longer the toaster but progress; no longer the magazine but togetherness; no longer the automobile but masculinity, happiness, or serenity. Kenneth D. Benne made the same point in a somewhat wider context when he described America as "a world where women wear uniforms and tend machines, men wash dishes and tend babies, libraries show movies and drug stores circulate books, bread is softened by chemicals from a munitions factory and spread with margarine made by soap companies." *

At the same time that these questions about its traditional values are being raised within business, the course of events is forcing a re-examination of others that seemed settled for several hundred years. These include values not customarily thought of as directly related to business operations but nevertheless of the greatest importance to them.

Man and Society

For centuries Western man knew, or assumed he knew, his place in society. As he conceived it, this was a given, established position determined by the feudal hierarchy and applied to all. Each had his trade, status, and role in his community, regulated even as to the order in which he walked in public and sat in church.

Though much of this still persists in our society, the need of people to express differences among themselves outgrew the limits of some of these older societies. Groups and individuals broke away; some found new lands. Societies built on the assumed equality of men rather than on the differences in their roles in life grew up. In these societies the rewards were for achievement, not birth; but even the Horatio Alger hero, archetype of the man who succeeds in spite of a low start in life, did so because his behavior conformed to a known and limited moral code. His long, patient, and honest effort at last achieved its blaze of rewards. Though his place in

* In an address to the Adult Education Association, Washington, D.C., quoted in the *Boston Herald*, July 21, 1955.

society was not established as in the older societies, any questions about the outcome which he and those like him asked along the way were more the pleasures of the hunt and the fun of getting there than the doubts of the displaced, the unplaced, and the rootless of modern times.

Thus, the average man in both these societies had his place in the community. He could devote his energies to tasks outside himself and his relations with others. He could and did attend to improving the environment in which his ancestors had struggled to survive. He built a better house and ate better food. He changed the face of the globe. So, not only a man's place in society but also his relation to the environment could be taken for granted. The assumption implicit in his thought and action was that he was master of his environment. Any doubts that he had about this he allayed one day out of seven by acknowledging his frailty and asking God for grace.

The New Knowledge

During these centuries, too, man's relation to knowledge was given: knowledge was to make men free. In respect to his relation to the environment, this has come true almost to the fullest extent of man's dreams. On the one hand, men have added measurably to the years of their lives; there is no question that in the future they will add more. On the other hand, it now seems possible for them not merely to dream of reaching but actually to reach the stars.

Though these results of several hundred years' effort are visible today, the assumptions about values underlying them are up for reconsideration as they have not been in all that period. About the turn of the century, the Cartesian principle that man is here and the world there, each separate and finite, was challenged in physics, where it had been king of kings. Einstein's theory of relativity, based on a very different assumption about man's relation to his environment, accounted for observable facts not otherwise explainable. This new idea of the relatedness of external fact to the frame of reference of the observer took hold at once in the arts and literature as well as in science to the great enrichment of our culture. In this respect, business and business education, often self-righteous in their statements of leadership, lag far behind.

Within the span of little more than 50 years the results of this new orientation for knowledge, previously idealized as an agent for freeing man, include the means for a more widespread enslavement of man than he had ever feared. Not only is death now possible for all of us by intent—an easy fact to live with, for who among us would so intend? Annihilation is just as possible by accident or, more frightening still because we cannot know the outcome, by mutation.

In respect to himself, the pursuit of knowledge has added to man's awareness of his determinism rather than to his freedom. C. G. Jung says that "medical psychology has furnished all the necessary empirical and experimental proofs" that man's conscious thought is counterbalanced by an unconscious.* In the Freudian view, this would be to say that what each of us is to be is, on the whole, fixed by the time we leave infancy, before thinking and knowing are important functions. Thus another of Western man's most treasured assumptions about his nature, Descartes' "I think, therefore I am," is open for reconsideration.† So too are our assumptions about the nature of a good and healthy society.

Thus, at the middle of the twentieth century man faces countless quandaries and ambiguities, not freedom and certitude. The three I have mentioned concern, first, man's conception of himself and his relation to others; second, his relation to the physical environment; and third, his relation to knowledge. In view of the importance of these relations in our daily lives, it is little wonder that tensions, doubts, anxieties, and violence characterize the scene at home and abroad when they are questioned. Many recent thinkers have recognized that something like this was taking place. Elton Mayo called the first chapter of one of his books "The Seamy Side of Progress." ‡ Erich Fromm shows an inverse correlation between progress toward democracy and acts of violence and alcoholism.§

---

* C. G. Jung, *The Undiscovered Self* (Boston, Little, Brown and Company, 1958), p. 83.

† Compare Charles S. Sherrington, *Man on His Nature* (Cambridge, The University Press, 1940).

‡ Elton Mayo, *The Social Problems of an Industrial Civilization* (Boston, Division of Research, Harvard Business School, 1945).

§ Erich Fromm, *The Sane Society* (New York, Rinehart & Company, Inc., 1955).

The Business of Business

How do these problems relate to the role of the business manager? Let me briefly describe a business situation where these questions are at issue:

> The people in Company X face these questions at many levels. Knowledge has changed their products, processes, and markets. The engineers doing advanced development work are all under 30 years old. The pace of new knowledge in their area is so rapid that the knowledge of men who finished their education only 10 years ago is already out-of-date. Men who ran machines are now run by them. Comparative oldtimers—the company is fairly new—who had bossed youngsters out of high school now find the latter telling them how jobs can best be done. Men who could not change their behavior had their jobs changed for them. To those who had struggled to maintain the belief that they were masters of their fate, this was perhaps the most wounding change of all.
>
> These problems, however, did not receive explicit attention in Company X, which was undergoing a tremendous expansion. The executives' excitement in planning new buildings and in anticipating new markets and profits masked these issues; in view of how little we know about them, this was perhaps wise. But the problems were there, evident in the many anxiety-producing reorganizations of the company and in the high grievance, turnover, and absence rates at all levels. The general manager, as capable an administrator as I have known, finally became weary of the endless struggle to maintain stability and went to what he hoped would be a quieter job. In the few years since, two others have tried his job and left.

As long as the values of the society in which business operated were unquestioned, business managers had a stable milieu in which to seek solutions to problems of productivity. It was entirely appropriate for them, so to speak, to attend to business, to provide the products. The conditions for effective work already existed. But once the values of this background began to change, the answers for business managers were not so simple. What had not been business tended to become business—and often with a whack.

Research shows that in all forms of life a stable base is necessary for assessing and taking action. The homeostatic mechanisms of the body, first studied at Harvard by Walter B. Cannon,* are instances in point. Just as these mechanisms provide inwardly the steady state necessary to the body for effective outward action, so too the values of society which I have illustrated provided managers with a stable foundation for business decisions. When this necessary pre-condition for outward action is upset on every hand, the mainte-nance of a stable state becomes a matter of the greatest importance. Here is the business manager's dilemma in mid-twentieth century: should he continue happily at what he knows best, managing for productivity alone, when the scene around him has shifted so greatly that this posture may leave him like an ostrich with his head in the sand; or should he accept, rather than avoid, the anxieties born of the changed conditions, and seek to work through these doubts and quandaries in order to make a contribution to the resolution of the distinctive problem of our times?

These are not questions that are likely to be settled soon; some may be with us for decades. Perhaps the task of working out new solutions will prove to be too difficult. From our studies, however, I have come to have great faith in the capacity of groups to survive. The problem as I see it lies not there but in the capacity of leader-ship to provide for continuing growth, change, and complication. No society has yet solved this problem, but that does not mean it cannot be done. If it can, research and education in business ad-ministration have an excellent chance of providing fruitful leads.

PARADOXES FOR MANAGEMENT IN A NEW SOCIETY†

During the past ten years researchers have continued to explore the relationship between the motivation, productivity, and satisfac-tion of employees in organizations. They have explored the effects of leadership practice on employee behavior and have carried on intensive work on the determinants of behavior in small work groups. On the whole, this research has produced findings which present paradoxes to the business leader. I should like to devote some attention to these paradoxes in this chapter, because in a

---

* Walter B. Cannon, *The Wisdom of the Body* (New York, W. W. Norton & Company, 1932).
† By Mr. Zaleznik.

curious way they point to the next step for managers in the development of more effective human relations. Let me first present the high lights of these recent research findings and an interpretation of their meaning for management practice.

One of the favorite questions in these investigations has been: what is the relationship between the productivity and satisfaction of employees? Because of the way early studies were interpreted, many people assumed that a causal relationship existed between satisfaction and productivity. They assumed that as you increase the employee's satisfaction, you also increase his productivity. To be sure, there were some early postwar studies which showed an association between high morale and high productivity, but along came some later ones with disquieting results which showed an inverse relationship between satisfaction and productivity. In several studies the investigators reported that the so-called happy workers are the low producers and the unhappy workers tend to be the high producers.

Sources of Satisfaction

This was upsetting to people who thought they had found a simple solution to problems of productivity and morale in the idea that high productivity results from keeping employees happy. This, therefore, is the first paradox facing the manager who is concerned both with the productivity of his organization and with the morale and satisfaction of his employees at all levels. What is a useful way for him to think about the relationship between productivity and morale in his organization?

In a research study which Fritz J. Roethlisberger, C. Roland Christensen, and I made,* we attempted to cast light on the apparently paradoxical findings about the relationship between productivity and satisfaction. We did not assume a causal relationship between productivity and satisfaction. Instead, we assumed that both factors are related to the motivation of the individual and the kinds of rewards he receives as a member of the organization. An individual comes to work in an organization to satisfy a variety of needs. We speculated that the satisfaction and the productivity of an individual

* *The Motivation, Productivity, and Satisfaction of Workers: A Prediction Study* (Boston, Division of Research, Harvard Business School, 1958).

bear a relationship to the degree to which he receives rewards that satisfy his psychological as well as his economic needs. While recognizing the subtle characteristics of human needs, we felt we could classify them into two broad categories: (1) those needs which tend to be satisfied by rewards from management or the formal organization of the company; and (2) those needs which tend to be satisfied by rewards from the small group, or the informal organization to which he is related.

In the first category—the management rewards—we typically think of the pay a person receives as the basic recompense through which he satisfies many needs. There are also other types of management rewards, like the opportunity for doing interesting work, job security, and fringe benefits. Presumably, and we speculated in this vein, the more a person is rewarded by management, the greater his motivation toward hard work and high production. Conversely, the less an individual is rewarded by management, the lower his motivation to work hard at his task and the lower his productivity rate. A similar statement can be made with respect to the determinants of satisfaction. The more an individual is rewarded by management, the greater his satisfaction; the less an individual is rewarded by management, the lower the expected level of satisfaction.

The second broad category of rewards are those associated with membership in the informal organization that exists in most work situations. Individuals satisfy many important psychological needs through their associations with others in a small, face-to-face group setting. For its well-accepted members, the group provides emotional support and security, prestige and approval, and the opportunity to fulfill a wide variety of roles in relation to other individuals. Our instincts toward gregariousness, our desires to reach out and communicate with our fellows, all these needs and many others are satisfied through group membership.

In continuing our research speculations, we felt there was considerable evidence from previous studies to suggest a relationship between an individual's position in the informal group structure and his motivation to produce. We also assumed from previous evidence a relationship between an individual's position in the informal structure and his degree of satisfaction, because in the rewards he receives through group membership, many needs are fulfilled.

In what way can a group influence an individual's productivity?

Any group exists because individuals conform to the norms and standards which maintain the unity and integrity of the group. Previous evidence on small work groups showed a tendency for the development of a group norm specifying a fair rate of output for individuals. Where an individual does not conform to this norm, he is generally subjected to disapproval and is punished through the capacity of the group to withhold its acceptance. We saw no logical reason why restriction of output *has* to exist in a group, but we were going on the *fact* of its existence as revealed in previous studies.

We hypothesized, therefore, that the well-accepted group members would be motivated toward neither high nor low production but more toward the group norm, which, again from past experience, we felt would approach but not exceed management expectations. In those cases where an individual had conflicts in his motivation toward productivity, or in those cases where the individual both belonged to the group and was favorably rewarded by management, we assumed that the control exercised by the group would lead the individual to conform to group norms and to avoid a high level of production.

The actual findings in this research substantiated many of our speculations but threw others into question. We found, for example, a very close relationship between the rewards a person received from the group and his level of productivity and satisfaction. Where an individual was accepted as a regular member of the group, he tended to conform to its output norms and to produce "on the line," or at a level neither particularly high nor low. He also tended to be relatively highly satisfied. Those workers who were not rewarded by the group in the form of regular membership produced at the extremes of high and low and tended to be relatively dissatisfied.

What kind of relationship exists between the rewards a person receives from management and his level of productivity? Among the regular group members we could not distinguish the rate of productivity and the level of satisfaction of those favorably or unfavorably rewarded by management. Among nonregular group members management reward seemed to have an effect opposite to what we expected. The high producers were those who received relatively low rewards from management; the low producers seemed to be those who were not accepted by the group but who were favorably rewarded by management. With respect to satisfaction, we found that those who succeeded in gaining acceptance from the group were highly satisfied whether or not they were favorably rewarded by management. On the other hand, those workers who had little or no acceptance from the group were on the whole dissatisfied whether they were favorably or unfavorably rewarded by management.

Small Group Relationships

The substance of these research findings suggests a second paradox for the business manager: that the rewards offered by management do not seem to have *sustained* motivational effects on the behavior of employees, but rather the sustained motivational effects seem to reside in the informal group relationships. The paradox lies in the fact that the very tools management ordinarily uses to motivate members of the organization *do not seem to motivate*.

The implications of this statement will become more evident as I review other paradoxical research findings. In a study of a middle-class, white-collar group in a research-engineering laboratory of a large industrial concern, Louis B. Barnes found that the engineers had sharply divided orientations toward their work.* Some of the engineers identified themselves with their professions as scientists and chemists. These people expressed interest in doing long-range research rather than projects of immediate use to the production department. Other engineers identified themselves with the values of the business organization of which they were a part. They were after advancement in the company and enjoyed taking on production assignments. This laboratory, incidentally, specialized in short-range projects of immediate use to production.

By and large, the professionals were isolated in the informal group relationships. They tended on the whole to be relatively dissatisfied, but they were generally the highest producers and the most competent members of the research department. The organizationals, those who identified with the values of the company, were very active in group relationships. On the whole, they were satisfied, but were not as productive or as competent as the professionals.

* Louis B. Barnes, "An Industrial Laboratory: A Small Group Study of Values, Behavior, Satisfaction and Productivity" (Unpublished Ph.D. thesis, Harvard Business School, 1958).

This research suggests a third paradox: the fact that people's values parallel those of the organization will not necessarily motivate them toward high productivity. In fact, this research suggests that attempts to alter the orientation of the professional may well work against increasing productivity and creativity.

Supervision and Productivity

In studies of patterns of supervision in relation to the productivity of work groups, researchers at the University of Michigan found that supervisors of work groups whose production was high provided general supervision, were person-oriented, and were not exclusively preoccupied with getting out production. On the other hand, the supervisors of work groups whose production was relatively low paid stricter attention to productivity, were more work-oriented, and provided closer supervision.* This finding suggests a fourth paradox: supervisors who are most directly concerned about production may well end up getting less production than those who pay less direct attention to output. In other words, the motivation to produce will not be instilled in employees through the pressures exerted by close supervision.

In some very interesting experiments on behavior in small groups being conducted at Harvard's Laboratory of Social Relations,† the experimenters have found a distinct tendency for individuals to specialize in the kinds of roles they play in a group. For example, some individuals tend to specialize in so-called task roles, in which they pay primary attention to the task or job the group has to perform. Other individuals tend to specialize in social roles, or those which generally keep group relationships harmonious and which

* Daniel Katz, Nathan Maccoby, Gerald Gurin, and Lucretia G. Floor, *Productivity, Supervision and Morale Among Railroad Workers* (Ann Arbor, Institute for Social Research, University of Michigan, 1951); also Daniel Katz, Nathan Maccoby, and Nancy C. Morse, *Productivity, Supervision and Morale in an Office Situation* (Ann Arbor, Institute for Social Research, University of Michigan, 1950), Part I.

† Philip E. Slater, "Role Differentiation in Small Groups," and Edgar F. Borgatta, Arthur S. Couch, and Robert F. Bales, "Some Findings Relevant to the Great Man Theory of Leadership," in *Small Groups, Studies in Social Interaction,* edited by Robert F. Bales, et al. (New York, Alfred A. Knopf, Inc., 1955).

tend to relieve the frictions that are likely to appear in any work group. The interesting aspect of this tendency toward specialization is the way individuals in task or social roles are perceived by other group members. The task specialists typically offer the most suggestions and contribute most to the completion of the task. On the other hand, they are not very popular or very well liked in the group. The social-role specialists are just the opposite. They are very popular and well liked, but they do not rank particularly high in contribution to task performance. These studies have also shown that few people are able to perform effectively in *both* task and social roles.

Task versus Group

These interesting findings corroborate many of our findings in actual work groups and lead us to a fifth paradox: healthy group and organizational relationships must fulfill two functions, (1) completing task goals successfully, and (2) securing and distributing to members the rewards and satisfactions which they require to sustain their membership and continued collaboration in the work of the group. Conditions seem to exist where an individual casts his lot in one or the other of these directions, either toward the task or toward the social aspects of the group.

The more group-centered an individual is, the more he may appear to be unrelated to the task of the group. He may receive rewards in the form of popularity and social approval, but he does not receive the rewards associated with task accomplishment. The more task-centered he is, the more estranged he may become from his fellows. He may receive the approval and rewards associated with task accomplishment, but will not necessarily receive the warmth and approval associated with group membership.

Let me cite one other set of research findings and pose the sixth in this series of paradoxes facing the manager as he looks to human relations research for some answers on improving his effectiveness. In the few studies which have attempted to evaluate the effects of human relations training, such training seemed to make little difference in the behavior of the supervisor. In fact, in one study * I

* Abraham Zaleznik, *Worker Satisfaction and Development* (Boston, Division of Research, Harvard Business School, 1956).

reached the conclusion that this training may have been making matters worse for the supervisor:

> The training suggested that the supervisor behave in a manner which differed considerably from the behavior of *his* supervisors and from the behavior generally expected of supervisors in the organization. From his point of view, while the training program suggested that he listen to his employees' problems, no one was listening to *his* problems. Although the training program suggested that he consider the human situation of employees at work as well as their rate of production, his boss considered *only* the production of his department and not the human situation with which the supervisor had to deal.

The paradox is this: human relations training, in many cases derived from research on the motivation, productivity, and satisfaction of individuals and groups, tends to lead in the direction of executive and supervisory behavior which is not sanctioned and supported within the total organizational environment.

Resolving Conflicts

These paradoxical research findings point to conclusions which I believe have important implications for business leadership.

First, the motivation of members of organizations is considerably more complex than the main instruments of motivation now in use suggest. Individuals seek to satisfy many needs as they work at their jobs. Attempts to motivate people through the simple management rewards of pay or job security will not have lasting effects. People do not work simply because they are being paid fairly. Similarly, attempts to motivate individuals through various devices such as music in the plant, house magazines, and other gimmicks will also have little effect on motivation, because these gimmicks do not satisfy the workers' needs.

Secondly, individuals working in the kind of organizational structure that is common today are frequently forced to make choices between the various legitimate goals they seek to reach. The conflicts which make these choices necessary are not inherent in the needs themselves, but rather are imposed on people by the patterns of organization we are using. The difficulty is that the alternatives which a person selects may fulfill some of his desires but leave others ungratified. This situation of conflict and frustrated purposes often results in the sacrifice of an individual's personal development and maturation to *his* detriment as well as that of the organization which seeks his contribution and his productivity.

For example, a person is likely to want to be associated with a group of his fellows, he needs a job which challenges him and gives him symbols of status, and he feels the urge for continuing self-development and self-realization. But to preserve the approval of his associates—his membership in the group—he may be forced to give up his desire to move ahead to a more challenging responsibility by the restrictions of today's type of social organization.

The present social environment in organizations heightens the conflicts. As the individual seeks to become a member of informal groups he finds himself cut off from opportunities for the development of his task competence. Group development in an organization is frequently characterized by strict lines for belonging or not belonging and by rigid adherence to norms which block individual development and group accomplishment. In such rigid groups a person has great difficulty discovering himself and his inner needs as well as his inner resources. Even if he should succeed in gaining some insight, which is the first step toward self-realization, his social environment may make it extremely difficult for him to be true to himself.

If, on the other hand, an individual emphasizes the development of job competence, he may very well jeopardize the communication with his fellows which maintains his sensitivity and his warmth, in short, his capacity for human experience. This task-oriented person runs these risks partly because most groups force a choice and partly because his task orientation may be a false escape from human involvement.

My third conclusion is this: present management concepts of motivation are relatively ineffective because they are aimed at needs which tend to become satisfied over a period of time. Most forms of motivation are aimed at man's economic needs. These needs are indeed important, but it is a mistake to treat them as the only ones man seeks to satisfy at work. After a person achieves some measure of economic security, the economic rewards do not motivate him in quite the same way. New needs arise. Man wants to belong to a cohesive group; he wants challenge in his work activity; he wants to find the route toward self-discovery and creativity. Furthermore, the traditional methods of motivation fail because they do not resolve conflicts between group membership, task achievement, and self-realization.

THE CONTRIBUTION OF HUMAN RELATIONS*

Human relations research and training have a contribution to make to the theme of this book: management's mission in a new society. Research can help to bring it down to earth by providing some facts on which to focus our thinking, while training can focus it on one aspect about which each of us can do something now if he so chooses.

What is the essential feature of our new society? For me it is the inability of its built-in ideas to cope with the march of events and problems. The obsolescence of today's conventional social wisdom— whether it be the conventional wisdom of conservatives or liberals, businessmen or academicians—is the most characteristic feature of our times.†

Such a daily exposure of inadequacy is anxiety-producing. It tends to excite an excessively vigorous defense of or attack on conventional wisdom or a complete withdrawal from the scene of battle. Experience has shown that neither of these resolutions is entirely satisfactory. For the individual they spell frustration; for the society they mean that little gets accomplished. We wait for the march of events—a major war or a depression—to compensate for the limitations in our conventional wisdom, and, as we all know, this is likely to be harmful as well as wasteful and inefficient.

Goal of Research

Research is a more efficient and rational way of changing our ideas before a catastrophe makes it imperative that we do so. Mr. Zaleznik gives us an example of this method. He takes an area, such as the motivation, productivity, and satisfaction of workers, about which the conventional wisdom makes many assertions. He

* By Mr. Roethlisberger.
† See John Kenneth Galbraith, *The Affluent Society* (Boston, Houghton Mifflin Company, 1958).

observes a small work group, and in terms of his study finds the conventional wisdom wanting. He calls his findings paradoxes. Being more intellectually stimulating and less anxiety-producing, a paradox can be rationally resolved. Findings in themselves are not paradoxical. Paradoxes exist and persist only in relation to certain fixed beliefs which vanish completely under a different set of assumptions. It is thus that new and better theories are born.

Let us note some of the other attributes of this method. Although it bears other conventional names, it can be called the method of limited withdrawal, of piecemeal attack, and of minimizing the risk of being caught napping on the intellectual front. This is not the method of an angry, apprehensive, or dogmatic man; it is the method of a bemused man seeking order in his universe.

Thus, in the midst of battle when verbal arguments are flying thick and fast, we do not find Mr. Zaleznik mounting his white charger and doing battle for or against the conventional wisdom: i.e., talking louder and faster about things he has never observed or never could observe and verify. Rather, like a good strategist of verbal combat, he starts retreating to a level where he can observe something against which his ideas and the conventional wisdom can be checked.

With the competence of a man who knows his business, he knocks six small but sturdy nails into the coffin of conventional wisdom about matters of worker motivation, productivity, and satisfaction. This is no wholesale massive onslaught; rather, it is a limited, piecemeal approach which in the long run has some chance of success. One good nail well placed has put some pieces of conventional wisdom permanently to rest.

Let us not be too optimistic. We must remember that the march of events and circumstances can deal heavier blows to the conventional wisdom of our times than a few facts of research. Nevertheless, research does minimize the risk of being caught short when the time comes. In suggesting research as a way for management to minimize risks rather than to maximize profits in the new society, I realize that I am choosing an idea that runs counter to the conventional wisdom of our times and is therefore likely to be unpopular. This wisdom asserts that the businessman is by nature a risk taker, so that the reduction of risk is abhorrent to his soul. Instead, the search for and glorification of risk and insecurity are

NEW DIRECTIONS IN HUMAN RELATIONS 271

attributes more natural to him. Nevertheless, I shall risk this un-
popularity and address my remarks to the way I find businessmen
behaving, rather than to their portrait according to the conventional
wisdom of the past.

Improving Practice

Human relations has more to offer the thoughtful executive than
some research findings against which he can test his preconceived
ideas. It can also help him to improve his practice in relating himself to others in a work group. This approach is not in itself research, but it does include one of its essential features—observation.

Human relations has always retained the small group as a major
focus of its studies. Let me cite some reasons for this:

(1) This focus has allowed theory and practice to be developed
together.

(2) The small group is something which can be observed easily.

(3) Besides offering excellent opportunities for concrete observation, the small group is the concrete unit in which much of the
world's work is done. Moreover, it is the unit in which men obtain
those rewards and satisfactions that make them willing to work.

(4) It contains and keeps together all the major dimensions with
which the administrator's job is concerned. It holds not only the
specialized tasks that need to be done if the group's purpose is to
be attained but also the individuals that are supposed to be doing
them. In it we can find not only the unique individuals who do the
work but also the relationships that are required and that develop
among them. It contains values and sentiments which each member
realizes in varying degrees. It includes followers and leaders, members of high and low standing, and members who like and dislike
each other. It contains norms of acceptable behavior by which the
regular members abide.

(5) All these dimensions exist together in one interrelated, organic,
living whole. Thus, the small work group is a little society; it is not
society in general, or in the abstract; it is a small, living, particular
social organism in which we are all intimately involved as members
or leaders.

(6) Thus, as a formal leader of a work group, the supervisor
or executive is not just a disinterested observer. He is also an involved member. This involvement brings in the most critical variables
of all—the administrator's assumptions, which often determine his
perception and feelings.

So the small group offers the executive or supervisor an opportunity for obtaining a better intellectual understanding of the medium in which he works. It also offers him a daily opportunity to practice and improve his skills in that medium. In the small group he can learn to make better clinical observation of his own behavior and the behavior of others under the burden of responsibility. He can see the fixed roles he plays and how he often fulfills his own needs through them more than the needs of the group. If he is interested, he can begin to become more perceptive of the roles that the group requires on different occasions to maintain its integrity so that it can secure its objectives. He sees how these contributions can be made without trying to fulfill all these roles himself. To do this he has to learn to "control" (retrain and re-educate) his feelings, which too often get in the way.

The answers to the major question that we are raising in this book, then, can be sought most fruitfully through this kind of hand-to-hand development of research and practice. Management's mission in a new society is not merely a matter for public proclamation or grandiose generalization; it is a subject for meticulous research that can result in better intellectual understanding and improved practices.

For the executive needs to understand not only his "relations to society" with a capital *S* but also his relation to society with a small *s:* the society with which he is intimately involved and which he can affect directly here and now. In this context, he can begin to correct and modify his behavior in the light of facts rather than in the glow of the conventional beliefs of his times. Here he can begin, for example, to understand the conditions of the "frozen groups" he often administers, the part he plays in these conditions, the more useful roles he might perform to assist in their unfreezing, and how he might go about performing these roles. At this level, his mission in the new society can become internalized in a code of professional competence. Short of this achievement, all we will get is grandiose talk and generalization.

The New Education

The development of such a code must become the objective of our business schools. Business education will have to do more than train managers in the conventional wisdom of business for the fixed, inherent, and traditional managerial roles of yesterday. The managers of the new society will need a new kind of education to provide the intellectual understanding and skills that the new society requires.

This new training will need strong support, because the going will be rough. If we go in this direction, we will have to give up many notions of executive behavior—of what the conventional wisdom asserts that it is or ought to be. It will require, moreover, the cooperation of the "long hairs," and several other species whom businessmen have traditionally tended to view with suspicion and even alarm. But although the going will be rough, what is the alternative? To go it alone is a bit of intellectual arrogance that the manager of the new society will no longer be able to retain if he is to remain its leader very long.

QUESTIONS AND ANSWERS*

From the floor: You seem to be minimizing the impact of management-controlled incentives on the productivity and motivation of the individual. Do you actually feel that this influence has been supplanted by others?

Mr. Zaleznik: When we use the term "incentive," we mean providing financial incentive plans of one sort or another. From the research evidence available, I would say that developing sustained motivation is, indeed, a more complex process than that. We need to develop a new concept and new means for dealing with the individual's motivation in an organization.

We have found that this phenomenon of restriction of output exists both in groups working on straight hourly wages and in those under piece-rate plans. Apparently these devices do not deal with the strategic variable of the person's position in the social structure of which he is a part.

From the floor: Shops are inclined to adjust their tempo to what the group will do. You will frequently hear a new member being told, "Let's not kill the rating."

* Businessmen present at the panel session on which this chapter is based raised certain questions which brought about the interplay of ideas reported more or less verbatim in this section.

Mr. Lombard: This whole matter of incentive motivation has been very much tangled up in the literature and discussions. I find it helpful to think of an incentive as something that someone offers to somebody else. It is external. I think of motivation as that which is within the person himself. Whether a person's motivation will be changed by an incentive is a very complex question. Certainly in a review of the research findings there is no evidence that there is a direct relation.

Mr. Roethlisberger: If a need is satisfied, it no longer motivates. When you have enough food, food is not going to be the most important thing to you. Now, many of the basic needs which you try to satisfy in industry are already satisfied. Therefore, you have done this part of your job. You have to fulfill other needs. There are other needs besides physiological needs for food, clothing, and shelter which these incentive schemes are not satisfying at all, such as social needs, status needs, and growth needs.

From the floor: How can management enter into the small social group and influence its objectives?

Mr. Zaleznik: Management is a small group, but management people do not recognize this fact. They do not consider their own group's social characteristics—whether it is healthy or sick, functional or disfunctional.

If the executive can change his own particular group, this change will have a spillover effect on other groups. In other words, worry first about your own group membership. Develop skills, observation, and behavior for it, and the effects will carry beyond it.

Mr. Lombard: The answer to questions like this is by no means clear. For instance, it is not certain that management will create more satisfaction, productivity, or growth by doing more for a work group. It may be much better to foster the group's development of its own way of working and living. There are so many unanswered questions here that a lot of research is going to have to be done in the next few years.

From the floor: Does your research work apply right up through the hierarchy to management?

Mr. Zaleznik: There have been fewer studies of actual management groups, but we think that the variables which we examine in work groups have general applicability. This is corroborated by the few studies which have been done in the middle-class white-collar group, in which there have been no shattering changes in variables yet, though there may well be.

From the floor: How valid will research measuring motivation and the other factors that have been discussed be in the future, when it has been pointed out that the type of work force which we are going to have in a few years will be scholastically quite different from the present one? In 20 years, 50% of the work force will have college degrees, and I think that job content is going to change rather rapidly. In other words, will research done today necessarily be very applicable 10 or 15 years from now?

Mr. Zaleznik: This question requires some examination. I don't know. But research is risk taking. You take certain risks, and you try to cover yourself by dealing with variables that have general applicability. In other words, you don't deal with your variables by trying to limit them to one kind of culture, one kind of technique, or one kind of group. As long as we cover ourselves in that way, certain aspects are bound to have some relevance. Now, the particular effects on motivation of the upgrading of the labor force would have to be studied in themselves.

From the floor: Are these groups that you speak of static, or do they change? And what about the fact that some groups are in the company and others outside? What about the question of the conflicts that are set up by differences that arise between the two?

Mr. Zaleznik: This question gets at the problem of multigroup membership. We are not members of one particular group, but of a number of them. And certainly in a factory there are overlaps. This is why we have to be very careful in making generalizations about what influences whom and how.

From the floor: It seems to me that we always emphasize *giving* things to people. Personally, I don't think that you can buy or beg in filling peoples' needs. For instance, it seems to me that most people have a relatively strong need for security derived from a feeling of the strength of authority. Have you made any studies on the effect on groups of good, old-fashioned, tough-minded discipline and high standards?

Mr. Zaleznik: I really don't know what you are talking about, since you are using completely nonoperational terms like "tough-minded."

From the floor: How can we approach the problem of training future managers in the area of group relationships?

Mr. Roethlisberger: It will mean changing our ways a good deal and doing more research. This would be costly, and there would be considerable risk involved. Too often we give approval to some of these ideas without seeing that, if we want to carry them through, more change from the traditional ways of doing things will be required than we realize.

Mr. Lombard: We must have people who are capable of addressing the problem of group membership in order to work through to increased productivity or satisfaction. That is going to require a different approach.

This problem of group membership, for an administrator, would come up around a complaint, or the administration of a budget, or something of that sort. Dealing with these problems effectively takes a capacity for conceptualizing and seeing new things in the present situation. This is a difficult idea to convey in training and education.

Mr. Zaleznik: The important factor is the executive's own behavior in the small group of which he is a part. Does he understand its social structure? Does he understand his own behavior patterns —what kinds of roles he takes in the group? Does he understand the effect of his behavior on other people? Is he seeking new kinds of involvement of the members of his immediate group? If he can answer all those questions affirmatively, there is no doubt that he is approaching the problem from the right direction. We are trying to give practical and immediate help in this area through the various kinds of training in group relationships which we are now developing.

THE ROLE OF MANAGEMENT IN
INFLATION AND RECESSION

*Bertrand Fox, Merton J. Peck, John V. Lintner,
and Warren A. Law*

BUSINESSMEN ARE USED to the terms, or the contrast of terms, *inflation-deflation* and *depression-recession*. In this chapter we have chosen inflation-recession intentionally.

We think that the threat of a major depression is far less than it was 20 years ago, and the possibilities of deflation, or serious deflation, are rather slim. We do think there are real possibilities or real threats in the inflation-recession alternative. Since 1939 consumer prices are up over 100%. Even during this last recession con-

Note: Mr. Fox, who makes the introductory observations, is Edsel Bryant Ford Professor of Business Administration and Director of Research, Harvard Business School; Mr. Peck is Assistant Professor of Business Administration, Harvard Business School; Mr. Lintner is Professor of Business Administration, Harvard Business School; and Mr. Law is Lecturer on Business Administration, Harvard Business School.

sumer prices have been up slightly. Some fell substantially, and a large number fell by small amounts. Over-all, even during the recession, however, there has been a continued increase in consumer prices as well as wages.

The type of inflation which concerns us most is the long-term creeping variety that moves up at a rate of 2%, 3%, or 5% during the year. We will not be talking about the kind characteristic of the immediate postwar period or the Korean War period. We are much more concerned with what is sometimes called the price-wage inflation.

We are going to focus, also, on the role of business and business decisions in inflation and recession. Of course, government has a major role here, and many other segments of the economy have real responsibilities. Businessmen, however, especially in large firms, have an important responsibility to think of the impact of their decisions beyond their firms.

During the war period 500 companies accounted for between 75% and 95% of the consumption of most of the basic raw materials. One thousand companies, in peacetime as well as wartime, probably account for at least 85% of the consumption of all materials. With such a concentration of influence, the actions of these 1,000 firms necessarily have a very important effect on the stability or instability of our economy. The businessmen who manage these companies, by taking into account the effects on the economy of their decisions, may contribute significantly to its stability.

THE OUTLOOK FOR THE WAGE–PRICE SPIRAL*

I would like to explore the implications of Erwin D. Canham's remark that "American business's most flagrant mistake in this decade is its failure to do its part to maintain price stability." † The problem of prices obviously cannot be discussed without looking at wages. Basically we have to ask how we can get out of the wage-price dilemma. In trying to answer this question, I shall examine:

> 1. The alternative ways in which price and wages can behave, in order to define responsible wage and price behavior.

* By Mr. Peck.
† See the chapter entitled "For a Revised Sense of Values," p. 75.

2. The possibility of achieving responsible price and wage behavior within the present institutional setup.

3. The nature of the government intervention that may occur if voluntary action fails.

What We Face

Essentially, we have four alternatives. Why the first, *continuing inflation*, should be ruled out as a solution has been well stated by Mr. Canham. Nevertheless, continuing inflation seems so inevitable that such people as Sumner H. Slichter urge that we concentrate on protecting as many as possible from inflation and attempt only to keep the inflation moderate—a policy based on the well-known saying, "If it's inevitable, relax and enjoy it."

The second alternative is *stable wages and a price level declining by 3% a year*. This is in many ways the most desirable outcome. Over the last 100 years output per worker has increased by 2% to 3% per year. With lower prices consumer incomes can purchase the increased output. Lower prices distribute the gains in productivity to everyone, and since progress is the product of society in general—scientists, managers, investors, workers—equity requires a widespread sharing through rough price reductions. I would rule out this solution on two counts. First, the present generation of union leaders is committed to a rising wage level. Secondly, can we count on the price reduction, or would we merely get the third alternative—*stable prices and stable wages?*

The 1920's show why this third solution is undesirable. In that decade the productivity gains were unprecedented, and with stable prices and stable wages profits increased. Such high profits, in turn, encouraged an investment boom, but as consumer demand was not increased by either lower prices or higher wages, it was impossible to sell the goods the new capacity could produce. The business spending on plant and equipment which had temporarily provided an increase in demand could not be sustained, and therefore when this stimulus to the economy was withdrawn, the crash of 1929 followed.

I conclude from this that an *increase in the wage level in line with the over-all gains in productivity* in the economy while prices remain stable is the most feasible policy, although not the most desirable. Lest I be accused of Walter Reutherism, let me add two points. Wages include all the fringe benefits: pensions, supplementary unemployment benefits, vacations, and so forth. Secondly, if output per worker increases by 3% a year and wages advance by 3% a year, the workers will not absorb all the gains of productivity. A simple arithmetic example will show this:

> Suppose that for the economy as a whole average hourly earnings are $2 per hour and average hourly output is $3. With about a 2% per year increase in productivity per worker, average hourly output would be $4 in 10 years—an increase of 33%. By the proposed standard wages should also advance 33% of $2, or $.67. The remaining $.33 of the $1 increase in hourly output should go into further investment or dividends.

The aggregate amount going to capital, of course, should rise because the increases in productivity are produced largely by an increased investment per worker. To realize the higher level of investment per worker we must increase the absolute amount of profits. Distributing the productivity gains, as in my example, will not necessarily leave us with the proper level of profits. Nevertheless, it is a simple criterion which operates in the right general direction and stabilizes the shares of labor and capital in national income, something characteristic of our economy in the past.

Prospects for Solution

But can this policy, a stable price level and wages increasing by 3% a year, be realized? In the past 10 years wages have gone up by 6% to 8% a year, as prices have, but the postwar pent-up demand and the Korean War boom were hardly auspicious for moderate wage increases and price stability. Even though the future may not contain such notable increases in demand, the concentration of productivity gains in certain industries jeopardizes the prospects for the future.

The American economy is divided by technology into the high-progress industries—steel, automobile, electrical, chemical, and metallurgical industries—and the low-progress industries—principally the services. The average gain of 3% is composed of gains of 5% in the high-progress industries and 1% in those that have shown low progress.

If we are to achieve a stable price level, then, wages in the high-progress industries must advance no more than the national average, and the excess in productivity gains must be passed on to the consumer in the form of lower prices. Price reductions here will offset the price increases necessary to maintain wages in other industries on a par with those in the high-productivity industries. Otherwise there would be such wide wage differences between the industries that it would become difficult to man the low-productivity industries. This is already apparent in the teacher shortage in the public schools. The continuing rise in prices of services, generally a low-progress sector, is another manifestation of this tendency.

The high-progress industries, however, share certain common features that make it questionable whether wage increases can be limited to 2% or 3% a year, and whether the balance of the increase in productivity can be passed on to the consumer in the form of lower prices:

- Most of these industries are highly unionized with a union leadership reluctant to accept the status quo in the distribution of income.
- Until recently, demand in these industries has been expanding, making it easy to pass on wage increases to the consumers.
- Competition in these industries has emphasized product improvement rather than price reductions, and this is where much of the productivity gains have been absorbed.

But the current situation is perhaps more encouraging. These industries were severely hit by recession, which may have emphasized the adverse effect of price increases on the sales volume. Unemployment is concentrated in these industries, and, although in many ways it is a national tragedy, it has reduced the bargaining power of the unions.

Still, I would not underestimate the difficulties ahead, nor the problems of the businessmen in such industries. It is all very well to assert that prices in the high-productivity industry should go down, but the individual businessman is often faced with intense product competition, and any price reduction may jeopardize his market share by reducing the funds for product development. It is all very well to say wage increases should be limited to 2% a year, but the individual businessman is often faced with powerful unions not content with such negligible gains.

Government Moves In

Nevertheless, I would argue that if some kind of solution for this wage-price spiral is not developed, government intervention is likely. In 1957 the House Banking and Currency Committee, the Senate Judiciary Committee, and the Joint Committee on the Economic Report held hearings on prices and wages. The discussion before these committees indicates the emergence of a common diagnosis that large and powerful corporations have raised prices and large and powerful unions have raised wages. The assignment of the major share of the blame varies with individual congressmen— some believe that it is concentration of economic power in large firms, others think that it is union monopoly, and still others adopt a "plague on both your houses" position.

In addition to a common diagnosis, a common remedy is emerging: formal public hearings on price and wage increases in the basic industries to enlist the sanction of public opinion against what might be classified as unwarranted increases. This has already been proposed, embodied in a bill introduced by Senator Joseph C. O'Mahoney several years ago.* Although legislative action seems far off today, it is a fact that sometimes only a five- or ten-year lag separates advocacy by a few and actual legislation. And the gap between public hearings and public control can be quite small. Furthermore, most of this legislation may be directed at the large firm rather than the large union, even though the problem may be more one of union than corporate monopoly. After all, if you cannot get legislation against James Hoffa, how could you legislate against Walter Reuther?

Therefore, I find myself in a dilemma. The best solution may not be achieved through responsible action by businessmen—they are locked in by their situation. And government intervention may well be more antibusiness than antilabor. Perhaps I am selling short both the economy and business administrators; the factors preventing price-wage spirals in the past may reassert themselves.

---

* See the *Hearings before the Subcommittee on Anti-Trust and Monopoly of the Committee on the Judiciary,* United States Senate, 85th Congress, 1st Session, July 9, 11–13, 16, 1957, Part 1 (Washington, Government Printing Office, 1957).

In the past 50 years businessmen have developed workable solutions to equally vexing dilemmas. In any case, developing a solution to the wage-price spiral will be an important part of management's mission in a new society.

STABILIZING THE ECONOMY *

There are many types of business decisions which have an important bearing on the matters of inflation and recession, but I shall concentrate on only three: *capital budgeting, production scheduling and inventory levels, and dividend policies.*

With respect to capital budgeting, I shall suggest that the tremendous increase in cash outlays on plant and equipment from 1955 to 1957 was a very significant factor in the resurgent inflationary pressure of the period. And I shall look at the over-all record to see whether the much-vaunted New Look of longer-range planning has as yet borne much fruit in stabilizing this dynamic segment of our economy.

As you may suspect, I shall suggest that it has not—business capital outlays have relatively been much more volatile and *de*stabilizing since the war than they were during the 1920's. The economy is undoubtedly more stable today than it was then, but this happy development has been in spite of, and not because of, the management of capital outlays by business. I will further suggest that in spite of the obvious difficulties, substantial progress in regularizing these outlays is not only possible but would make an important contribution to our national objectives of more consistently high levels of income and employment. It would help achieve greater stability in price levels and a more dynamic and a more consistently growing economy, free of unwanted and positively undesirable inflationary pressures.

On the other hand, in this context of stabilization and growth I will point out that inventory fluctuations are becoming relatively smaller than they have been in the past. Improved methods of production scheduling and inventory management in business, as well as structural changes in the economy, have contributed to this favorable development. Finally, business management has contributed importantly to the stability of the economy by its modern

* By Mr. Lintner.

dividend policies. Newer techniques point the way to further progress in stabilizing inventories and capital budgets. The need is particularly great in the capital budgeting area, and I will devote most of my attention to these outlays.

Capital Outlays and Inflation

The important impact of fluctuation in capital outlays on levels of income and employment—the so-called business cycle—is quite generally recognized. The effect of fluctuations in plant and equipment outlays on inflationary pressures and price levels seems to be much more generally misunderstood or overlooked. The recovery from the 1953–1954 recession provides an excellent illustration of the impact of sudden changes in capital spending on price levels.

The low point of the last recession was reached in the summer of 1954, but, as often happens, plant and equipment expenditures continued to decline to the end of the year. By that time consumer spending had already begun to pick up, but apart from a very sharp and early increase in consumer durables—especially automobiles and housing—the increases in other sectors were quite gradual and relatively unexciting. The boom in the automobile market began to wither within the year, and housing shortly thereafter.

The really major continuing thrust in the whole recovery was in business plant and equipment expenditures, and secondarily in state and local outlays. Capital outlays were increased 5.5 billion—28%—during 1955–1956. In the following years, instead of falling off as consumer durables did—or merely holding steady as nondurable goods did in real terms—these business capital outlays kept growing, until by late 1957 they were up a total of $12 billion, or some 44%.

After 1955, consumer spending simply moved with the growth in income from a percentage standpoint and fell behind the increase in dollar income. Contrary to the common impression, consumers were saving more, not less, after 1955. Both consumer disposable incomes and spending increased about 22% over the three years —less than half of the increase in business spending. The support to rising incomes and employment from other sectors was generally much smaller than that from capital spending, and in no case was it as well sustained.

This early vigorous push of capital spending soon led to near-capacity operations, increased prices, and much improved profits for suppliers. The insistent push for still more output led managements to grant wage increases greater than current increases in productivity. Increased unit costs were reflected in still higher prices, and, more importantly, primary increases in wages and materials prices then gradually worked themselves through other sectors where the pressure of demand was not so strong, and where the increases in productivity were smaller or negligible, thereby raising unit costs and requiring price increases in these other industries as well.

In this way, a strong cost pressure for price increases spread throughout the economy. In this connection we may note that the big upward push in industrial prices began in mid-1955 and continued through 1956. The consumer price index did not begin to move until the late spring of 1956, and, due to its usual lag behind wholesale prices as well as special factors affecting food prices, it kept on rising after wholesale prices stabilized early in 1957 —and, incidentally, even after they had turned down sharply in late 1957.

Let us take a little longer perspective. After the great increase up to 1957, capital spending fell by nearly 25%. By the end of 1958, adjusting for price levels, outlays were no larger in absolute units than in the early postwar years, even though the economy was nearly half again as large in real terms.

What I am suggesting is that the situation would have been much healthier all around if some of the large investments in 1955, 1956, and 1957 could have been anticipated and made in 1954—thus lifting the floor of that recession and reducing price pressures in the following years—and if some of the plants and equipment pushed through in 1956 and 1957 in the face of short supplies, rising costs, and a high volume of debt financing could have been deferred to 1958 and 1959. After all, those are the years when they are going to be needed. If these steps had been taken the recent recession would not have been as bad as it was, and there would have been less pressure on prices in the preceding boom.

Roller-coaster Spending

The economy, of course, needs added capital plant and facilities in order to grow, and we should try to keep our production capacity a little ahead of rising demands for output in order to maintain or improve our growth and to prevent inflation. A shortage of capacity in the face of strong and insistent demands for goods is the best of all prescriptions for inflation. But—by the reverse of the same token—surging increases in capital outlays that produce widespread excess capacity over current demands for goods is a potent prescription for recession and unemployment (if not for deflation). Roller-coaster capital budgeting weakens the over-all stability of the economy, stimulates price increases, and raises wages on the upswing. All this contributes importantly to a progressive decline in the value of the dollar, because, for a good many reasons, we can no longer expect general price and wage reductions in a recession to offset the increases of the preceding upswing, and there may be no counterbalancing reductions at all.

We have all seen and heard a lot about forward planning, professionalization, and increased staff work in this area of capital spending. I know from my own field observations and from the more extensive surveys on this front by the McGraw-Hill Publishing Company, Inc.,* that a rapidly increasing fraction of companies, not counting utilities, have 5- to 10- and 15-year projections and targets where none existed 10 years ago. Such people as Neil H. Jacoby and Sumner H. Slichter have urged this as one of the major contributions of private business to postwar stability.

This poses the question: just how much has private business contributed to economic stability by way of improved capital budgeting practices? We have already seen that the surge in capital spending was a primary inflationary factor in the 1955–1957 boom. And after more or less serious excess capacity began showing up quite generally, the major cutback in capital spending played a major role in the recent sharp recession. The cutbacks were just as large percentagewise in 1957–1958 as they had been a decade earlier in 1948–1949, in spite of the presumed improvements in capital-budgeting practice in recent years. Under the kindest sort of interpretation, there is no progress toward stabilization demonstrated in this postwar comparison.

But let's take a longer look. Using producers' durable goods (excluding plant for which no separate data are available) we can get comparable figures back into the 1920's. From 1923 to 1929

---

* See the annual *Survey of Business' Plans for New Plants and Equipment.*

there were two recessions and two expansions. The two expansions of the 1920's—mid-1924 through 1926 and early 1928 to mid-1929—showed increases of 25% and 33% in producers' durable outlays. The two recent expansions—1950 to mid-1953 and 1954 to 1957—were 43% and 44% in current dollars and 28% each in real terms. After correcting for prices, the upswings in the 1950's have about the same order of magnitude of those of the 1920's. But on the downside, there are notable and unfavorable differences. The declines in 1923–1924 and from late 1926 through 1927 were 14% and 13%; the 1953–1954 decline was about the same in real terms (14%), but the cutbacks in 1948–1949 and in 1957–1958 were both 25% in real terms—roughly twice as severe.

In short, not only is the stabilizing effect of such efforts hard to find in the record of the last year as compared to 1948, but even more strikingly perhaps, the 1948–1949 and 1957–1958 cutbacks were roughly twice as large as those in the mid-years of the 1920's. And we may note that this was true not only of the cutbacks as a per cent of previous peak rates, but also as percentage of the gross national product.

On the basis of the record, the internal planning of private business on capital outlays has not yet produced any greater stability in this crucially important dynamic sector of the economy. If anything, the investment outlays of private business have been a greater source of instability—a greater destabilizer—in the postwar economy than in earlier periods of generally favorable business conditions. We do have an inherently more stable economy, but on the basis of the objective record private business in its capital-budgeting outlays has hindered rather than helped the effort. No one is urging businessmen to put the needs of the economy before the real best interests of their own companies—to engage in a private *counter*cyclical capital budgeting policy. But there are major possibilities for a *more non*cyclical, longer looking, type of capital budgeting for numerous types of important outlays, such as new products and programed replacements, where the greater cyclical stability of capital outlays would be entirely consistent with (and often contribute to) the self-interest of the firm and its employees and stockholders—as Melvin G. de Chazeau has well brought out.*

* "Can We Avoid Depression in a Dynamic Economy?" *Harvard Business Review,* July–August 1954, p. 37.

Inventories

In contrast with heavy capital outlays, the swings from inventory accumulation to decumulation in the last recession were *not* any larger than in the 1948–1949 recession (approximately $11.5 billion in each case). And since the stocks of inventories and the volume of total output had been growing rapidly over the decade, the *percentage* fluctuations have been falling rapidly over the postwar period—and have been very much smaller than they were during the 1920's. The shift in inventory investment was 8½% and 6½% of the gross national product in the two recessions of the 1920's; it was only about 5% in 1948–1949, 3% in 1953–1954, and only a little over 2½% in 1957–1958. Although this improvement is in part attributable to certain structural changes in the economy, private business itself can take a good part of the credit because of the adoption of improved procedures and policies in the handling of inventories.

Dividend Policy

Finally, the dividend policies followed by most leading corporations have made an important contribution to the stability of the economy. Our research on dividend policies indicates that most firms have a reasonably well-defined, normal payout ratio which is in the nature of a target or an ideal. Outside of utilities, most companies will gradually adjust their dividends toward this target payout ratio when earnings are changing markedly, but actual dividend payments will be stabilized by the gradualness of the adjustment. This relative stabilization of dividends has several important and favorable consequences. It obviously serves to stabilize consumer incomes from dividend payments, but perhaps still more importantly it means that business-retained funds are an important "shock absorber" between fluctuations in the gross national product and disposable incomes. In addition, some of our other research seems to indicate very strongly that stock market prices generally depend much more closely on cash dividend payments than they do on reported earnings or even normalized earnings. The stabilization of dividends thus serves as an important influence tending to help stabilize the stock market. This of course does not mean that psychological swings of buoyant optimism or otherwise do not have a very important influence on market prices; I am simply pointing out that with all the important psychological and other factors being what they are, the stabilization of dividends helps to make the market more stable than it would otherwise be. A clear instance of this was provided early this year when the maintenance of dividends was very much in line with what would be expected on the basis of those dividend policies shown in our research, and this maintenance of dividends was surely one of the reasons why the market remained as high as it did. And to the extent that the level of the market does influence the decisions of business and consumers, any degree of stability added by way of the dividend policies of business must be counted on the plus side.

Any full appraisal of the stabilizing effect of dividend policies on the economy must, of course, take account of the reverse side of the coin—to the extent that dividends are stabilized the fluctuations in retained funds are made greater, and this may serve to increase the fluctuations in business capital outlays. Time does not permit going on into this matter here, but one thing is clear: whether these reverse effects are important depends on the capital-budgeting policies of business firms.

Business has continued dividend policies which have contributed to the stability of the economy, and it has progressively adopted policies which importantly reduce the destabilizing effects of inventory fluctuations. The record on capital budgets, if anything, has deteriorated. I am enough of an optimist, and I have enough faith in the ingenuity of American businessmen and the contribution which can be made by research and serious attention to the problem that I believe real progress toward stability can be made in this difficult area of capital budgeting, as it already has in the other two areas I have discussed.

CONSUMER INSTALLMENT CREDIT AND INSTABILITY *

Under the direction of the Federal Reserve Board, a study of consumer installment credit has recently been concluded.† As is often true of works by economists, this study—comprising 6 vol-

* By Mr. Law.

† Board of Governors of the Federal Reserve System, *Consumer Instalment Credit* (Washington, 1957).

umes and 1,800 pages—discloses more areas of disagreement than agreement. On one point, however, there was general agreement. The dozens of economists contributing to the study conceded that changes in availability of consumer credit have contributed to economic instability. Moreover, consumer credit is particularly likely to add fuel to the inflationary fire because it creates added demand for goods, but, unlike some credit to businessmen, does not eventually lead to any increase in supply.

There is no doubt that extension of consumer installment credit has been highly erratic over the postwar years. Here, for example, are the changes since 1950:

1951	+9%	1955	+26%
1952	+25%	1956	+2%
1953	+7%	1957	+6%
1954	−2%	1958	−5%

I do not wish to imply that these fluctuations in consumer credit cause turning points in business activity. This is far from proved. But they do intensify fluctuations having their origin elsewhere.

In an upswing, the availability of credit permits consumers to purchase durable goods in anticipation of an increase in their incomes and to make up for purchases postponed during a recession. This expenditure, in turn, has what economists call multiplier and accelerator effects on other types of spending. That is, increased consumer demand for television sets not only increases the producer's demand for machinery to produce television sets but also increases incomes of workers in the television industry, which they in turn may spend for more consumer goods, ad infinitum.

The outstanding example, of course, is automobile credit, which comprises almost half the total consumer installment credit outstanding. Almost $5 billion in automobile credit was extended in 1955, and automobile sales increased a phenomenal 42% over 1954. The following year they declined 28%. Without attempting to trace the effects of these ups and downs on the rest of the economy, let me merely point out that the automobile industry purchases about 42% of all the sheet steel consumed in the United States, 24% of the bar steel, 60% of the rubber, and 28% of the zinc. Sales of automobiles, tires, batteries and accessories, and service station supplies comprise about 12% of our gross national product.

Of course, it may be argued that these fluctuations in automobile sales reflect changes in demand for automobiles rather than in credit availability. However, it is significant that cash automobile sales in 1955, the boom year, increased only one sixth, while credit sales increased one half.

In a downswing, cyclical declines in income are magnified by the stock of debt outstanding, since repayment of debt forces people to decrease the fraction of their incomes spent on current consumption. The magnitude of this problem is seen in the fact that payments on installment debt in 1957 were 11% of total disposable income (an amount greater than payments on mortgage debt, rent, life insurance, and annuities combined).

General Credit Controls

It seems clear that consumer credit is a significant factor in the business cycle. The same comments might be made about almost any type of credit, however, and the pertinent question here is whether general credit control, of the type exercised by the Federal Reserve Board in recent years, is sufficient to offset the destabilizing effects of consumer credit. It is my belief that general credit controls are inadequate for this purpose.

The facts cited above support this conclusion. In a period of severe credit restraint (1955–1956), consumer credit terms were markedly relaxed, and record amounts of installment credit were extended. In 1955 consumer installment credit extensions were $39.1 billion, exceeding the previous record by over $7.6 billion. In 1956 extensions were even larger.

Why did credit restraint by the Federal Reserve Board fail to curb consumer credit? There are several possible explanations, which are perhaps best examined by considering commercial banks and sales finance companies separately.

Role of Banks

Part of the explanation, of course, is that banks were extremely liquid at the beginning of the period and were able to obtain additional loanable funds (and thus mitigate Federal Reserve Board action) by selling short-term governments. Between December 1954 and February 1957 commercial banks increased all types of loans by $18.8 billion, while reducing holdings of governments by $12.3 billion. This is a continuing problem of credit control. As business declined, banks increased their holdings of governments by more than $7 billion in 1958, which means that the Federal Reserve Board has its work cut out for it when it attempts to tighten credit.

Of course, there are limits to a bank's willingness to sell its government securities, and once liquidity has been reduced to the danger point, Federal Reserve policy becomes more effective. But even then there are reasons for believing that consumer credit suffers less than other types.

To begin with, consumer credit is very profitable to banks. A 1955 survey showed a ratio of net income (after gross installment credit expenses) of 5.29%. In view of the relatively favorable loss experience with consumer loans, even in the depression of the 1930's, it is possible to argue that the consumer is treated unfairly in the credit markets.

Moreover, there is the matter of overhead. Installment lending is usually handled by a separate department with specialized employees. To utilize this investment efficiently requires a large volume of consumer credit activity. Finally, banks are subject to considerable pressure from automobile and appliance dealers, regular customers who depend on credit for their sales and who threaten to go elsewhere (particularly to sales finance companies) for accommodation if the bank is recalcitrant.

Sales Finance Companies

These companies are under the same pressure as banks. Their profits, which are usually large, are based on volume operations, and there is constant pressure to increase volume to spread the overhead. Dealer pressures are also important.

Unlike banks, however, many sales finance companies are also under pressure from manufacturers. These are the so-called captive finance companies—wholly owned and operated as subsidiaries of manufacturers. The growth of these firms has been remarkable. At the beginning of 1949 there were only 19 captive finance companies. Today there are at least 69. Their primary purpose is sale of the parent company's product, and their actions are influenced more by merchandising requirements than by credit conditions.

Let me cite two examples. In 1954–1955 General Motors Corporation faced a serious threat from Ford Motor Company for leadership in the automobile industry. Its subsidiary, General Motors Acceptance Corporation, had recently declared in a policy announcement: "GMAC's current experience shows that where down-payments on new cars are less than one third, repossessions are disproportionately higher, as dealers are well aware."

Shortly after this statement, GMAC's policies were changed and the percentage of transactions involving down payments lower than one third almost doubled. A dealer testifying later before the Subcommittee on Antitrust and Monopoly stated that early in 1955 he began losing sales to GM dealers because of financing, although his own finance company had always been competitive in the past. GMAC, he asserted, was taking automobile paper that in the past it would not have taken.

Similarly, in 1956, when the Federal Reserve Board was tightening credit continuously, General Electric Company announced a liberalization of financing terms. At a press conference the president of GE praised the Federal Reserve policy of restraint but announced at the same time that the GE credit company was helping those feeling the pinch.

Thus, when credit tightens, the position of the consumer borrower seems relatively secure. Admittedly, as banks dispose of governments in a falling bond market and sales finance companies are forced to pay higher costs for their funds, they may react by increasing interest rates on their consumer loans (although bank interest rates are notoriously sticky). This has little effect, however. Installment buyers are apparently insensitive to changes in finance charges, and maturities may be lengthened a little if necessary to offset the effect of higher finance charges on monthly payments. This is what happened in 1955, when the median maturity of new automobile loans increased from about 24 months, with one-third down payment, to about 30 months, with one-fourth down payment.

Return to Selective Controls

What is the solution? The one most commonly offered is a return to selective controls over consumer credit, similar to the controls over margin requirements for stock market loans. During

World War II and the Korean conflict the Federal Reserve Board had the power to control consumer credit specifically (the famous "Regulation W"), but Congress did not extend this authority when it lapsed in 1952.

There are economists on both sides of the proposal that the Federal Reserve Board again be given stand-by controls over consumer credit. The most common argument against it is that the proper role of the Federal Reserve Board is merely to control the total available supply of credit rather than to allocate it among various alternative uses. Selective controls, this argument runs, are discriminatory and give monetary authorities too much power, enabling them, for example, to decide that consumers should increase purchases of automobiles and decrease television purchases— as in a socialistic, planned society.

This argument can be overdone. It ignores the fact that general credit controls of the type presently used are also discriminatory. They weigh heavily on a few sectors which are disproportionately sensitive to credit conditions. Residential construction is perhaps the best example, although some types of state and local government spending and smaller businesses which rely heavily on borrowed funds should also be included. In contrast, businesses which finance themselves from internal funds and consumer borrowers are shielded from the impact of general credit restraint. Thus it may be argued that general credit controls discriminate in favor of consumer credit. If so, then selective controls over consumer credit might not only make credit policy more effective but might also make its incidence more equitable. In short, the sharp distinction between general credit controls and selective controls is an oversimplification.

Another objection to selective controls is that they are difficult to administer and enforce. The Federal Reserve study mentioned previously contains a detailed survey of problems that arose during World War II and immediately thereafter, when selective controls on consumer credit were in effect. A major difficulty was that lenders other than commercial banks had to be controlled.

One student of the problem has suggested that the solution is to apply controls at the "wholesale" rather than the "retail" level (as was true of the old "Regulation W"). That is, he has suggested

that the Federal Reserve Board establish variable collateral requirements on new loans by banks to nonbank installment lending institutions. Thus sales finance companies, when borrowing from
banks, would be forced to post varying amounts of consumer installment paper as collateral. By raising the requirement above
100%, the Federal Reserve Board could restrict credit in this area.
This suggestion has some defects, and is merely indicative of possible approaches to the problem. But where there is a will, there
should be a way.

The point is simply that present general credit controls do not
regulate consumer credit. In order to control this type of credit in
a boom, general credit would have to be tightened so drastically as
to have disastrous effects on other sectors more sensitive to existing
methods of control. Under these conditions the Federal Reserve
Board needs to operate with a scalpel rather than an ax.

Is there any alternative to selective controls, which would certainly
be received with something less than enthusiasm by lenders? Perhaps the answer is self-restraint by the lenders themselves in any
future boom of the 1955 variety. Lacking such restraint, we shall
probably see renewed demands for more effective controls over consumer credit.

QUESTIONS AND ANSWERS*

From the floor: What can the individual businessman possibly
do to help curb the inflationary process and remedy the recession?

Mr. Fox: Sumner H. Slichter has said that any individual business really is too small a part of the economy to feel that it ought to
take this broader responsibility. I can't agree with him. It is the action of individual businesses, trade unions, governments, and so on,
large or small, which accumulates into inflationary pressure, and
since the actions of larger organizations have the greater effects,
they should be aware of them.

Wage negotiations are one important area of responsibility. Take,
for example, a business that is fortunate enough to be one of those
whose productivity is well in excess of the national average. As a

* Businessmen present at the panel session on which this chapter is based
raised certain questions which brought about the interplay of ideas reported
more or less verbatim in this section.

result of that better-than-average productivity, it can negotiate a wage arrangement with its union that grants increases in wage rates in excess of the increase in the national productivity average, and is able to afford these increases because of its own productivity. It may, however, be helping to set a pattern that others cannot follow except by raising prices. It has always seemed to me that with a system of rounds of wage increases, the initial pressure comes on the industry that has a greater ability to pay in the sense of rates of productivity. If such an industry gives in to the extent of granting what it can afford to pay, perhaps without raising prices, when this could not be maintained throughout the economy, its act generates inflationary pressure as it spreads through the entire system.

Another area is consumer credit. This is not limited to banks and finance companies. If individual firms, in the granting of credit— consumer credit, perhaps extended through subsidiaries in the form of installment credit, or sometimes business credit—loosen up their credit terms at a time when this will push demand beyond what can be sustained, that, again, is going to have an inflationary effect.

In the capital expenditure area, even if we can't conceive rationally of anything resembling a countercyclical investment policy, we can imagine a fairly long-term plan of capital expenditures that would maintain the level of capital expenditures on a reasonably stable basis. In this way we can put a floor under industries producing capital equipment. I think this would have a major stabilizing effect.

So even though the action of a single firm can have little impact by itself, the *aggregate* of actions may be inflationary or stabilizing and contributes to the total.

From the floor: Our principal plant is located in a city where there are very large General Electric, General Motors, and steel company operations.

We are unionized, of course, and I would like to have somebody tell me how in the world I can do anything other than meet the wage levels of the three largest employers in the community.

Mr. Fox: I don't think you can.

From the floor: Therefore, my job is to achieve greater productivity for that higher wage level. That is quite an order, because I think the steel corporations and General Electric and General Motors are well-managed industries.

Furthermore, the largest single item that goes into our product is steel. On a certain morning I received a letter from four different steel companies saying that on the next Monday their price of steel would go up $4.50 a ton. There is not a single thing in the world I can do about it. Isn't it wonderful to be able to write your customer a letter like that and have it stick? We have to go out and *sell* our product!

It seems to me that the very large companies in this country have to assume a great responsibility. If they do not recognize and assume that obligation, I see no possibility whatsoever of stemming inflation.

From the floor: Actually, there are only about 10 or 15 companies in that list of 1,000 mentioned by Mr. Fox that call the shots. We are at the mercy of those 10 or 15 companies today. I bet you every man who occupies a position relatively comparable to mine will testify that he is under their thumb.

From the floor: I would like to correct the impression that the managements of steel, auto, and other big companies that are wage setters enjoy raising prices and wages, and that we do not exercise control in the wage area. I don't think there is any industry that has taken more strikes than steel. But the minute the strike begins, our customers start crying at the government, insisting that we end the strike and give them the steel they need. So big strikes become political, and are unthinkable in election years—which, after all, are fairly frequent. Finally, our government and our people will not stand for mass unemployment. With that kind of background, how can steel, auto, or any other industry stand up to strikes? Basically, that is our problem.

My company is doing two things that I believe are constructive. We are stepping up our education program—that is, the intracompany program—and we are paying major attention to getting the hourly employees and the nonexempt salaried employees more thoroughly aware of the problems that confront the country and particularly our own company.

Perhaps more important, we have decided as a matter of basic company policy to become active in politics, even to the extent of specific political action. We have designated one of our senior officers to study the important political issues of the day, and we shall seek to get our people to support the right side of that cause.

From the floor: As workers increasingly own stocks and become aware of management's policies, I think they will look beyond the immediate bargaining issues to the social problems we have been discussing here. Their single-minded belief that the best and immediate benefit is income derived from wages will be diluted.

I think what industry is doing in making shares available to workers on time payment plans or to mutual fund groups, tends to ameliorate the situation over a long period of time.

SMALL BUSINESS IN
OUR NEW SOCIETY

A. D. H. Kaplan

QUESTIONING THE POWER OF SURVIVAL OF SMALL BUSINESS in our increasingly complex business structure has figured prominently in the public opinion and policy of this nation at least since the turn of the century. The dreaded prospect of small business fading out of the economic picture has not materialized, and there is reason to believe that, through the recurrent fears and the measures taken to allay them, the stamina of small business in the American economy will continue to reassert itself. The question is how to maintain a continuous alertness in the adaptation of small business to changes in the economic climate, rather than how to prepare for its demise.

The problem of adaptation to a changing economic climate may be seen in the attempt to find a meaningful definition of small business. Anyone who has made the attempt to set down the pertinent criteria has been made aware of the difficulty of finding a

Note: Mr. Kaplan is Senior Staff Member of the Brookings Institution.

common denominator for roughly 4 million American enterprises
that may be put in the small business category. Before World War
II the Department of Commerce used, for census purposes, such
upper limits as sales of $50,000 a year for retailing and services, and
100 employees for manufacturing. Even these arbitrary limits bring
more than 99% of all firms under small business. The upper limits
of small business size have been raised, for purposes of financial aid,
in postwar legislation. Absolute size limits have been relaxed, moreover, to take account of the relation of size to type of industry—a
little fellow in steel or petroleum may be no smaller in sales or
assets than a firm of major influence in clothing or carpets.

Where the enterprise is neither clearly small nor clearly huge,
there is some merit in basing its classification on whether its management is in essence "proprietary" or "corporate." Thus, disre-
garding legal form, the enterprise may be regarded as small business
when the proprietor or the partners themselves constitute both the
ownership and the management. When the business has reached
the dimensions that require a management corps employed by the
corporation to direct its policies and operations—a group clearly
differentiated from the ownership—it certainly belongs to the big
business category.

Why the chronic national worry about small business, the state
of its health, its chances of retaining a significant role in our progressively more massive economy? Apart from particular problems
of small business firms, the general answer that comes most readily
to mind is: small business is important because it rests on an approach to economic democracy which is vital to our way of life. It
is the economic symbol of the significance we attach to individual
opportunity and initiative—the willingness to risk one's capital on
confidence in one's ability successfully to meet competition in the
market. If we do not have these, the American system as we know it
will pass into history.

This is all very well, but one is struck by John Davis's remarks in
his chapter of this book—and by those of his fellow panelists voicing
a widely held view—as he faces up to this issue in relation to the
small farmer.* His day has gone, it is said, and the sooner everyone

---

* See the chapter entitled "Converting Farm Problems into Business Opportunities," p. 224.

recognizes it the better off we will all be, farmer and consumer alike. Maybe, in this age of complex technology, fixed costs, specialization, and mass distribution, the day of the small businessman has gone too. Maybe he just does not serve a real function any more, regardless of our sentimental attachment to him.

The record of small business does not, to my mind, justify such fatalism either as to its present or its future. New business entries, currently numbering close to 400,000 a year, point to the persistence of the widespread urge to self-employment and personal risk taking even in this age of impressive growth in large-scale enterprise. The new entries outnumber the annual discontinuances to maintain the historical ratio of business firms to the general population.*

The small business has itself become larger. The $3,000 to $10,000 venture before the war has its counterpart in the $10,000 to $30,000 investment required to open the corresponding type of entry today. Like the minimum wage, the minimum size for a successful business start and efficient operation has been rising. Yet the higher investment requirements for a small business have apparently not stopped the historical rate of inflow; moreover, it has not caused the rate of business failures to reach the norms of the 1920's.

The nonincorporated section in the national income accounts, which roughly reflects the performance of small business, has shown an increase in the dollar value of small business's contribution to the national output of goods and services which is not significantly out of line with the rate of increase in business as a whole. The income originating in nonincorporated firms (nonfarm) increased from under $40 billion in 1947 to over $65 billion in 1957, according to Department of Commerce estimates.† Percentagewise, the net income of business proprietors appears to have declined over this period, while the share for compensation of employees of unincorporated enterprises has risen—reflecting the postwar increase in number of employees per enterprise in the small business sector.

* The U.S. Department of Commerce estimates 4.323 million business firms in operation as of December 31, 1957, which means 25 firms per 1,000 of the population. The corresponding (necessarily less reliable) estimate for 1900 is 1,645 firms, which would give 22 firms per 1,000 persons at the beginning of the century.

† National Income Supplements, U.S. Department of Commerce, Survey of Current Business.

Small business has been treated to sporadic injections of government aid through loans and guarantees and some types of relaxation in taxes and reporting requirements, as compared to big business. Such public measures to ease economic pressures on small enterprises point to the need for developing more systematically the appropriate institutional facilities in financing and technical assistance which are now inadequately available to small business. Small business will require access to the investment market through channels which are better adapted to its needs than those offered to big business through the already established organizations of investment banking.

It is notable that small business with its myriad facets can seldom speak for itself as a class. Some small business enterprisers will be the severest opponents of other small businessmen on such matters as changes in the patent laws, resale price maintenance, agency affiliation with large suppliers or distributors, and so on. By the same token, any suggestions for the improvement of small business as a whole tend to be confined to those few generalized privileges (such as lower taxes) to which the favorable reaction is not even confined to small business. Under these circumstances, perhaps the most important factor in providing greater opportunities to small business is to make provision for a high degree of versatility and flexibility in the public facilities designed to meet its varied requirements.

On this score I have found it illuminating to look into some of the ways in which the strengthening of small business has been fostered in various countries outside of the United States. Possibly one or two examples may also serve to freshen our thinking on the issue of whether small business is in danger of being "socialized" or deprived of its essential independence and self-responsibility by public measures in its behalf.

Small Business Abroad

Throughout the world, at least outside the Iron Curtain area, the urge to self-determination and economic progress has been finding expression in efforts to improve the economic effectiveness of small-scale industry.

In Japan the emergence of democratic processes within the

business structure is evidenced by a gradual emancipation of small industry from the traditional dependence on the wholesaler who furnished the materials for the work to be done, or on the larger industrial and distributing organization from which the small local factories got their subcontracts or sub-subcontracts. Under the Smaller Industries ... Cooperative Law of 1949, the smaller enterprises have pooled their skills and used assessments on their incomes or obtained outside capital to obtain modern equipment and technical guidance to improve their productivity. As of November 1955, approximately 60% of small-scale industry in Japan was represented in a total of 34,914 voluntary cooperatives ranging from local groupings of atomized units to regional and national federations. Government assistance to private financing, as well as technical managerial guidance, is supplied by the Smaller Enterprise Agency (in the Ministry of International Trade and Industry).

India, formally committed to the development of a socialist economy, has sought to make a more secure place for small-scale crafts and local enterprises, notably in "cottage industries" suitable to agricultural communities. The government has undertaken to market the output for the small producers through publicly sponsored selling cooperatives. More substantial local industries have been aided in obtaining capital for improved equipment.

Closer to the American scene we find in Canada the Bank for Economic Development, which started out before the close of World War II, with the initial capital furnished by the Bank of Canada, to meet the requirements of new and growing industries for types of financial and technical assistance that were not available through the regular banking and investment facilities. During the 14 years of its existence, the Bank for Economic Development has provided some instructive lessons in suiting the type of financing to the requirements for optimum development of the client. It has apparently been free to make long-term loans, to take stock for its investment in the firm, to delay the start of interest payments and take adequate compensation later, to give and charge for qualified managerial guidance as well as financial assistance.

England has had two similar institutions since 1945 to implement the MacMillan Report calling for more suitable financing of small business needs. One of them, the Industrial and Commercial Finance Corporation, through its subsidiary EDITL (Estate Duties Investment Trust, Ltd.) also makes provision for the small enterprise to finance its survival by helping it to meet inheritance taxes or other obligations when its owners pass on.

In some ways I find the approach of the Netherlands to the assistance of small business as instructive a one as can be found. The Netherlands has probably had as long an experience as any Western nation in government ownership and operation of public utilities and in governmental economic intervention in the economic life of the nation. In terms of permissive legislation, there is little one might expect of a socialistic regime that the Dutch government does not have the power to do—from creating new land by pushing back the sea to acquiring specific industries for government management, controlling entries into business, or organizing business and labor federations. Nevertheless, the postwar years have seen a trend toward more private enterprise rather than less. This has happened, apparently, at a time when the government has been provided with, and has used as needed, a complete list of facilities for paternalistic intervention in the affairs of private business—particularly for aid to small business.

As far back as World War I, the Dutch government made credit grants to middle-class (Middenstand) businessmen who had met with financial difficulties in times of economic stress, as in the depression of the 1930's or during wars which shut off normal markets. These were regarded as incidental relief dictated by special circumstances. The more comprehensive attack on the problem of maintaining the efficiency of small business as a contributor to national economic progress began after the experience of the 1930's.

It appeared to the government that, aside from special crisis situations, small firms had need of short-term credit to meet liquidity troubles, long-term credit to finance investments, and expert advice in matters of business economics and accounting. In meeting this problem the government, and occasionally the municipalities and trade associations or chambers of commerce, founded Regional Security Funds and centers for economic advice.

The types of facilities currently available in the Netherlands, other than the special credits mentioned above, include:

> *Business Equipment Credits*—to facilitate the acquisition, extension, and renewal, improvement, or repair of operational equipment.

Mortgage Credits—to permit building or purchase of business premises on mortgage loans up to 85% of total value.

Establishment Credits—to facilitate the establishment of a business in a new building or development in need of such facilities.

Takeover Credits—to assist qualified persons to take over an established business, in industries that have their own Special Guarantee Funds.

Economic Cooperation Credits—to assist small business in acquiring joint facilities for production, distribution, research, or in mergers, to increase the efficiency of operation of undersized firms.

The interest in this list lies not so much in the ground it may cover as in the careful screening of applicants for credit-worthiness within the intent of the measure. Most of the facilities provided are in the form of government guarantees of bank loans or loans by the membership of an industry. The government's responsibility is to provide the excess of the credit over what could be obtained without its help. The combination of comprehensive permissive legislation and the application of sound banking principles consistent with the liberal purposes of the measures has apparently not resulted in abuse of the credit aid.

An illustration of the climate in which the program operates may be supplied by a reference to the administrator of the program for guaranteed personal loans:

In the Ministry of Economic Affairs, the division which governs the guaranteed credits program for small business men is under a Director General for Middle Class Trades (D.G. voor de Middenstand). The guaranteed loans are made for the government only by the Middenstandsbank, which has its main office in Amsterdam and branches in other cities. The Director General, in The Hague, is a government officer with a wide knowledge of the problems and sincere concern for the effectiveness of the program of making loans available to meet situations not met by the private banks. But in Amsterdam the Director General also serves as a member of the board of the Middenstandsbank, where the borrower will pay the going interest and commission on the loan, and may even have his loan turned down by the banker who is also the Director General.

The Middenstandsbank is essentially a private bank covering the whole field of commercial banking; only a minor part of its business is in the guaranteed loan field. The privilege of making guaranteed loans, as far as one could tell, is not sought by the other commercial banks. There is no apparent concern about a conflict of interest in the person of the Director General, nor any concern about the handling of the guaranteed loans by only one private bank.

The Netherlands serves to exemplify the point that the availability of permissive legislation to aid small businesses need not be at all inconsistent with the application of sound banking principles or the prevalence of a mutually desirable working relationship between business and government to strengthen an important area of private enterprise.

Place of Small Business

Before we would go as far in measures to aid small business as other lands have, many Americans would want to be convinced that our use of more government aid would really be directed toward increasing efficiency and competitiveness of small business. Here they may have in mind the readiness of small business in some lines to seek protection under fair trade laws, or the heavy turnover in the small business area, amounting in any one year to roughly a fifth of the firms in operation. Why do they quit? Is it because they cannot match the efficiency of the large corporation? All this assumes, of course, that one can measure efficiency against the desire to enter or step out of business. The important consideration may be that the opportunity to enter or to quit is itself an aspect of economic liberty for which the turnover is not too high a price for society to pay. That need not prevent us, however, from encouraging more adequate preparation for the trial of entrepreneurship in our fast-moving economy.

It might be argued that it is important for our total society—economic, social, and political—that we maintain a certain percentage of our labor force as self-employed. Here is an outlet for people who dislike routine and security, a leavening of the community loaf that is needed if we are to continue to be a free and enterprising community. We want to keep the gates open so that someone who wants to try his hand at entrepreneurship can do so. This is part of the privilege of being an American that most of our citizens probably deem worth preserving.

Some observers maintain, further, that we can continue to get a good "fit" for all types of buyers and markets only if we have the flexibility and pioneering in small experiments that small business provides. Furthermore, the little fellow can function as a gadfly, even a pacesetter, in quality, price, style, and service. Small business has a subtle impact on the total society that is not easy to measure, but we have many examples of the effect of enterprising little companies on their big brothers. They have been breeding grounds for ideas which have later been picked up by the giants that can carry them forward on a grander scale.

Somehow, over the years, small business has been remarkably able to roll with the punches and to keep coming back in spite of all that has happened to replace the small enterprise in particular industries and functions, or otherwise to place obstacles in its path. Maybe these obstacles have had something to do with its resiliency, its ability to withstand adversity. I think that small business has justified our confidence that it will find ways to keep going in the next ten years, even though we do not know exactly what the pattern may be. It seems reasonable to expect that as big business gets greater its needs for outlets in small business, for supplies at the small and medium-size business levels, will likewise develop.

The kind of thinking that turned blacksmith shops into filling stations is going to continue. From the standpoint of all of us, including big business, it is important that it be so. To strengthen the possibility, we must make sure that small business gets the kind of people who know how to use their minds, who know something of the techniques of decision making and are capable of assuming responsibility. We should encourage men of superior talents to go into smaller firms, and we should not be afraid of government action to strengthen the position of the small, entrepreneurial enterprise. Government help to small business, if focused on the improvement of its economic performance, is not inconsistent with free enterprise.

POWER AND MORALITY IN BUSINESS

Benjamin M. Selekman

THE RELATIONSHIP BETWEEN POWER and morality presents an issue of the utmost urgency for business managers. The lesson of history is unmistakable: no person and no group has held power very long unless it was sooner or later invested with moral values and moral purposes. Empires, kings, and dictators may have enjoyed tremendous power and cut a wide swath for a while, but were dethroned or defeated when their self-aggrandizement and self-seeking betrayed the fact that they lacked moral purpose.

Businessmen face this ancient truth and familiar dilemma. Here is a vast new profession: management. No group in history has wielded the power that management in the typical corporation does today. A handful of people hold sway over standards of living, chances to work, and the welfare of the community, the nation, and the world.

Note: Mr. Selekman is Kirstein Professor of Labor Relations, Harvard Business School.

In the typical corporation, one or two or perhaps a half dozen people embody within themselves the three major functions with which any kind of authority is endowed: legislative, executive, and judicial. The managers make policies, administer them, and execute them. If anyone questions them, the same managers sit in a judicial capacity over themselves. And, unlike a democratic government, this group is self-perpetuating. It is small and cohesive. The day is gone when executives were controlled by the majority stockholders or a leading family. Furthermore, the board of directors—theoretically outside representatives—consists largely of a management group or people whom management selects, as Erwin Canham reminds us in his chapter.*

This tremendous power is a new phenomenon in human history, but despite our inexperience with it, it has on the whole been remarkably well exercised up to now. This high degree of responsibility is due to many factors—including, I believe, the professional business schools, the attack on business, particularly in the 1930's, and, of course, the caliber of men who have assumed leadership in our enterprises.

Balance of Forces

But there is another, more important, explanation: the development of a balance of power. This is a familiar constellation of forces in society. When any nation or group within a nation gains great strength, other nations or interest groups naturally mobilize their power to check the first group and meet it on equal terms.

In the case of American business, government and labor have grown in strength, in the first instance to regulate corporate activity, and in the second to bargain with management on a plane of equality. After the Great Depression, with its mass unemployment and suffering, the political reforms of Roosevelt and Truman dominated the American scene. At the same time the unions marched in, seized property, called sit-down strikes, and did battle for what they considered to be their rights. It is no coincidence that the expansion of professional management coincides with the growth of unions and government regulation.

The point is that a balance of power is the natural outgrowth of

* See the chapter entitled "For a Revised Sense of Values," p. 75.

fear of too much untrammeled might for any one group. Even if businessmen were all angels—and they are not—they should expect and accept this as a perfectly natural phenomenon and learn to live with it, just as labor may expect to face government regulation if its growth of power threatens or seems to threaten the national welfare.

Thus, balance of power produces more than just stability; it leads to a greater morality than power that is unilateral. For power in itself is amoral. It is simply the bringing together of energy, whether it is the energy of nature, machines, or mind and skill. It is man who gives morality—or immorality—to power, and this morality comes out of struggle, suffering, and adversity.

Sometimes moral standards arise out of the conflict released when a group of men abuse their power—as happened in 1929 and the 1930's. During those years misleading investments created artificial wealth and a boom in speculation; as a result, a reform movement arose. On other occasions new codes are written after a long period of jockeying for position. But come they will, one way or another, and no group should be so blind as to fail to accept their inevitable appearance.

Thus, the moral exercise of power is enhanced by the pushing and pulling of various forces in society. Without the pressure of unions, government, and farmers, the business community might well find itself reverting to a kind of jungle law of untrammeled competition.

It was this counterpressure that forced American management to re-examine and justify its behavior. Management turned its attention to social responsibility because it was being challenged by labor and government. For, after all, this new emphasis on moral and social responsibility dates from the 1930's, the very time when business found itself under attack. Until then, business had been largely dominated by the ideology of the nineteenth century, as stated by the often-quoted Adam Smith and elaborated by David Ricardo and Thomas Malthus.

According to this doctrine, self-interest should be the dominant motive for man. In the very nature of things wages tended to remain at a subsistence level. The price of labor was fixed by the market; labor was a commodity. Malthus added the grim theory that population grew faster than the available food supply, so most people were bound to live on thin margins and some even to starve. The Darwinian theory of the survival of the fittest accentuated this brand of economics. The rich became rich because they were "fitter," and employers and those who occupied positions of power did so because this was the order of nature. To give public assistance to the poor was tantamount to defying nature. It was degrading, demoralizing, and created dependency. If there must be outdoor charity, it should be carried on by private agencies. Otherwise it was best to put the poor in almshouses.

One of our problems today is to find a new philosophy. Nineteenth-century thought was basically the businessman's ideology, and we do not yet have a substitute for it. We talk about social responsibility, but we have found no solid ideological content to replace this older one.

We are having trouble making the change partly because the nineteenth-century approach had much to justify it from a practical point of view. The theory stimulated the creation of our great material wealth, the development of the resources of the continent, and the building of great industries. It served us well for the great war emergencies in which we were to be engulfed. When the West was threatened by Fascism and Nazism, it was the machine tools which the old, rugged individualists had built that were turned to making war materials.

Search for Legitimacy

I have pointed out that the Great Depression and the attack on business by labor and government—an attack crystallized into regulatory legislation of wide scope—projected a new world demanding a new frame of reference. Out of adversity, out of attack, came the search for a new and realistic moral justification. Business, like any power system, was driven to look for a basis of legitimacy. All power groups strive mightily to be accepted as legitimate, as having the right to govern. The quest for legitimacy is an old theme in political and constitutional history.

But, you may ask, why is it important to establish morality in the use of power and legitimacy in the field of economic administration? The answer is a practical one. No matter how good their intentions, business managers cannot win acceptance for their professional conduct unless they establish a moral basis for their actions. Businessmen must give moral value to power because the minute they organize it, they begin to deal with, and are dependent on, other human beings. Investors, customers, employees, all become involved, establish interests, and exert moral pressures which can be translated, as we have seen, into political pressures.

Thus businessmen must find an appropriate moral framework within which their power can operate. But this is no easy matter. The fulfillment of moral goals is a difficult task, as history amply demonstrates. We all subscribe to the Sermon on the Mount, but find its application very difficult. This is the eternal struggle of man, as it is his eternal aspiration.

For man is both sinful and virtuous; he is both saintly and demonic. These qualities are all built into us. In addition, businessmen face certain tense situations all the time. For example:

> Morally, a human is an entity in himself. He is God's son. His dignity is all-important. He has a right to fulfill himself and live in the community. In view of this, the businessman has a responsibility to provide maximum employment, good wages, healthy working conditions, and a higher standard of living. But man as labor is also a cost. Hence an employer may have to lay off his employees or shut down a plant on which a whole community depends and move it elsewhere because of lower cost or easier accessibility to markets or raw materials. This is a fearful undertaking, but the businessman must face this issue every day.

Let me phrase it this way: the technical must is what you have to do to be competitive, to survive, to succeed, and the ethical ought is what you ought to do because of the human beings involved, human beings whom you have attracted to work for you, whom you have tried to interest, and from whom you have sought loyalty. These same problems arise, though not quite so sharply, in relation to the community and customers.

The problem is further complicated because its solution demands that we share power—a very difficult task for most people. Managers want to be charitable and benevolent; these are old virtues. But when the workers are organized and the unions come in to negotiate and bargain, that is not so easy. Unilateral power is sweet, all the more because for a great many years industry enjoyed it.

When the unions came along in the 1930's, they were very aggres-sive. In changes and shifts of power, aggressors are not polite. Power is raw and destructive. When it is not shared gradually, the people who suddenly achieve power can be and usually are rough.

Thus, assuming social responsibility is not easy; it must be worked at. What guidelines can we find as we try to implement it?

To begin with, the manager as leader must convey integrity in all his behavior. He cannot convey moral values unless he believes in them and lives them. As I talk with managers on trips around the country, and as I read business literature, I see three principal shortcomings that threaten the moral position of businessmen and public acceptance of their right to exercise their great power. Un-less executives overcome these faults, the search for a moral basis for the use of power may be taken out of their hands and the de-cision made by other groups.

Self-Righteousness

One of the chief dangers is self-righteousness, an unfortunate trait which expresses itself in many ways. Let us look at two com-mon instances.

1. Management tends to take all the credit for increased produc-tivity. In meeting after meeting executives tell how *they* have achieved the great record of American productivity. In so doing, they deny labor and everyone else any part in this magnificent achievement. Often they are explicit in assigning labor a minor role, if any at all. But they forget that unless workers are around to fix a machine when it breaks down, production ceases. Moreover, they overlook the primary role played by scientists and engineers, who uncover the secrets of how to harness nature's power—steam power, electrical power, and now nuclear power.

Of course, management does fulfill a strategic role. Most products would stay in the laboratory if businessmen did not get the money together, build a factory, form a sales organization, employ workers, and market the products. But even if we agree that management is a leading factor in increasing productivity, it is self-righteous to claim the complete credit and deny others their fair share.

Self-righteousness arises from many causes. Perhaps it is a reac-tion to criticism, especially unjust criticism. But one of the penalties of power is the exposed position which it involves, and those who have power should expect to be scrutinized and attacked. Oftentimes these assaults are rough and jarring, but that is the nature of the society.

Whatever the dynamics of self-righteousness may be, it is a malicious and destructive attitude. One of the values businessmen ought to build as leaders of men is a sense of community. Productivity is a team operation under management direction; so is controlling inflation. Both are cooperative undertakings. Managers ought to be leaders in giving people credit for their contributions. Only by so doing can they create a community. Moral leadership to which people will respond depends on a sense of mutual respect and unity. Self-righteousness is divisive and harmful for all of the parties involved.

2. Management tends to put all the blame on labor for inflation. This disturbs me greatly because it is alienating labor—and not the union leader, who may use this talk as propaganda, but the working man at the bench, who is chasing an increased cost of living. He responds to our merchandising appeals and goes into debt to buy all our fancy new products. He is advancing his standard of living faster than he can afford to, due to our good selling. So when we tell the bricklayer, the carpenter, the miner, or the steelworker that he is responsible for inflation, he says, "Look at my grocery bill, my rent, my clothes, my shoes. My wife is always after me for a little more money."

Let us stop to look at *his* side of the story. For the first time in years the working man has had a good labor market. Full employment is a recent phenomenon that began with the war period. For most of his life the working man has had to scrounge around. Like every executive and every professional man, the worker also would like to get a break. When he gets $.10 or $.15 an hour more and business tells him he is responsible for inflation, the accusation has a divisive and destructive effect. Executives not only enjoy large basic salaries, but also new lifetime contracts, stock, retirement funds, escalator clauses, and so forth. When such an executive tells his workers that they are responsible for inflation, it just does not ring true. For example:

> A company president who was making quite a large salary visited one of the plants and stopped to talk with the workers. He sounded

off on the danger of inflation. After he was through, he was told, "Mr. X, we'll make you a proposition. You resign from your job, and we'll hire you as our negotiator. You did pretty well for yourself."

Cynicism

The second danger is cynicism—the very negation of morality, since it rests on a basic distrust of man. If you believe that man is wholly self-centered, predatory, and corrupt, you cannot convey a moral attitude, and you cannot expect people to respond to your leadership.

One disheartening example of cynicism is the businessman's attitude toward labor leaders. He persists in saying that every labor leader is a politician and corrupt, despite the great and courageous efforts labor has been making to clear racketeers out of the labor movement. The unions have set up committees of ethical practices, and have expelled the most powerful union of all, the Teamsters Union which is the hub of a complex matrix of human and economic power.

It took great courage for George Meany, Walter Reuther, Al Hayes, and other labor leaders to come to grips with this problem. The underworld had moved in, a not uncommon phenomenon when a new movement is struggling to be born and then suddenly becomes powerful. Bootleggers from the 1920's and Communists muscled in, and real trouble spots developed. Both Walter Reuther and his brother were shot at when they tried to clean out the numbers rackets in the automobile plants, and we are all familiar with the difficulties created by the Communists. It is not easy to straighten out a situation like this, particularly when the "good guys" are so intertwined with the "bad guys." Nevertheless, labor is determined to go through with the clean-up even if it destroys itself in the process of doing it.

Executives also tend to look down their noses at politicians, even though we ourselves are all politicians. Anybody who tries to appeal to any mass of people is in politics; when we advertise, we ask for votes, for preference for our commodities or services. Like all politicians, we do not mislead, but we exaggerate. The differences between politicians and businessmen are of degree, not of kind.

Businessmen treat intellectuals cynically, too, and thus destroy people on whom they depend for ideas on how to organize our institutions and how to understand human behavior. We waste our capital when we take a destructive attitude toward intellectuals, for we block their insights, which can help us. When they produce good ideas, they make us think more rigorously. We cannot afford to be contemptuous of these people who have the intellectual potential to strengthen our skill and power.

Perfectionism

The third great danger that I see is our assumption of perfectionism, our tendency to give the public the impression that we have all the answers to the world's problems. Businessmen make too many promises and claims in areas where they lack the technical capacity to deliver and where, moreover, attempting to make good on their commitments may interfere with their survival in a competitive world.

From reading current business literature on the professionalization of management, one might well conclude that the businessman now has statistical tools to solve almost any problem that comes up. It is, of course, true that many advances have been made in techniques such as data processing and methods of statistical analysis. What businessmen fail to make clear to the public, however, is the crudity of these devices, which are really only in the early stages of development. Without intending to, perhaps, businessmen have conveyed too strong an impression of their ability to deal with both business problems and the ills of society generally.

Management runs a great risk when it conveys an exaggerated notion of its skill in handling the problems of modern society. The greatest danger is that the public may take management at its word and expect it to be able to work miracles both inside *and* outside the walls of its plants.

The truth of the matter is that we do not yet know how to stabilize markets and prices, how to control the business cycle, how to expand overseas production, or how to unscramble the problems of big government. Yet we often talk as if we did, urging people to put everything in our hands and trust us. The disillusionment will be all the stronger when the public finds out that management is all too human. We have only to look at the contrast between the 1920's, when the businessman was a hero, and the 1930's, when he was the villain, to see the dangers of perfectionism and the speed with which the public can change its attitudes.

Constitutionalism

What should we do to avoid cynicism, self-righteousness, and perfectionism? How can we develop the moral attitude which is indispensable for leadership? We must have a check on our own power, a constitutional framework, and if we are wise we will take a lead in constructing it ourselves. In the historical, classic way, people exercised power through constitutionalism. In government, justice takes the form of constitutionalism; perhaps business too can create organizational machinery which will provide a system of checks and controls. I do not want to suggest a blueprint, because in the beginning we ought to remain flexible.

The kind of constitutionalism I have in mind is exemplified by management's response to some aspects of trade unionism.* In the 1930's we saw sit-down strikes, seizures of property, and mass picketing. In the 1950's, as we look at the General Motors or Ford agreements, we can see that management has acquired know-how in negotiating these agreements and in administering them. The grievance machinery, particularly, with its outside arbitration, has developed as a judicial system. Here is a constitutionalism which companies assumed under pressure and which has satisfied the demands of the opposition. We have, in effect, a nongovernmental constitutional system to supplement our national political one.

The way management handled the problem of discontented foremen represents another good example of constitutionalism. During the war, foremen were forgotten men, squeezed between top management with its pressure for efficiency and aggressive unions putting the heat on for relaxation of discipline. They had to organize to protect themselves and, in fact, actually called a strike in Detroit and elsewhere. Finally, management established policies and rules defining the rights and duties of foremen and giving them status. Managers used the "legislative process" to deal with this group of people in the corporate community, and bound themselves—again

* See the chapter entitled "How Effectively Are Management and Unions Living Together?" p. 238.

under pressure—by certain rules and regulations. It is interesting to note incidentally, that management may have to go through the same process shortly with technicians and scientists.

Another area for constitutionalism is the board of directors. How should we give adequate representation to the stockholders? How can we have a check on management? What techniques can we work out to make the board of directors a really effective governor?

Management has one particularly tough problem to resolve in creating a constitutional system for itself. Unlike a political government, it cannot allow itself to be ousted. Somehow, businessmen have to set up checks on themselves, provide for an opposition, and do it without the kind of election machinery which could depose them.

If management is to remain in control, it must limit itself constitutionally, and it must create a moral atmosphere for leadership. It must avoid self-righteousness, cynicism, and perfectionism. It has an obligation to be just and equitable. And, like all great governors of men, great executives must so conduct themselves that they convey the impression to everybody that righteousness prevails within their realms.

QUESTIONS AND ANSWERS*

From the floor: I agree with many of your points, but I disagree with a couple of your basic assumptions. When you assume that power and morality are mutually essential, I think you imply that there is an absolute morality. You overlook the fact that morality changes and that absolute power either conforms to the moral climate or changes the moral climate to legitimatize what the power is doing.

From the floor: Is there a moral issue in management's determination to take every legal and legitimate means to keep the men in its company from becoming unionized?

Mr. Selekman: No, I don't think there's a moral problem involved here, because entry of a trade union is now a matter of due process. It's all spelled out. Every employer has the right to present

---

* Businessmen present at the panel session on which this chapter is based raised certain questions which brought about the interplay of ideas reported more or less verbatim in this section.

his case to the workers before they vote. If the manager does anything wrong, he runs afoul of the law. There are limits to what he can do, but as long as he obeys the law as administered by the National Labor Relations Board, he's all right.

From the floor: Suppose he finds a technicality in the law by which he can prevent the entry of a trade union. Does it now become a moral problem?

Mr. Selekman: Each side has its lawyers to protect it. If the manager doesn't do anything underhanded and operates within the framework of the law, he is behaving correctly. I should say, though, that morally the wage earner has a right to have an organization to represent him. This organization, as I have said, is a necessary check on our unilateral power and our judgment. It helps us to do the right thing and to work justice.

From the floor: Why should the worker have an organization? Can't he attain his goals through his own efforts?

Mr. Selekman: Unions are a natural evolution of constitutional government. I'm a great believer in supplementary constitutional systems, because I don't want to give all power to the central government. But—and this is the key—if these supplementary constitutional systems are to come into being and work, managers must think of themselves as governors of men.

Part Three

A CASE STUDY IN BUSINESS
RESPONSIBILITY

BUSINESS AND ITS RESPONSIBILITY
TO NATIONAL DEFENSE

To bring some of the issues raised at the Conference into sharper relief, the participants saw a film depicting a business problem which had strong overtones in the area of community responsibilities and relationships. The movie, written and produced at the Harvard Business School, tells the story of a company which was hit by a pair of government decisions in the defense area. Though the incident is fictional, it is based on facts drawn from a number of firms which have gone through a similar experience.

The script by itself cannot convey the story in all its dimensions, but it should serve to give readers of this book some feeling for the incident and for the decision which faced the president of the Athena Electronics Company. In determining what should be done in the face of project stretch-outs and payment delays imposed by the government, Chuck Thompson had to measure the extent of his firm's responsibility to the national defense effort as well as the normal business issues.

The discussion sessions which followed the film produced a number of ideas, some of which are summarized in this chapter.

—The Editor.

THE ATHENA ELECTRONICS COMPANY*

The Athena Electronics Company is a medium-sized manufacturer, primarily engaged in the production of commercial electrical and electronics products. Like so many other companies of its type, Atelco is also involved in military production. For example, one of its more promising defense projects is Medusa, an advanced-design, solid propellent intermediate-range missile, somewhat similar in appearance to the test vehicle from which it was evolved. It is with the future of Medusa that this incident is primarily concerned.

Like many companies which do both military and commercial business, Atelco had organized its defense activities into a separate division under Vice President James Brown, who was assisted by a staff which included Richard Herndon, Director of Military Relations, and Dan Bauer, Comptroller. Within the Defense Systems Division, the more important projects were assigned to project managers. Responsibility for the Medusa missile had been delegated to Alford Smith, who directed the activities of a team of scientists and engineers, headed up by Darcy Martin, Chief Engineer.

Yet, as is usually the case in controversial situations having a direct bearing upon policy, final decisions must still be made by corporation presidents such as Atelco's Charles Thompson, acting on the advice of senior executives like Walter Jones, Corporate Treasurer.

It was with just such a situation that Jim Brown became involved on September 17, 1957.

(*Office of James Brown, Vice President, Defense Systems Division.*)

TELEPHONE OPERATOR: I'm still trying to locate Mr. Herndon for you, Mr. Brown.

BROWN: Have you tried the guidance laboratory?

* Copyright, 1958, by the President and Fellows of Harvard College. Case material of the Harvard Graduate School of Business Administration is prepared as a basis for class discussion. Cases are not designed to present illustrations of either correct or incorrect handling of administrative problems.

OPERATOR: I'll ring them now. (*Simultaneous with this, Herndon enters.*)

BROWN: No, cancel the call, Operator. Mr. Herndon just walked into the office.

HERNDON: Morning, Jim. (*Sits down.*)

BROWN: Morning, Dick. I was just going to give you a call.

HERNDON: I'm afraid I have bad news. The Air Force just called us to advise us that they're stretching out the Medusa Project. It's to be just about cut in half for this next year, or in other words, we'll get approximately the same amount of money we got this past year.

BROWN: Oh, that is bad news. Did they give you any reasons? With whom did you talk, Dick?

HERNDON: Well, understand, there's nothing official, but I talked with Colonel Johnston, the Air Force Medusa Project Officer. Paper work on the stretch-out hasn't caught up yet, but he thought it best to advise us what's in the wind.

BROWN: Is there any doubt in your mind that they really mean business?

HERNDON: No, I think this is probably the real thing. Of course, we've had alarms before but I would guess that since they're going over the program pretty carefully, this time they really mean business.

BROWN: Well, I think what we ought to do is to probably get Al Smith and Darcy Martin in here to talk this over. (*Picks up phone.*) Miss Homer, could you come in a minute, please? And, on second thought, I think it might be a good idea to have Dan Bauer in here, too.

MISS HOMER: (*Enters.*) Yes, sir?

BROWN: Miss Homer, I wonder if you would put a call through to Al Smith, Darcy Martin, and also Dan Bauer and ask them if they could come in for a few minutes?

MISS HOMER: Has Mr. Smith returned from his trip yet?

BROWN: Yes, he got back early this morning.

(*Miss Homer exits.*)

BROWN: You know, what I can't understand about this, Dick, is why on earth they would stretch out the Medusa Project at this particular stage of the game. If we have to go back to an ex-

penditure level of $10 million for this coming year, it's going to
slow down this program from 24 to 36 months. And that's going
to mean that Medusa, like so many other weapons, will be obsolete just about the time we get it into operation. Why do they
do these things to us?   ‘

HERNDON: Well, you know as well as I do it's a matter of their
having overprogramed in past years. As a result, they can't keep
up with all the contracts they've got now without getting a big
bulge in the appropriations and expenditures. You know they
didn't do as well appropriations-wise as they expected. Budget
ceilings, I guess, have an effect here, too.

(*Knock on door. Martin and Bauer enter and sit down.*)

BROWN: Morning, Darcy, Dan. Sit down, will you please? Dick
came in this morning and gave me a bad piece of news that both
of you ought to know about right away.

BAUER: Well, I've got some bad news too.

HERNDON: Well I had a chance to talk with Al Smith just before
I came in here so he knows what's up. I wonder if Darcy and
Dan do too.

(*Martin and Bauer nod heads "No."*)

BROWN: Well, I think before we proceed, it would be a good idea
if I had my secretary come in to take some notes. (*Picks up inter-
office phone.*) Miss Homer, could you come in, please, and bring
your book? Let me see if I understand this problem, now. (*Miss
Homer enters.*) Oh, fine, Miss Homer. Miss Homer, would you
sit down and take notes of our conversation, please? (*Miss Homer
sits down beside Brown's desk.*) As I understand it, this is the
situation. Dick got an informal call this morning from the
Medusa Project Officer. And he advised Dick that the Air Force
was going to cut the project by approximately one half within the
next year.

BAUER: Does that mean that they're going to cut it now, or as of
the fiscal year beginning in June?

BROWN: They're going to cut it right now!

BAUER: And is this a half of what we're scheduled for or half the
rate we're going now or what?

HERNDON: As I got the picture from Colonel Johnston, it means an
immediate cutback in the authorizations so that we don't spend

more in the next 12 months than we spent in the past 12. Since we've been expanding and building up, it means a cut from where we are now.

BAUER: Well, if you figure out our current rate of expenditures on an annual basis, it comes out to about $14 million a year. So that we're . . . (*Interrupted by a knock. Smith enters.*)

BROWN: Morning, Al.

SMITH: Sorry I'm late.

BROWN: That's all right. Will you sit down, please?

(*Smith sits down.*)

BAUER: So as I was saying, we're spending at about the rate of $14 million a year on this project now, so that if we're going to stay within the ceiling of $10 million for the coming 12 months, we're going to have to cut well below that. I guess this is as good a time as any to give you this piece of news I've got. This TWX just hit my desk. Let me read it to you. It says, "Current Department of Defense Fiscal Accounting Policies have imposed an austere expenditure limitation upon this Command. As a result, it appears that reimbursement of contractual obligations must be deferred until the second half of fiscal year 1958. Every effort will be made to ameliorate the present situation. However, the possibility of processing vouchers for payment prior to December 31, 1957 seems rather remote."

BROWN: Wait a minute! Does this mean that payment is going to be delayed on work already completed?

BAUER: It looks that way, because in this next paragraph here they specify that not only will payments be withheld on future vouchers received through December 31, 1957, but it may also be necessary to defer them on vouchers that we've already submitted to them. And then, of course, there's this usual business about reluctance to employ this method, which was reached only after exhaustive efforts to explore other means. They sincerely hope that our reaction will be favorable and cooperative, and voluntary concurrence is essential to the maintenance of their fiscal position, and so forth, and so forth. I'll see that you guys get copies of the thing.

BROWN: Oh, that's pretty rough. It's all very well for the Air Force to talk about maintaining its sound fiscal position, but what about our sound fiscal position? Dan, let's pass up this question of payment for the time being. What I think we ought to do right away is to figure out what this is going to mean to us from the standpoint of time, our manning tables, our subcontractors, and all the rest of it on the Medusa Project. It's just possible that we might be able to salvage something from the situation.

MARTIN: Well, I can tell you one thing. If we have to cut back below $10 million, it means we're going to have to let a lot of people go. Not only that, but we're going to have to cut back on some of our outside developmental work. If this goes deep enough, it can wreck the contract.

SMITH: There's always the possibility that we may be able to get this decision reversed up the line somewhere, especially since we haven't received any official notification.

BROWN: Well, I'm willing to give that a try, Al. But yet, on the other hand, I have the feeling that this cutback and stretch-out are part of a general pattern that the Air Force is going to have to go through. You remember what happened on the Navajo Project. They canceled it out completely after they put a lot of money into it. The fact of the matter is, the Air Force just doesn't have the money for which they're committed for their projects, and they especially don't have this money if they're going to stay within the appropriations limit and particularly within the new expenditure ceiling they had given to them by the Department of Defense and the Bureau of the Budget. Dick, I'd be very much interested in knowing what happened to the Perseus Project. I certainly would feel better if I knew that it was being stretched, too.

HERNDON: I haven't heard a thing, Jim.

SMITH: Oh, they couldn't cut us and let Perseus go ahead. Theoretically, Medusa is infinitely more advanced in terms of performance.

BROWN: Well, they might, you know, Al. The people over at Air Research and Development Command like Perseus more than they do Medusa because Perseus is surer. The thing that worries them about the Medusa Project is that a lot of the work we're doing on guidance and countermeasures is entirely new. It constitutes a breakthrough in the state of the art.

SMITH: Perseus is sure, as you say, but Medusa will be a much better weapon, if it will actually do the things we hope it will.

BROWN: That's a very big "if," Al. I'm afraid the Air Force may not want to spend the type of money they are and have been on Medusa in the face of that sort of contingency. Incidentally, I think that the rest of you might be interested in some film footage that Al brought back this morning. It's a test of a prototype engine somewhat similar to the one they're using on Perseus. Al, would you mind going out and getting the projector for us, please?

SMITH (*Goes to get projector*): Darcy, would you mind helping me with this screen? (*The two men set up the projector and screen.*)

BROWN: I think you all know that the main problem which they had on Perseus for a long time was the engine. And I have a distinct impression that that's pretty well licked now, mostly from the experimental work which they've done on both the Titan and Atlas Projects. Of course, I still think we're ahead. You know that Perseus was liquid-fueled, and we all know the advantages of a solid propellent in this respect.

SMITH (*Seated by projector*): Would you turn the lights off, Dan? (*Scenes of missile footage follow.*)

SMITH: Would you turn the lights on, please, Dan? (*Turns off projector.*)

MARTIN: Dick, this alleged superiority of Perseus over Medusa (*Rolling up screen.*), how strongly do the people over at ARDC feel about this? (*Puts away screen and sits down.*)

HERNDON: Well, you know how it is, Darcy. Both weapons have their sponsors at ARDC and at the Pentagon. The Perseus supporters are pretty enthusiastic about it, and they think they can have it operational by 1962. We promised 1963, but there's always the chance that we won't have the guidance or countermeasures by then. With limited funds, I think some people in the Air Force would probably take a chance on a sure thing rather than on a contingency like ours, even though, if the contingency pays off, they'll end up with a lot better weapon.

BAUER: Yeah, but what I want to know is, even if we do get this program restored to its original $20 million figure for the coming months, how are we going to finance it without any advance payments between now and January 1? I can hear Walt Jones screaming and yelling about that one now. He's going to want to expand the commercial products division and cut down on the defense systems division. He'll argue, and in some respects I must say he'll be right, that our profit margin is greater in commercial products, and at least we know when we are going to get paid for them.

SMITH: Well, undoubtedly what is going to happen is between now and the first of the year we're going to have to go to the banks and borrow money to carry on not only the Medusa Project but a lot of our other government work as well. That'll mean getting money somewhere at about 4½% to 5% interest, which, as you know, is not allowable cost under present government contract regulations.

BROWN: Well, I can just hear Thompson and Jones and all the rest of them—see them shaking their heads and saying, "We told you so." You know they've been worried for a long time that we've been becoming much too dependent on defense business, and that sooner or later somebody was going to pull the rug out from under this division. And it looks right now that that's exactly what the Air Force has started to do. And I know very well that the reaction is going to be pretty unfavorable. No, the question is, I think, what are we going to do about it? Or to be more specific, what should we recommend to Thompson and the rest of them?

HERNDON: One thing I think we ought to do, Jim, is for you and me to go down to Washington and see if we can't find out some information in greater detail and also see if we can't try to do something. Perhaps we can get them to reverse their decision so that we can at least be able to operate at our present level, or maybe we'd even be able to pry some funds loose by January 1.

BROWN: I don't know, Dick, before I went off on a hunting expedition like that I would feel obliged to talk to Thompson. I think we ought to give him the benefit of our views on it and also tell him what we think the impact of this will be on us from a developmental, manufacturing, and money point of view. I don't know, but his reaction may be that we should wash out the whole thing before we get in any deeper.

SMITH: I don't really see how we can do that. We're into it pretty far already. And if our development work pays off, this is going to be a pretty important weapon not only to national defense but to Atelco as well. Why, it will be the biggest manufacturing job as a prime contractor that we've ever had.

BROWN: That's true, Al. But it won't be unless we can get somebody in the Pentagon to let us carry out our development program more or less on the basis of our original schedule.

MARTIN: Look, Jim, if you can give me a couple of days I can have some of my people put together some rough estimates as to what will happen if we have to cut back by about half. At least we can get some idea about what this will mean to us in terms of people, facilities, subcontracts, and so on.

SMITH: Maybe with $10 million we could keep going on the parts of the program that have a long lead-time like the research and development on the guidance and countermeasures, so that slippage on the program will be minimized. I don't know exactly how much leeway we have here, but it would certainly be worthwhile taking a look at it. There are certain people here at the plant that we simply can't let go if the project is to go ahead at all.

BROWN: OK, well I tell you what you do. You, Al, and Darcy try to get the information now as fast as you can. In the meantime what I'll do is try to work out an appointment with both Walt Jones and also Thompson, and I suggest that in a couple of days we try to go over and meet with them. Some of us can go over and give them the bad news and also give them our recommendations on what we think the corporation should do. Of course, the more information we have, and the more facts we have, the better. I'll have my secretary call you in a couple of days and let you know when we'll be meeting. Thanks very much.

(*Herndon, Martin, Bauer and Smith leave.*)

(*On September 19, two days after the meeting in Jim Brown's office, Corporation Treasurer Walter Jones met with President Thompson in the latter's office.*)

THOMPSON: Jim Brown and some of his people from Defense Systems will be over in a few minutes. They've got some bad news for us. Medusa Project has been stretched out.

JONES: I knew it!

THOMPSON: There's also a likelihood that there may be some postponements on the payment on the contract until after the first of January.

JONES: That is serious. Government's slow enough paying the way it is. But if they're going to slow down still further, we'll have to go into the banks in order to borrow money. We'd have to borrow something like $2 million between now and the first of the year on Medusa alone, to say nothing about what we'd need for the other government projects. I don't need to tell you that I've never been too enthusiastic about these defense contracts. The more I see of them and the way the government behaves, the less I like it. Seems like it's just one crisis after another. In March it was the termination of that Navy contract; then we all broke our necks getting that Project Olympus contract; now it's Medusa that's in trouble. If our profit on the Defense Systems Division were better, perhaps I might feel a little happier about it.

THOMPSON: Well, I know that you haven't felt too enthusiastic about government work, and I've had some doubts about it myself. While it's true that the margin on our sales is only 3%, on the other hand, considering our modest investment in defense systems, it provides a yield which compares favorably with that of the commercial division. Moreover, I think you'll have to acknowledge also that we have a public responsibility to use our know-how in this area.

JONES: This is all very true. But looking at it from the stock-holders' standpoint, where are we?

THOMPSON: Well you'll have to admit that work of this kind presents us with an opportunity to do some very advanced research and development work which conceivably might have some important payoffs in the commercial area. Obviously, a point of view like this might be difficult to prove with paper and pencil, but I have a strong feeling that aside from the national contribution it could be making, it also contributes in two aspects to the company: first, in terms of product diversification and secondly in earning power.

JONES: Yes, this would be true if we could bring it along to the point of putting it into production, and if we don't go broke doing it, and if the government doesn't renegotiate our profits anyway.

THOMPSON: Well, it won't do any good to sit here and grouse about the government; they've got their problems too.

(*Knock at door. Thompson's secretary enters.*)

SECRETARY: Mr. Thompson, Mr. Brown and the people from the Defense Systems Division are here. Shall I show them in?

THOMPSON: Would you, please? (*Secretary ushers in Brown, Smith, and Bauer. Secretary leaves and closes door.*) Good morning, Jim. How are you today? Nice to see you, Dan, how are you?

JONES: Morning, Dan, Al.

(*The men nod, murmur appropriate greetings.*)

THOMPSON: Won't you sit down?

(*The men seat themselves.*)

BROWN: Well, as I told you over the phone, Chuck, we've received some bad news on Medusa. The project is going to be stretched out and generally cut back to about one half of what we contemplated for this next year, beginning at once. And to make matters worse, Dan here has just received word from the Air Force of curtailed payments between now and the first of the year so they can get their expenditures down to the $18 billion ceiling. You both may recall that this was the limit which was placed upon them by the Department of Defense and the Budget Bureau. You see, this is all part of the effort to stay within the $275 billion debt ceiling which the government is already approaching. Dan and Al and I were talking over the situation at some length, and we're pretty much in agreement as to what we should do about it.

THOMPSON: Fine. Why don't you go ahead and tell us what you had in mind.

BROWN: Well, first of all, we worked up some figures on what the impact of the cutback would be. Al did most of the work on these, and I think he's in a better position than I am to explain them. Al, why don't you go ahead?

SMITH: As far as we can see, with the ceiling of $10 million expenditures for the next 12 months ...

THOMPSON (*Interrupts*): Why don't you put it on the chart, Al?

SMITH: OK. Fine. (*Gets up and goes to flip chart in corner of Thompson's office. Writes figures on it as he explains to men ...*) Well, this is where we are now. I'll give you the figures we've

worked up. Give you the expenditure level, personnel, and delivery dates. Our expenditure level now is about $14 million.
And we have about 500 people assigned to the Medusa Project.
And our current delivery date is 1963. Now, if we're forced to
hold to this $10 million ceiling, we're going to have to cut about
half of our Medusa people as soon as possible. That is, about
250 of the scientists, engineers, and the small number of shop
people who have been working on the project. However, we can
still retain enough personnel to keep going on the really crucial
research and development necessary to push the state of the art
if Medusa is going to go ahead. Now, on the outside, a pro rata
cutback would bring our research subcontract and vendor items
down to about $2.5 million.

THOMPSON: What happens if you do cut that deeply?

SMITH: Well, as I see it, it will be a delay of about 2½ years, or
about 1965 or 1966.

THOMPSON: Why?

SMITH: Because we would be cutting into our basic research and
development on the guidance and countermeasures so deeply.
However, with this $10 million, plus an extra $1.8 million, we
should be able to reduce their slippage factor substantially so
that essentially it would mean a cutback of about a year, or a
delivery date of roughly 1964. Now, this is a brief summary of
the figures we've worked up—if there are any further questions,
I'll be glad to try to answer them as we go along.

BROWN: I have one question right at the outset. Can we possibly
get that amount of money, the $1.8 million, from the Air Force, or
will we have to put up that amount of money on our own in
order to keep pushing on that project and to keep slippage at a
minimum?

THOMPSON: Well, that's a possibility, but go ahead.

BROWN: Well, I'm going to be frank. As far as I can see, if Medusa
slips by 2½ years, it's going to be overtaken by other, even more
advanced weapons. And on that basis, the Air Force will end
up buying Perseus and then probably buying for a later date, say
1966 to 1970, some even more advanced weapon than Medusa.
I don't know. Obviously, we can't be sure of this whole thing,
but that's roughly the way we size it up.

THOMPSON: What about the 250 people that you cut back from the Medusa Project? Can you absorb them into the Defense System? As I understand it, you were still hiring people—scientists and engineers—last month.

BROWN: Well, that's true, but we stopped hiring the first of the month. And of course there's the possibility that in the projected layoff of 250 people not necessarily those involved only on the Medusa Project would be involved. Of course this would naturally mean that there would have to be shifting around of people and their assignments within the division.

THOMPSON: What happens to our subcontractors? The university for example?

BROWN: Well, they'd have to cut back too. We haven't had a chance yet to figure what the termination costs would be but we know there'd be some.

JONES: Yes, this stop-and-start business gets pretty expensive. What kind of level would you have to come down to in order to hold to the $10 million ceiling for the year?

BAUER: Seven and a half million dollars if we begin to cut back and lay off right away. That's from our present level of $14 million.

THOMPSON: Well, as I understand it, if you have another $1.8 million, you can save the slippage and the time schedule and keep Medusa as an advanced weapon, leading into a possible production contract?

BAUER: That's the way we size it up.

THOMPSON: Then we either have the choice, as I said, of going to the government for the money or risking our own, gambling on the fact that we'll be reimbursed for our R & D investment and eventually earn a profit on the production contract itself.

JONES: Well, aside from that, how do you suggest we finance the project over the next few months?

BAUER: We'll just have to go to the banks. I'd estimate that at the peak of our effort we'd be into them for $2 million on this project alone. Then if the government decides to hold back on payments on other projects, why the amount could go up substantially. We haven't heard anything from the Navy as to what they're going to do on Project Cutty Sark, for example. If they hold back payment, the Division is going to be on the hook for perhaps as much as $5 or $6 million before the end of the year.

JONES: In the face of that kind of a demand for borrowed money, you're suggesting that perhaps we ought to lay out $1.8 million of our own on the gamble that we can keep Medusa alive and bring in the production contract?

BROWN: Well, Walt, as I've said, we'll certainly try to get it from the Air Force first, but if we can't get it from there, or if we don't put up the amount that is necessary ourselves, then I think we have to make our minds up that Medusa is dead. At least it's pretty much dead as a production item if our estimates are correct. Oh, it's true that I think the Air Force will probably keep the program going on a developmental basis, just because many of the ideas which we're pioneering on will be useful for other systems and other weapons. But that will amount to only a few million dollars a year. I would very much doubt whether we would ever get into production on the missile itself.

THOMPSON: Two points, Jim. Have you ever been able to find out whether we are in direct competition with Perseus, and second, are they getting cut back too?

BROWN: Well, I haven't been able to find out specifically whether we are in direct competition or not, but on your second point, it's my judgment that Perseus is too far along to be cut back. I'm not sure, Chuck, whether you've had a chance yet to see the film footage that Al brought back showing the Perseus engine and the prototype test firing.

THOMPSON: Yes.

BROWN: It gives you a pretty good idea of how far along they are.

THOMPSON: Yes I did, Jim; I had a chance to see it. All very interesting, but it doesn't give us too much to go on.

BROWN: Well, Al and Dick Herndon and I were planning to go down to Washington tomorrow night in the hope that we could get some idea of what this cutback is going to mean. Undoubtedly, the Perseus competition is going to be a factor in this situation. In fact, if it weren't, the Air Force would almost be forced to go ahead full blast on Medusa. As it is, with Perseus a fairly sure thing, I'm afraid they have some doubts about our missile.

THOMPSON: Frankly, I think I'd have real trouble selling our board on the idea of putting $1.8 million of our own money in a thing as conjectural and as far in the future as the Medusa production contract. If we had it in our pockets, that'd be something of another color. But with the situation so uncertain, not only in the Air Force, but in the defense program as a whole, frankly I must confess that I'm rather skeptical as to whether we'd ever get our money back.

BROWN: In our judgment, it's a reasonable gamble, although admittedly it's far from a sure thing. Furthermore, there's a chance that we can get much of this money recognized as allowable under a development contract.

THOMPSON: Well, if we are to believe what we hear, there's a strong likelihood that defense expenditures during the next few years are more likely to be down than up, partly due to technical budgetary considerations and partly due to the economy drive.

SMITH: Of course, if the Russians or someone else were to start another Korea, or if they were to come forward and announce some dramatic new breakthrough, that might change the picture very radically.

THOMPSON: Well, as I said, there's a strong likelihood that the defense budget is going to continue to be very tight for the next several years. When I was in Washington last week, all the talk was about economy and the curtailing of expenses and in the military, the duplication and the waste. It's really been built up into quite a hassle, partly because people feel that way and partly because certain elements in the business community itself have been fanning the economy flames and getting the people to put the heat on their senators and congressmen.

BROWN: Well, I know that's the general pattern, but on the other hand, Chuck, the whole picture can change very quickly. I don't think we should forget for one moment that what we have here is a very critical project. In fact, so far as I'm concerned, while this is a very conjectural matter, if we do what we think we can do, we'll not only end up with an extremely fine weapon, but we'll have one which will also be a real contribution to the combat capability of the Air Force. I think that given an adequate amount of time and a reasonable amount of money we ought to be able to demonstrate that. Of course, we're back to the old question, do we get the time and the money?

THOMPSON: I'm fully aware that we have an obligation not only as citizens but also because the Defense Department and the Air Force are important customers, and they're in a tight spot right now. Nevertheless, there are certain limits beyond which we cannot go and still protect the interests of the company. As Dan has pointed out, we may be in the banks for something in the neighborhood of $2 million. And under the regulations which disallow interest payments on borrowed capital, that in itself is a rather substantial contribution. Personally, I have serious doubts as to whether we should grubstake the government during this next year for $1.8 million just because perhaps they have been unable to live within their appropriation or because they're trying to undershoot an arbitrarily set debt ceiling. And then there's Walt's point that perhaps the equivalent of our money invested in commercial product development, at least for the short haul, conceivably might have a very attractive payoff.

JONES: It certainly would! And furthermore, our Commercial Products Division people have some pretty interesting ideas of their own coming along. This, of course, will mean that their research and development demands will be considerably higher for this coming year than they were last year. It's O.K. making allowances for the problems of the government, but I can't see carrying them on our shoulders. We aren't that big, and we just don't have that kind of money. Furthermore, the profits on their business are much lower than they are on our commercial products. I, for one, have real doubts about the wisdom of putting any more of our money into the Defense Systems Division.

THOMPSON: Al, do you have a run-down on those figures which you gave us on the flip board a few minutes ago?

SMITH: No, I just have some pencil notes here. I'm having a memorandum typed up for you and Walt as to just what they look like. It should be over in the next hour or two.

THOMPSON: Good. I'd like to take this up with the Executive Committee on Tuesday morning. And if you can be there, Jim, I'd like to have you there too.

BROWN: Well, as I told you earlier, I was planning to go to Washington with Dick Herndon and Al.

THOMPSON: Well I know. But I think it's also important if you can get some additional information on this matter, Lord knows we could use it. Furthermore, I'd like to have you there to answer the questions which might come up during the meeting. I must acknowledge that I really don't know what I'm going to recommend to them on this. If you can call me not later than Monday afternoon, I'd certainly appreciate it.

BROWN: O.K. I'll give you a call from Washington if we hear anything definite.

THOMPSON: In the meantime, if you and Dan would get together and make a strong pitch to the Air Force and get some sort of relief on our money so that we get paid on these curtailed-progress payments I think that's extremely important. Furthermore, I think that if you can get any sort of a change in the regulations so that we can get our money on interest payments that we have on our contract it would be very helpful.

JONES: Dan and I will get together on that as soon as we break up here.

THOMPSON: One more thing. Anything in the wind on new business which might take up the slack on Medusa?

BROWN: Yes. We can't be sure, but we hope to be able to get the contract on the Project Southern Cross. As you know, we've been battling this out for some time with General Aircraft and Electronics. It's my understanding that the work on phase one of the project program hasn't progressed too satisfactorily, and therefore we stand a better than even chance of getting the work on phase two. This will start up slowly, but it should do quite a bit toward offsetting the impact of the Medusa cutback if that stands. In our opinion we think that probably we'll be able to employ about 150 on the Southern Cross Project approximately three months after it starts. And that would take care of about 60% of the people laid off on the Medusa Project. That should help quite a bit.

JONES: And will we get paid for any of it?

BAUER: Now look, those invoices don't even go in until the end of November or early December, and the freeze is off the first of January, so we'll get paid all right, and we'll get paid on time.

THOMPSON: Jim, have you heard anything about any other cutbacks or terminations that might be pending?

BROWN: No, we haven't heard of any, but there might well be some.

THOMPSON: All right. Let's leave it here. I'll see you on Tuesday morning, Jim, and meanwhile I'll be expecting to hear from you Monday afternoon from Washington.

BROWN: O.K. Fine.

THOMPSON: Good luck.

BROWN: See you then.

THOMPSON: Thanks a lot, gentlemen.

BROWN: Goodbye ...

* * * * *

Mr. Thompson's Problem

What should Atelco President Thompson recommend to the Executive Committee on the Medusa project? He tells his executives frankly that he is not sure which way he should move. "We have the choice," he says, "of going to the government for the money or risking our own, gambling on the fact that we'll be reimbursed for our R & D investment and eventually earn a profit on the production contract itself, or letting the program go by the board."

As he ponders the question after his associates depart, he will have to break apart several kinds of issues in his mind. This will not be easy, for they are thoroughly "intertwingled"; each impinges on the other, and the answer to one partially determines and is determined by the decisions made on the others. But, recognizing the somewhat artificial and arbitrary nature of the divisions, the disturbed Mr. Thompson might ask himself:

• Strictly from the business standpoint, is the investment of this $1.8 million a good risk?
• Should Atelco continue in the defense business at all?
• What responsibility do we have to the security of the nation?
• Can some sound long-range pattern of relationships between government and private business be worked out?

Too Big a Risk?

To many managers, the investment of $1.8 million for a company of Atelco's size does not seem like an unwarranted risk. As one observer put it, "A company as big as this grows by taking broad strokes, not by being penurious. After all, you build a business by taking risks." While it is true that Atelco may not be reimbursed, may never get the production contract on Medusa—if, to be sure, Medusa ever gets produced at all—and may have to foot the bill for interest charges, the lure of the $750 million job is an enticing one. Furthermore, the company is in deep on Medusa already, and another expenditure might have the effect of justifying everything that had gone before.

The facts are not all neatly lined up on one side of the issue, though. This is a specialized project, and difficult to convert if it goes sour. The profit margins are low. Perseus, though not as advanced a weapon, is due to be operational sooner, and is further along. Defense production contracts by no means always go to the firm that has done the basic development work. And the onrushing economy wave, so much in the picture in September 1957 when the story took place, might very well result in major and permanent cutbacks.

In deciding whether the investment is in the immediate self-interest of Atelco, Thompson will also have to look at the spin-off possibilities in the research for the commercial products division. He will need to evaluate the future benefits of the advanced work his firm is doing in terms of other weapons systems yet to be launched. His treasurer, the professional "no man" of the group, will have to tell him what the impact of the delayed government payments will be and how much the nonreturnable interest charges will run. Is it really only $1.8 million he is considering here, or is the total sum involved in the whole operation going to add up to a considerably larger figure?

He will have to ask himself about the technical people involved. "Can we find places for them if we cut way back? If we let them go, will we be able to replace them with men of equivalent talent in the future when another project is undertaken? Possibly we should invest the money and keep Medusa breathing just to hold onto them until we need their high skills again later. On the other hand, what will happen to their morale if they find that we have virtually given up on Medusa as an ultimate production item?"

Some managers have argued that the government is just like any regular customer who gets into trouble occasionally and should be helped out. Like the commercial end of the company, being on good terms with potential and actual customers is a good insurance policy. Finally, once out of a fast-moving area like this, how quickly and easily can a firm get back? If you do not keep going, are you not in danger of slipping so far behind the competition that catching up would be a real chore?

Drop Defense Business?

The company treasurer tells Thompson that he's never been too enthusiastic about these defense contracts. "The more I see of them and the way the government behaves," he says, "the less I like it. Seems like it's just one crisis after another." So the president, impelled by Jones' critical attitude and the seriousness of this two-pronged crisis, might well take a look at the whole defense business of his company.

The profit margins are small, as Walt Jones so vigorously points out, and the vagaries of doing business with Washington are made obvious enough in the case. Then there is the frustrating fact that to a businessman the government's problems are artificial ones. They are created only partly by economic necessities; after all, everyone can understand a customer who runs into a spell of heavy going. In dealing with the men from the Potomac, though, the business manager gets snaggled in all kinds of pressures which he does not understand. Why is there an arbitrary debt ceiling, and why does the administration refuse to get it lifted? Why the sudden, indiscriminate economy drive? Why this constant blowing hot and cold on projects? And how does it happen that the government overcommits itself and then finds the bills all coming due at the most inconvenient times?

But Thompson has to look at the constructive side, too. As he indicates, the return on investment is good because Uncle Sam is so deeply involved in the construction of facilities. The risks are of a different character from those in civilian business. Then, for an electronics company, the question arises whether it is possible to ignore defense contracts, since so much of the work in that field is wrapped up in military activities. In some companies—possibly Atelco itself—the bulk of the research is, in effect, subsidized by Washington, and the commercial products division benefits from the spillover.

If the production contract on Medusa is a serious possibility in Thompson's thinking or his recommendation to the Executive Committee, the issue of "how much defense business" is sure to be troubling him. After all, a three-quarter billion dollar contract—the largest Atelco has ever had as a prime contractor—is going to have a sharp impact on the entire firm. It will call for a new look at the balance between civilian and government business, and force a restudy of the company's objectives.

It may be that this re-examination is long overdue at Atelco, anyway. Possibly the managers have no clear policy on government business, have never accepted the difficulties that accompany it and prepared for them both organizationally and psychologically. Conceivably they have drifted into this line without really thinking the matter through, and now need to take a fine reading on their position. As some people have suggested, doing regular business with the government is a perfectly normal operation, in contrast to the developmental work in which Thompson's firm is participating. Perhaps they should concentrate on lining up some of the run-of-the-mill jobs instead of the mercurial weapons systems contracts.

Responsibility to Nation

But Chuck Thompson cannot get far into the question of whether to do any business with Washington at all, and if so, how much and what kind, without hitting straight into the issue that a number of observers see as the heart of his problem: what is his responsibility to the nation as a whole?

Here he has a weapon that promises to be one of the most effective available to the Air Force, and, as he says to Jones, "I think you'll have to acknowledge that we have a public responsibility to use our know-how in this area."

One businessman, commenting on the problems of Mr. Thompson, had this to say:

> If a company has spent a large amount of money and energy and acquired a great deal of special skill in the development of hardware which is directly of benefit to the national defense and national interest, it has a certain moral obligation not to let that know-how, equipment, development, and knowledge decay from lack of use. We need these weapons for our very survival, and a businessman should be willing to make this kind of contribution—especially

when this part of his business has been built largely by public funds, anyway.

So far so good, but the difficult task is to find how far this public responsibility is to carry you. Another executive put it this way:

> When you raise the "national interest" as an abstraction, an ideal, there is no doubt about your acceptance—verbally—of the idea of responsibility. But the wicket gets a little stickier when you try to pin this down to a real situation and implement it. You have to draw the line between doing these things in a going concern and just not being a going concern much longer. Thompson had better make sure that he does not maneuver himself right out of business, for in that case no one wins. As a matter of fact, I could make an argument for the proposition that the most responsible step Thompson could take is to worry about his own company and build it up just as strongly as he possibly can. Our real national interest is best served by keeping our business big and healthy.

The matter of "how far" this public responsibility should be carried in real life has another twist, too. Is it the businessman's job to decide between missiles, or the Air Force's assignment? Why does Jim Brown suggest that Atelco should determine whether and how much Medusa is needed? In a case like this, shouldn't the company go along with the Defense Department's judgment? Not necessarily, say some, because this judgment is likely to be formed with only half the facts, after a lot of political pulling and hauling, and on the basis of budgetary considerations rather than need.

Be that as it may, Thompson cannot duck this issue. Either Atelco has a responsibility or it does not; if it does, someone has to determine just how far that obligation goes.

Business-Government Relationships

Finally, Thompson should be worrying—even if he is not—about the long-range pattern of business-government relationships. How can the obvious communication breakdowns be avoided? Is there some way that the government can run its part of the operation with a little clearer understanding of what happens on the other end of the line? Can the wrinkles in the legislation and administrative decisions be smoothed out on issues like deferred payments, interest charges, reimbursements, construction contracts, and so on? Can profit margins be made more realistic, the role of competition clarified, and real incentives established? Can real, continuing liaison be constructed?

Maybe the answer to this whole situation is to turn over the development and production of weapons to the government and keep private business out of it. This policy has worked fairly successfully with government arsenals; perhaps we should expand that kind of arrangement and let business go back to doing business.

Or maybe businessmen should abandon the profit motive for the duration of the crisis, throw away their usual bench marks, and, virtually, join the army. Perhaps they should scrap incentives and do the job for altruistic reasons just because it has to be done.

Without casting judgments on either of these two positions or any variations thereof, the thoughts of one leading executive with extensive wartime Washington service is apropos here. "To do the impossible production job needed in World War II," he said, "we did not abandon all the traditional dynamics—or even the forms— of the American business system. Quite the contrary, we worked to get the self-interest and the patriotism of the manager and his firm moving in the same direction as the national need."

This is indeed a challenging task, though one with which business managers are not unfamiliar. More and more they have been seeking, within their companies, to find, define, and harness the peculiar interests, drives, and skills of the individuals who work for them in order to build a functioning team for the benefit of all. No one would claim that we have managed to do this on a national level between companies; the relationship of the individual firm to the government and to the whole society is a great unmarked area for exploration. Charting and colonizing it is a large part of management's mission in this new society.